# Chicken Soup for the Soul®

# Country Music

*Chicken Soup for the Soul: Country Music*
*The Inspirational Stories behind 101 of Your Favorite Country Songs*
Jack Canfield, Mark Victor Hansen, Randy Rudder. Foreword by Ken Kragen.

Published by Chicken Soup for the Soul Publishing, LLC  www.chickensoup.com

*Front and back cover photograph courtesy of Getty Images/Iconica: Zia Soleil. Interior illustration courtesy of iStockPhoto.com/dra_schwartz.*

*Cover and Interior Design & Layout by Pneuma Books, LLC*
For more info on Pneuma Books, visit www.pneumabooks.com

Distributed to the booktrade by Simon & Schuster. SAN: 200-2442

**Publisher's Cataloging-in-Publication Data**
*(Prepared by The Donohue Group)*

Chicken soup for the soul : country music : the inspirational stories behind 101
  of your favorite country songs / [compiled by] Jack Canfield, Mark Victor
  Hansen, [and] Randy Rudder ; foreword by Ken Kragen.

     p. : ill. ;  cm.

A collection of 101 stories written by famous country songwriters and singers about the genesis of their hit songs and their personal stories, often never told before, about the lyrics for their award-winning hit songs.
  ISBN: 978-1-935096-67-2

  1. Lyric writing (Popular music)--Literary collections.  2. Lyric writing (Popular music)--Anecdotes.  3. Country music--History and criticism--Literary collections.  4. Country music--History and criticism--Anecdotes.  I. Canfield, Jack, 1944-  II. Hansen, Mark Victor.  III. Rudder, Randy.  IV. Kragen, Kenneth.  V. Title: Country music

PN6071.M87 C455 2011
810.8/02/0357                              2011922319

PRINTED IN THE UNITED STATES OF AMERICA
on acid∞free paper
20 19 18 17 16 15 14 13 12 11                01 02 03 04 05 06 07 08 09 10

www.ChickenSoup.com

# Chicken Soup for the Soul® Country Music

The Inspirational Stories behind
101 of Your Favorite Country Songs

Jack Canfield
Mark Victor Hansen
Randy Rudder
Foreword by Ken Kragen

Chicken Soup for the Soul Publishing, LLC
Cos Cob, CT

# Contents

Foreword, *Ken Kragen* ...................................................... xi

Introduction .................................................................... 1

1. 16th Avenue, *story by Thom Schuyler* ............................ 5
2. All-American Boy, *story by Bobby Bare* ........................ 8
3. Almost Home, *story by Craig Morgan* ......................... 12
4. American Honey, *story by Hillary Lindsey* .................. 16
5. American Made, *story by Pat McManus* ...................... 19
6. American Saturday Night, *story by Ashley Gorley* ........ 24
7. Back When We Were Beautiful, *story by Matraca Berg* ..... 27
8. Believe, *story by* Craig Wiseman ............................... 30
9. Bobbie Ann Mason, *story by Mark D. Sanders* ............. 36
10. By the Time I Get to Phoenix, *story by Jimmy Webb* ...... 39
11. Can't Be Really Gone, *story by Gary Burr* .................. 42
12. Coward of the County, *story by Billy Edd Wheeler* ....... 45
13. Delta Dawn, *story by Alex Harvey* ............................ 50
14. Desperados Waiting for a Train, *story by Guy Clark* ..... 54
15. D-I-V-O-R-C-E, *story by Bobby Braddock* .................. 57
16. Everlasting Love, *story by Buzz Cason* ....................... 60
17. Everything Is Beautiful, *story by Ray Stevens* ............. 64
18. Gentle on My Mind, *story by Betty Harford* ............... 67
19. Ghost in This House, *story by Hugh Prestwood* ........... 71
20. Golden Ring, *story by Bobby Braddock* ..................... 74
21. Gone Country, *story by Bob McDill* .......................... 77
22. Good Ole Boys Like Me, *story by Bob McDill* ............. 80
23. Green, Green Grass of Home, *story by Curly Putman* ..... 83
24. Halfway Home Café, *story by Ricky Skaggs* ................ 87

25.  Harper Valley PTA, *story by Tom T. Hall*..............................90

26.  Have You Forgotten? *story by Darryl Worley*.........................94

27.  He Didn't Have to Be, *story by Kelley Lovelace* ......................99

28.  He Stopped Loving Her Today, *story by Curly Putman* ........103

29.  Here in the Real World, *story by Mark Irwin*......................106

30.  Hey Cinderella, *story by Suzy Bogguss*................................109

31.  Highway 40 Blues, *story by Larry Cordle* ...........................113

32.  Holes in the Floor of Heaven, *story by Billy Kirsch*..............116

33.  How Do You Get That Lonely? *story by Rory Feek* .............120

34.  I Believe, *story by Skip Ewing*.........................................124

35.  I Can't Make You Love Me, *story by Mike Reid*....................128

36.  I Fall to Pieces, *story by Harlan Howard*............................132

37.  I Hope You Dance, *story by Tia Sillers* ...............................137

38.  I Love the Way You Love Me, *story by Victoria Shaw*..........144

39.  I Run to You, *story by Tom Douglas*...................................147

40.  I Was Country When Country Wasn't Cool,
     *story by Dennis Morgan*...................................................150

41.  It Matters to Me, *story by Mark D. Sanders* .......................153

42.  Jackson, *story by Billy Edd Wheeler*...................................156

43.  Jesus Take the Wheel, *story by Hillary Lindsey*...................160

44.  Johnny Cash Is Dead and His House Burned Down,
     *story by Larry Gatlin*.......................................................164

45.  Letting Go, *story by Doug Crider*......................................167

46.  Little Rock, *story by Tom Douglas* ....................................170

47.  Live Like You Were Dying, *story by Craig Wiseman* ............173

48.  Long Black Train, *story by Josh Turner* ..............................177

49.  Long Black Veil, *story by Buck Wilkin*................................182

50.  Love, Me, *story by Skip Ewing*.........................................185

51.  Mamas Don't Let Your Babies Grow Up to Be Cowboys,
     *story by Patsy Bruce*.......................................................188

52.  Man of Constant Sorrow, *story by Dan Tyminski* .................191

53.  Marie Laveau, *story by Bobby Bare* ...................................196

54.  Maybe It Was Memphis, *story by Michael Anderson* ............199

55.  Mississippi Squirrel Revival, *story by Buddy Kalb*................204

56.  Mr. Bojangles, *story by Jerry Jeff Walker* .............................208

57. Murder on Music Row, *story by Larry Cordle* ....................212
58. My List, *story by Rand Bishop* ...............................216
59. My Son, *story by Jan Howard* ................................220
60. Not That Different, *story by Karen Taylor-Good
    and Joie Scott* .................................................223
61. Old Dogs, Children and Watermelon Wine,
    *story by Tom T. Hall* ..........................................227
62. Old Hippie, *story by David Bellamy* ..........................231
63. On Angel's Wings, *story by Karen Taylor-Good* ..............237
64. Online, *story by Chris DuBois* ..............................241
65. Reuben James, *story by Alex Harvey* ........................245
66. She Thinks I Still Care, *story by Dickey Lee* ...............249
67. Simple Man, *story by Charlie Daniels* .......................252
68. Smoky Mountain Rain, *story by Dennis Morgan* ...............256
69. Somebody's Prayin' *story by Ricky Skaggs* ...................259
70. Something in Red, *story by Angela Kaset* ....................262
71. Southern Voice, *story by Bob DiPiero* .......................266
72. Strawberry Wine, *story by Matraca Berg* .....................270
73. That's Just About Right, *story by Jeff Black* ...............273
74. That's My Job, *story by Gary Burr* ..........................277
75. The Cape, *story by Jim Janosky* .............................281
76. The Dance, *story by Tony Arata* .............................285
77. The Devil Went Down to Georgia,
    *story by Charlie Daniels* .....................................289
78. The Famous Lefty Flynn's, *story by Jamie Johnson* ...........293
79. The Good Stuff, *story by Craig Wiseman* .....................296
80. The Grand Tour, *story by Norro Wilson* ......................301
81. The Highwayman, *story by Jimmy Webb* ........................304
82. The House That Built Me, *story by Allen Shamblin* ...........307
83. The Most Beautiful Girl, *story by Norro Wilson* .............311
84. The River, *story by Victoria Shaw* ..........................315
85. The Song Remembers When, *story by Hugh Prestwood* ..........318
86. The Streak, *story by Ray Stevens* ...........................322
87. The Thunder Rolls, *story by Pat Alger* ......................327
88. This One's for the Girls, *story by Hillary Lindsey* .........331

89. Time Marches On, *story by Bobby Braddock* ........................ 334

90. Unanswered Prayers, *story by Pat Alger* .......................... 337

91. Uncle Pen, *story by James Monroe* ................................ 341

92. Walk on Faith, *story by Mike Reid* ............................... 344

93. Walking Away a Winner, *story by Bob DiPiero* ................... 347

94. What A Difference You've Made In My Life,
    *story by Archie Jordan* ......................................... 350

95. Where've You Been? *story by Jon Vezner* ......................... 353

96. Wichita Lineman, *story by Jimmy Webb* ........................... 358

97. Wind Beneath My Wings, *story by Larry Henley* ................ 361

98. You Had Me From Hello, *story by Skip Ewing* ..................... 365

99. You Won't Ever Be Lonely, *story by Andy Griggs* ................ 369

100. You're Gonna Miss This, *story by Ashley Gorley* ................ 373

101. You've Got to Stand for Something, *story by Aaron Tippin* ...... 377

Meet Our Authors ..................................................... 380

Song Lyric Copyrights ................................................ 383

Photo Credits ........................................................ 395

About Chicken Soup for the Soul ...................................... 397

# Foreword

As the former president of both the Country Music Association and the Academy of Country Music, even I have always been intrigued by what inspired or motivated these songwriters to create such wonderful, memorable songs.

Managing country stars like Kenny Rogers, Trisha Yearwood, Travis Tritt, Diamond Rio and Collin Raye certainly gave me a behind-the-scenes look at the creative process, but with the exception of Travis and my friend, singer/songwriter Skip Ewing, most of my artists' songs were written by others and it has never ceased to amaze me how varied and interesting are the stories behind their many hits.

Travis Tritt once said, "Country music is the soundtrack for our lives" and I've seen that over and over again. All of us have experienced things in our lives that reflect the lyrics of so many of these songs. I think that's why we are so fascinated by what it was that moved the writer to put those words into a song.

I remember many years ago a young songwriter who was living in my guest room wrote a #1 song about a difficult situation I was experiencing in my personal life. (I thought perhaps he should have paid *me* royalties on that.)

Another thing I love about this book is it brings to the forefront so many great writers who rarely get the recognition they so richly deserve. It's eye-opening to see how many songs we attribute solely to the artist who performed them rather than the writer who created them. Most people think Willie Nelson and Waylon Jennings wrote

"Mamas Don't Let Your Babies Grow Up To Be Cowboys" when it actually was Patsy and Ed Bruce. And Collin Raye is so identified with "Love Me" that it's easy to think he wrote it when, in fact, it was the work of Skip Ewing and Max T. Barnes.

Of course, the writers have other compensation. I once returned from Europe with my client, the late John Hartford, and in his mailbox we found a package with dozens of royalty checks for his Glen Campbell hit, "Gentle On My Mind." They totaled nearly $100,000 and John and I sat on his living room floor and tossed the checks up in the air as we laughed and celebrated this unexpected windfall.

A few years back I produced an award-winning television special called *A Day In The Life Of Country Music* where we sent 24 different film crews out to follow country stars for 24 hours. What struck me when I looked at the footage from that show is how much of a star's day is spent just like the rest of us, being a real person, living a real life, rather than the glamour and glitter we all associate with stardom. I guess that's why they sing songs that remind us all of what we're going through in our own lives.

Speaking of producing, I'll never forget the moment, sitting on the set of Kenny Rogers' first *Gambler* movie, when his co-star, Bruce Boxleitner turned to me and said, "The next film you guys should do is Kenny's current hit, 'Coward of the County.'" I called CBS that very day and made a deal to make that song into a television movie. At first Kenny resisted doing the project, but eventually he went ahead and delivered what I still consider his best ever acting performance.

The story in the song "Coward of The County" was so strong that the picture basically wrote itself. Still, I always wondered what had inspired the songwriters to create it and how they came to call the villains in the piece the Gatlins. I was particularly curious because Kenny toured often with Larry Gatlin and his brothers and kiddingly referred to them when he sang the song. In these pages you'll learn the true story of how Billy Edd Wheeler and Roger Bowling decided to use that name in the song.

Another song in this collection that I was closely associated with is Hugh Prestwood's brilliant "The Song Remembers When," which my then-client Trisha Yearwood recorded. Reading Hugh's description of how he came to write that song reminds me of what wonderful poets so many of our best songwriters are. He mentions loving Robert Frost, Edwin A. Robinson and Emily Dickinson and taking direct inspiration from a poem by Anne Sexton. He also talks about how he drew directly on things he was experiencing at the time. As he talks about driving through the clouds in Denver and hearing one of his own songs on the car radio, the images of the beautiful video Trisha did for the song comes to mind.

The story Jon Vezner tells about what brought him to write "Where've You Been?"—a song that became such a huge hit for Kathy Mattea—will literally make you cry. His publisher did exactly that when he played it for her. Music means so much to us. We don't just listen to it; we work out to it, make love to it, sing along with it, and relate to it in so many ways. Jon's journey with this song also is illustrative of the serendipitous nature of getting a song recorded.

Reading Alex Harvey's explanation of how he adapted co-writer Barry Etris' "Reuben James" is also quite a revelation. He drew on his and his father's experiences and adapted them to the song. I was managing Kenny Rogers when Alex's persistence finally paid off and Kenny sat down and listened to Alex and his music. It shows you writing a song is only part of the game. You've got to really believe in yourself and your material and keep plugging away to make something happen.

Also, don't miss reading Alex Harvey's story of how he came to write "Delta Dawn" with Larry Collins. Artists are often motivated by tragedies or hard times, but this one will take your breath away. No wonder so many artists recorded that song. It truly came from Alex's heart and as he said, "it literally wrote itself." I've heard the same thing many times from writers but this one makes a total believer out of me.

Collin Raye had a #1 hit with the Karen Taylor-Good and Joie Scott song "Not That Different" several years before I began managing him. Still, I got to hear the song over and over as Collin performed it at show after show and audiences sang along to these moving lyrics.

That's one more reason I love reading the story of how these two ladies collaborated on the song while living far apart in two different cities and how Joie eventually moved to Nashville on a dare.

And I guess it is a songwriter's dream to have a hit the size of Curly Putman's "Green, Green Grass of Home." There have been something like 700 different recordings of that song worldwide and he's still writing away for (Sony) Tree Publishing 45 years later. But these are just a few of the 101 stories in this book.

I've been waiting a long time for someone to assemble a book like this. My cowboy hat's off to Randy Rudder, Mark Victor Hansen and Jack Canfield for the incredible work that went into gathering and editing the treasure trove of delightful and revealing stories that make this book such a terrific read.

You'll laugh, you'll cry, you'll be amazed and entertained. The next time someone says, "I wonder why they wrote that?" you'll know right where to go to get the answer. And if, by chance, you're one of those people who love to write music and lyrics, you'll get all the motivation you could ever ask for in the pages of this book. Enjoy it.

~Ken Kragen

# Introduction

As a long-time music journalist, I have always been fascinated by two questions: *What makes a song a hit?* and *Where do song-writers get the ideas for songs?* What are those intangible factors that cause one song to resonate with listeners across cultures and continents, and another equally strong song to fade into obscurity? Throughout the course of talking with the songwriters included in this collection, I discovered there are perhaps as many possible answers to that question as there are songs and songwriters.

The late Bill Monroe, Father of Bluegrass, spoke of the "ancient tones" that reside in our collective unconscious and are passed down from generation to generation through folk songs, lore, and—who knows?—possibly even genetically. In this collection, Bill's son James tells us more about the inspiration behind his father's classic bluegrass fiddle standard, "Uncle Pen."

Jimmy Webb, writing on what is possibly the shortest, yet most covered, song in his amazing catalog, says it is still a mystery to him why "Wichita Lineman" has been so popular. "It's a lonely, romantic, prairie gothic image," he says of the lineman working on the plains. "I definitely tapped into it and used it with 'Wichita Lineman,' which is also, of course, a love story about a guy who can't get over a woman." Webb reveals he wasn't even finished with the song when he sent it to the studio for Glen Campbell to hear—that he intended to add another verse and chorus later, but the song was arranged and recorded before he knew it.

Southern literature and poetry certainly have a solid place in inspiring country music lyrics as well. Alex Harvey ("Delta Dawn") credits Robert Frost and Carl Sandburg, along with French street poet Rimbaud (who influenced Bob Dylan's writing), as having a big impact on him. Bob McDill is a fan of author Robert Penn Warren and playwright Tennessee Williams, and credits them for having influenced his songwriting. McDill alludes to "those Williams boys: Hank and Tennessee" in "Good Ole Boys Like Me."

It's also surprising how often William Faulkner pops up in country music lyrics. The bard of Oxford, Mississippi is alluded to in both Pam Tillis's "Maybe It Was Memphis" (written by Michael Anderson), and Tim McGraw's "Southern Voice" (written by Bob DiPiero and Tom Douglas.)

A number of other songwriters in *Chicken Soup for the Soul: Country Music* noted the influence of film and theater on their writing. Tony Arata wrote Garth Brooks' hit, "The Dance," after seeing *Peggy Sue Got Married.* John Hartford wrote "Gentle on My Mind" after he and his wife Betty watched *Dr. Zhivago* together one evening in 1966. And Billy Edd Wheeler, while a graduate theater student at Yale, wrote the Johnny Cash/June Carter Cash classic, "Jackson," after reading *Who's Afraid of Virginia Woolf?* Go figure that one.

According to many of the writers in this collection, the songwriting Muse often manifests at the oddest times and in the oddest places. Tom T. Hall finished "Old Dogs, Children, and Watermelon Wine" on the back of an airplane barf bag on his way home to Nashville from the 1972 Democratic National Convention in Miami, inspired by an old gentleman he met in the hotel bar the night before. Larry Henley finished "Wind Beneath My Wings" on a piece of scrap paper while sitting in a fishing boat. And the number of hits that have been written on bar napkins is legion.

As far as what makes a song a hit, Jimmy Webb says in addition to the obvious factors, such as the quality of the melody, the lyric, and how well the song fits a singer's voice, everything from the level of humidity in the studio to the way the song sounds in an automobile can affect how far a record makes it up the charts.

The popularity of songwriters clubs like Nashville's Bluebird Café, and television shows like PBS's *Austin City Limits* and *Legends and Lyrics* attest to the fact that many music fans of all genres share my curiosity about the inspirations behind songs. So here are the stories behind 101 classic country songs, spanning five decades, by some of Nashville's top tunesmiths. They are songs born of dreams, joy, pain, anger, love found, love lost, family, faith, courage, pity, compassion, and honor. They are, as many songwriters say, "life set to music." Happy reading.

I would like to thank a number of people in Nashville who went above and beyond the call of duty to help put me in touch with many of the songwriters included in this collection. They include Gerilynn Pearce at Universal Music Publishing, Aaron Mercer at Sony/ATV Music Publishing, Kissy Black and Dawn Delvo at Lotos Nile Marketing, and Vanessa Davis of Splash! Public Relations, and Taylor Lindsey.

I would like to thank my wife Clare Rudder and daughter Abigail for being so supportive during this project, and my mother Jane Rudder, who has always been my biggest fan. I also want to thank Bob Jacobs and Leigh Holmes at Chicken Soup for the Soul Publishing for giving me this opportunity and for their tireless efforts in helping me assemble the manuscript, photographer Alan Mayor for coming through with so many photos, and all my friends at Joy Church International in Mt. Juliet, Tennessee. I am truly a blessed man.

~Randy Rudder

# 16th Avenue

*Story by Thom Schuyler*
*Song written by Thom Schuyler*
*Recorded by Lacy J. Dalton*

I remember quite vividly where I was when I wrote "16th Avenue." My wife and I had just settled into being married and had our first child. We had bought a little bungalow near the 100 Oaks Mall area in Nashville. It was late one Friday night and I was just picking around at home. I really didn't even have an idea. It wasn't one of those songs where I thought, "This is a great idea. I can't wait to start writing." I didn't even know what I was doing! I just started writing the song.

I scribbled down probably three verses and then I thought it was too much of an "industry" kind of song. It didn't really have the structure of a commercial song. It didn't even have a chorus. So I just threw it in the desk drawer.

About three months later, I played it for my publisher, Even Stevens. He was working with Eddie Rabbitt then, and he had a publishing company on Music Row. He asked me if I was working on anything, and I told him yes, but I didn't think it was very commercial. I played it for him and his eyes got as big as saucers. He said, "Where did that come from?" and I told him I didn't know. He said, "Well, work on it some more."

I'm an absurdly practical guy. I was prepared to come to Nashville, and I had a little bit of money saved, so I never really stayed at any of the boarding houses on Music Row or lived in my car or any of the things mentioned in the song, but I would observe other people who did and listen to their stories.

Once I had finished the song, we did a little demo of it. There was a guy named Jerry Smith, who has worked with a lot of new artists over the years to help them get their start. He was plugging some songs for Even Stevens and Eddie Rabbitt and he took "16th Avenue" and another song I had written called "My Old Yellow Car" down to producer Billy Sherrill's office at Columbia. He came back and said that Billy liked them both, but "My Old Yellow Car" was his favorite.

Two or three days later, Billy called me at the publishing house and asked me if I would come down to his office and visit with him, which was quite a thrill for a young writer like me. He was very generous with his time and he ended up recording both of those songs with Lacy J. Dalton, a singer he was producing then.

They used "16th Avenue" to open the Country Music Association Awards Show in 1982. Lacy came out and sang it, and they did this really wonderful montage of downtown Nashville photos, and cats walking around with guitar cases and things like that on the screen behind her. It was a very nice piece, and then Columbia put it out as a single. It really had its run on big radio in the early part of 1983.

From time to time, when I hear it, I'm reminded what a great recording it was, and how well it was produced and how great her vocal was. It's only been recorded twice as far as I know. Maybe there are certain songs that need to be recorded only once and should be remembered in their original form.

Honestly, to this day, if there is any one thing I've done in this town that I am associated with, it's that song. I still think of it as an insider song. It did get into the Top 10, and it was a big record for Lacy, and it still gets played a lot, but I've had bigger hits. I've had number ones, but people don't always remember them. But they remember this song. Some people call it "the songwriters' anthem," and that's quite an honor.

# 16th Avenue

From the corners of the country, from the cities and the farms
With years and years of livin' tucked up underneath their arms,
They walked away from everything just to see a dream come true
So God bless the boys who make the noise on 16th Avenue.

With a million dollar spirit and an old flat top guitar,
They drive to town with all they own in a hundred dollar car,
'Cause one time someone told them about a friend of a friend
   they knew,
Who owns, you know, a studio on 16th Avenue.

Now some are born to money. They never had to say survive
And others swing a nine pound hammer just to stay alive
There's cowboys, drunks and Christians, mostly white and
   black and blue,
They've all dialed the phone direct to home from 16th Avenue.

Oh, but then one night in some empty room where no curtains
   ever hung,
Like a miracle some golden words roll off of someone's tongue,
And after years of being nothing they're all lookin' right at you,
And they for awhile they'll go in style on 16th Avenue.

Hey it looks so uneventful, so quiet and discreet,
But a lot of lives were changed there on that little one-way street,
'Cause they walked away from everything just to see a dream
   come true,
So God bless the boys who make the noise on 16th Avenue.

# All-American Boy

Story by Bobby Bare
Song written by Bobby Bare
Recorded by Bobby Bare
(under the name of Bill Parsons)

I grew up in southern Ohio, and I knew I had to go somewhere else to do something with my music. I couldn't get anything going in Portsmouth, Ohio. I was too chicken to go to Nashville, because that was where all my heroes lived. I didn't think there was room for me down there, so I decided to go to L.A. I was in Portsmouth one night and I saw a guy with a Palomino Club bumper sticker on his car with California plates and a Nudie suit who said he was going to L.A. So, my steel guitar player and I decided to go with him. I was always pretty loose like that. That was how I wound up on the West Coast. This was in 1954 and I was 19 years old.

In 1958, I wrote "All-American Boy" about a rock and roll picker getting drafted into the Army. I recorded it a few days before I went into basic training in Fort Knox, Kentucky. I was doing a demo on my old buddy, Bill Parsons, back at King Studios in Cincinnati. There were about fifteen minutes left in the session and I'd been working on this song. It was an old "talking blues" kind of thing. We spent most of the time doing a song on my friend and then I put it down real quick, left the studio, and went off to join the Army.

This record label in Cincinnati, Fraternity Records, heard it and put it out and, within days, it was the biggest record in America, and here I was in the Army! And since Bill had booked the session, his name was on the record. It was my voice on the record, but my name wasn't there!

I was drafted about six months after Elvis went into the service, so when the song hit, everybody thought it was about him. When it hit #2 on the charts, Bill called me up, scared to death, and said, "What am I going to do?" I said, "Just ride it out. Buy yourself a car or something. It will be forgotten in six months anyway."

He said, "They want me to do the Dick Clark show in Philadelphia." And I said, "Well, do it. You're going to be lip-synching anyway. You can lip-synch me as well as I can lip-synch me." So he went to Philadelphia and lip-synched my voice on *American Bandstand*, and then they had a big party for him in New York.

That was about the only hit that Bill had, as far as I know. I think a lot of people knew it was me anyway. It was probably fortunate that my name wasn't on the record though, because I would have been labeled a novelty singer and it might have killed my career. I never would have had big hits like "Detroit City." I would have been a one-hit wonder.

# All-American Boy

Gather 'round, cats, and I'll tell you a story
About how to become an All-American Boy
Buy you a guitar and put it in tune
And you'll be rockin' and rollin' soon
(recite) Showin' off, hittin' hot licks, and all that jazz

Well, I bought me a guitar a year ago
Learned how to play in a day or so
And all around town it was well understood
That I was knockin' 'em out like Johnny B. Goode
(recite) Hittin' them hot licks, yeah number one

Well, I'd practice all day
And up into the night
My papa's hair was turnin' white
'Cause he didn't like rock 'n 'roll
He said, "You can stay, boy
But that's gotta go
(recite) He's a square
He just didn't dig me, at all

So I took my guitar, picks and all
And bid farewell to my poor ol' pa
And I split for Memphis where they say "Y'all"
Them swingin' cats are havin' a ball
(recite) Sessions, hot licks.
They dig me

I was rockin' and boppin'
And I was getting' the breaks
The girls all said that I had what it takes
When up stepped a man with a big cigar
He said "Come here cat
I'm gonnna make you a star
(recite) I'll put you on Bandstand
Buy you a Cadillac
Sign here, kid."

Well, I signed my name and became a star
Havin' a ball with my guitar
Driving a big long Cadillac
And fightin' the girls off my back
They just kept a comin'
Screamin,' yeah. They like it.

Well, I picked my guitar

With a great big grin
And the money just kept on pourin' in
But then one day my Uncle Sam
said, (knock, knock,, knock) "Here I am."
(recite) Your Uncle Sam needs you, boy
I'm gonna cut your hair off
Ah, take this rifle, kid.
Gimme that guitar…

# Almost Home

*Story by Craig Morgan*
*Song written by Kerry Kurt Phillips*
*and Craig Morgan*
*Recorded by Craig Morgan*

I was talking to my wife on the phone one day and she was complaining about me being on the road so much. I told her, "Just relax. It won't be long. I'm almost home." I thought that might be a great song idea, so I wrote it down.

A little later, I sat down with Kerry Kurt Phillips and we started writing it. We beat it around for a month or so. We were taking it from the relationship angle. Then, I was driving into Nashville one day to try to write with Kerry some more, and there was a homeless guy standing on the Demonbreun Street Bridge near Music Row, holding up a sign. I told Kerry about it when I saw him. I said I felt sorry for the guy. He knew the guy, who was in pretty bad shape, and he said, "Yeah, that old boy's almost home." And we looked at each other and said, "That's it."

It took us three or four sessions to get it down. Kerry is a pretty particular writer. We wrote it three or four different ways, trying to figure out exactly what we wanted it to say. The lines about running through the cottonwood trees and the Calico Creek came from him. Calico Creek is an actual creek near where he grew up. I wrote the lines about walking down an old dirt road, past a field of hay that had just been mowed, being chased by the honeybees, drip-drying in the summer breeze. I was reminiscing about my boyhood growing up in Kingston Springs, near Nashville. I can still smell that hay every time I sing that song.

"Almost Home" was the 2003 Nashville Songwriters Association Song of the Year, and it is still one of the most requested songs. A gentleman told me at a show once that before his father-in-law passed away he had requested the song be played at his funeral.

Kerry and I never discussed what was meant by "almost home," but, as I found out later, we might have looked at it differently. To me, I just thought he was going back home in his dream, but in Kerry's mind, he was ready to pass on. But that's what's great about co-writing: two different writers bring two different perspectives to a song.

It got pitched around. George Strait had it on hold for a while. I hadn't planned on cutting it myself. Then one day, I called my producer and said, "We just wrote a great country song." And I read him the lyric over the phone. At the time, he had some land over in Hickman County, forty-two acres of which I wanted. He told me he would trade me those forty-two acres in exchange for publishing on that song. I said, "Well, if you think it's that good, maybe I'll just hold onto it."

Trace Adkins and I almost got into a fight about it at the Opry one night. I was there in my dressing room and he came and stood in the doorway. He filled it plumb up, of course, since he's about 6'6". He said, "I want to know how the hell you got that song, 'Almost Home.' I should have cut that thing."

I said, "Are you kidding me? How do you think I got it?"

He said, "Do I look like I'm kidding?"

I thought we were fixing to come to blows there for a moment. I said, "I wrote it."

He said, "Well, I'll be damned." But we got over it. We're good friends now.

# Almost Home

He had plastic bags wrapped 'round his shoes
He was covered with the evening news
Had a pair of old wool socks on his hands

The bank sign was flashing "5 below"
It was freezing rain an' spittin' snow
He was curled up behind some garbage cans

I was afraid that he was dead
I gave him a gentle shake
When he opened up his eyes
I said, "Old man, are you ok?"

CHORUS:
He said, "I just climbed out of a cottonwood tree
I was runnin' from some honey bees
Drip dryin' in the summer breeze
After jumpin' into Calico Creek
I was walkin' down an old dirt road
Past a field of hay that had just been mowed
Man I wish you'd just left me alone
'Cause I was almost home..."

Then he said, "I was just comin' round the barn"
'Bout the time you grabbed my arm
When I heard momma holler, "Son hurry up."
I was close enough for my old nose
To smell fresh cobbler on the stove
And I saw daddy loadin' up the truck
Cane poles on the tailgate
Bobbers blowin' in the wind
Since July of '55

That's as close as I've been

CHORUS

BRIDGE:
I said, "Old man you're gonna freeze to death"
Let me drive you to the mission
He said "Boy if you'd left me alone
Right now I'd be fishin'"

CHORUS

# American Honey

*Story by Hillary Lindsey*
*Song written by Hillary Lindsey, Shane*
*Stevens, Cary Ryan Barlowe*
*Recorded by Lady Antebellum*

I was on a trip to Gatlinburg in the Smoky Mountains with Shane Stevens and Cary Barlowe. While we were there, we saw a sign for American Honey whiskey, so that's where we got the title.

We started writing it while we were still there in Gatlinburg. We wrote the lines, "She grew up on a side of the road /where church bells ring and strong love grows." We all grew up in the South. Cary is actually the son of a former preacher. Shane is from North Carolina, and I'm from a tiny town in Georgia, so we had a lot in common as far as our upbringing.

As the story unfolded, we realized that it was a story about all three of us growing up and missing our innocence and wanting to get back to that. There are a lot of metaphors. It's not really a straight-ahead kind of song. It's more allegorical, which is kind of cool because it lets the listeners read into it whatever they want.

We all get wrapped up in our jobs and, as songwriters, you worry that you're never going to write another song or another hit and, before you know it, you act like you're old and out of ideas, when you're not. If you allow that to happen, you can worry yourself into oblivion. The innocence and the freedom and the lightness that comes with being young and not knowing so much — and missing that — is what we were going for.

We just did a work tape and sent it over to Paul Worley, Lady Antebellum's producer, who flipped over it. We weren't sure it was going to get cut until later on. They actually had their first album close to being wrapped up, so we weren't sure it was going to happen. We were hopeful, but just thought it might have been too late to get on the album. But the band loved it and they decided to add it at the last minute. The next thing we knew it was cut, and then it was a single, and then it hit #1. I love it when it happens that way!

# American Honey

She grew up on a side of the road
Where church bells ring and strong love grows
She grew up good
She grew up slow
Like American honey

Steady as a preacher
Free as a weed
Couldn't wait to get goin'
But wasn't quite ready to leave
So innocent, pure and sweet
American honey

CHORUS:
There's a wild, wild whisper
Blowin' in the wind
Callin' out my name like a long lost friend
Oh I miss those days as the years go by
Oh nothin's sweeter than summertime
And American honey

Get caught in the race
Of this crazy life
Tryin' to be everything
Can make you lose your mind
I just want to go back in time
To American honey, yeah

Gone for so long now
Gotta get back to her somehow
To American honey

CHORUS

# American Made

*Story by Pat McManus*
*Song written by Pat McManus and Bob*
  *DiPiero*
*Recorded by The Oak Ridge Boys*

I grew up in the Pittsburgh area and started writing songs when I was about 10 years old. I used to write them for my brothers' girlfriends. My brothers would claim they wrote them. Then when they broke up with the girls and started dating new ones, I would just change the girl's name in the song so it would fit the next girlfriend. They weren't paying me anything, so I wasn't going to write a new song every time they broke up with someone.

I really wanted to break into the entertainment business, but I didn't know how, so I studied broadcasting at Columbia School of Broadcasting. I thought that would get me in the door to show business, but I realized later that I really just wanted to sing and write songs. I quit broadcasting school and moved to Nashville in the early 1970s.

The first few weeks in Nashville, a couple of really bizarre things happened to me. I was staying in a boarding house near Music Row, paying them something like $5 a night. One night I went to listen to some music in a little lounge in a hotel on Broadway. While I was there, I asked if I could audition to play. I figured if I could pick up a few bucks, I could pay for my room and something to eat and that would allow me to keep writing songs full-time.

A few days later, I was singing there and a lady who was listening to me introduced herself and said her name was Joan Edwards. She said, "I think you are really going to do well in this town, and I want to help you." I was just blown away, but a little skeptical, too. She told me I needed to stick it out and then she said she wanted to give me enough money to pay my bills for the next six weeks or so and asked me how much that would be. I said I didn't know exactly, but I guessed it would be about $500. Then she left.

The next day, I was at the boarding house and the landlady called me down and said someone was there with a package for me to sign. It was a delivery courier and he had a letter from Joan with a check in it for $500. So I walked to a nearby bank—I walked everywhere then because I didn't have a car—and they looked at me a little skeptically because I was dressed kind of grungy and had an out-of-state license and had a pretty big check to cash. Just then, the manager walked by and said, "Is there a problem?" When he saw the name on the check, he said, "That's from Joan Edwards. It's good. Cash it." So I had my expenses taken care of for a while.

Then, a few days after that, I just happened to be walking by the RCA building. I saw some musicians going into the building, so I just walked in behind them like I knew what I was doing. When they got to the end of the hallway, they turned right and I turned left. I went to the first office that had a light on, and I knocked. The guy inside told me to come in and he asked me what I wanted. I told him I just wanted someone to listen to my songs. He said, "How did you get in here?" and I told him what I did. He said, "Sit down. Anybody who's got the guts to do that has to want this pretty bad."

So he listened to my songs said he liked a few of them. I later found out he was the president of RCA Records! He later agreed to buy ten of my songs for $100 each and half of the publishing rights. So I had $1,000 plus the money I had gotten from Joan. That made $1,500, which was a lot of money back then! It was like God or an angel was just leading me by the hand those first few weeks.

I moved to L.A. for a few years after that and had a few pop songs recorded, including by The 5th Dimension and a singer named Carl Graves, but I eventually came back to Nashville and started writing for Bob Beckham at Combine Music. This was where Kristofferson and Billy Swan and a whole slew of other writers had worked.

One day I came into the Combine offices and Bob DiPiero was there writing. He and I had been getting together two or three times a week to write. He was up on the third floor of the building, which they had converted to writing rooms and a kitchen.

Bob said, "I got this idea and I really want to write it with you, but I don't know where it's going exactly." I told him I was on my way to sing a jingle for Natural Light beer over at Buddy Killen's studio and I couldn't stay. "It will just take a minute," he said. I called the studio and asked if they could wait a few minutes and they told me it was okay. So Bob said to me, "Here's the idea. It seems like everything I buy is from another country, but my girl is 100% red-blooded American" or something like that. So we came up with the lines, "My baby is American made / born and bred in the USA."

I went and sang the demo for Natural Light beer and came back to the Combine offices later, where we continued working on it. We weren't sure we could use brand names in the song because we had lines like, "I got a Nikon camera, a Sony color TV," etc., but then we realized that it would be like free advertising for the products so we didn't think they would have any problem with it. We finished the song in a few days and then started pitching the demo.

Later we heard that the Oak Ridge Boys were interested and wanted to put it on hold and we said "Sure." They changed the melody just a little bit and then said they wanted to sing it on the road to see how it played live before they recorded it.

They came back after a few weeks and said they wanted to record the song. Not only that, they wanted to name their album *American Made* and call their next tour the "American-Made" tour. That was how great the audience reaction was. This was 1983, during the Reagan years, so patriotism and things like that were becoming hip again, and the crowds just loved it.

They put out a whole line of merchandise to go along with the tour: hats and jackets and T-shirts. And when the single was released, it debuted in the 30s, I think. That was one of the first times that a song debuted that high, and it eventually hit #1 for two weeks.

Later, there was an executive from the J. Walter Thompson ad agency who heard the song on the radio and decided it would make a great jingle for Miller Beer: "Miller's made the American way, born and brewed in the USA" was how it went. They had a group that sounded like the Oak Ridge Boys sing the jingle and they made several other versions sounding like other pop stars that were hot at the time. The single and album sold well and the song even became one of BMI's Million-Airs (a million times aired on radio), but I think we made more money over the long haul from the jingle than we did on the record royalties and airplay. That was pretty ironic considering the day I wrote the song I had just sung a jingle for Natural Light, which is made by Anheuser-Busch!

One of my favorite memories from this song happened the next year, when Bob and I went to Fan Fair (now called CMA Fest), which was held at the Tennessee State Fairgrounds. As we were walking back to our cars after seeing one of the shows there, we saw a man and his wife walking toward us with American-Made T-shirts and hats. We didn't say anything, but as we passed by them, we saw the guy reach down and pat his wife's bottom and he started singing, "My baby is American made." Bob and I just looked at each other and laughed. You can't pay for moments like that.

# American Made

Seems everything I buy these days
Has got a foreign name
From the kind of car I drive
To my video game
I got a Nikon camera
A Sony color TV

But the one that I love is from the U.S.A.
And standing next to me.

CHORUS:
My baby is American made
Born and bred in the U.S.A.
From her silky long hair to her sexy long legs
My baby is American made.

She looks good in her tight blue jeans
She bought in Mexico
And she loves wearing French perfume
Everywhere we go
But when it comes to the lovin' part
One thing is true
My baby's genuine U.S.A., red, white and blue

CHORUS

# American Saturday Night

Story by Ashley Gorley
Song written by Ashley Gorley, Brad Paisley,
and Kelley Lovelace
Recorded by Brad Paisley

**B**rad came up with the idea for this song, and he nailed the chorus: "French kiss, Italian ice / Spanish moss in the moonlight / just another American Saturday Night." Once we got there, it set the stage for the rest of the song. From there, he and Kelley Lovelace and I took off with it. Kelley and I had been working on it for a couple of days, and then we got together with Brad just to see if all of our cultural references were fitting right. We finished it at Brad's house about 1:00 or 2:00 in the morning. He's a late-night writer. I've left his house at 4:00 or 5:00 in the morning several times.

After we finished the song, that became the name for the album and then the tour, so the concept really caught on from there, and it also became a #1 single, too.

We were really proud of the fact that it went to a deeper level, beyond just the typical "redneck, Saturday night bonfire" kind of song. It was really more about the idea of a typical New York street fair where all these different cultures come together. We all came up with the different ideas, whether it was the toga party, or the Brazilian leather, or the Canadian bacon, or the German car — it was just about celebrating all the different influences that make America, America. You can get a little taste of the world in about three hours in some neighborhoods like that.

Brad loves coming up with those new ideas, or maybe a new take on an old idea. That was a record where he wanted to depart a little bit from just using gimmicks or silliness, and it's pretty apparent from the singles they've come out with. When you're writing a lyric, it's tough to be clever, but not necessarily funny, to make it a fun song, but to be thoughtful at the same time. He played the song at the Capitol on the Fourth of July, too, so that made it pretty special.

When they started talking about doing the video, Brad called me up and said he wanted me to be in it. He said he wanted Kelley and I to make cameo appearances in it, but I was in London, so I called him and said, "Ah, man, I can't. I'm out of the country." So nothing else was said about it, and the next thing I knew I saw a copy of the video and he has my head superimposed on some guy at the toga party wearing this blue, Elvis-looking leisure suit. He got my head off the Internet somewhere and cut if off and put it on this guy's body. My kids have it on their iPods and they get a big kick out of it. I don't know whether he was getting back at me for blowing off his video or what, but I thought it was hilarious when I saw it.

## American Saturday Night

She's got Brazilian leather boots on the pedal of her German car
Listening to the Beatles singing "Back in the USSR"
Yeah, she's goin' around the world tonight
but she ain't leavin' here
She's just going to meet her boyfriend down at the street fair

It's a French kiss, Italian ice
Spanish moss in the moonlight
Just another American Saturday night

There's a big toga party tonight down at Delta Chi
They've got Canadian bacon on their pizza pie
They've got a cooler for cold Coronas and Amstel Lights
It's like we're all livin' in a big ol' cup
just fire up the blender, and mix it all up

It's a French kiss, Italian ice
margaritas in the moonlight
Just another American Saturday night

You know everywhere has something they're known for
Oh, but usually it washes up on our shores
My great, great, great, granddaddy stepped off of that ship
I bet he never ever dreamed we'd have all this.

You know everywhere has somethin' they're known for
Oh, but usually it washes up on our shores
Little Italy, Chinatown, sittin' there side by side
Live from New York, it's Saturday Night!

French kiss, Italian ice,
Spanish moss in the moonlight
just another American, just another American
It's just another American Saturday night

# Back When We Were Beautiful

*Story by Matraca Berg*
*Song written by Matraca Berg*
*Recorded by Matraca Berg*

This song was a result of two separate conversations that I had fairly close together. My grandmother came to visit me and we had a girl's day out and had lunch together. She was having such a good time. At one point, she stopped in the middle of eating and looked at me. I'll never forget the look on her face. It's hard to describe, but it was kind of like wonderment and surprise. She said, "I still feel like a girl on the inside. And when I look in the mirror, it's a shock to me because I *don't feel* this old."

I had the exact same conversation with my husband Jeff's mother a couple of months later. We were talking about Jeff's parents. They were very much in love and his father looked like a movie star, too. They were a great-looking couple. His father died when he was still pretty young—he was in his fifties. She was showing me pictures of them when they were out dancing at clubs and going to dinner and things like that.

I actually had the line, "Back When We Were Beautiful" scribbled down as a possible title in my idea book, but I didn't know what it was going to be about. I thought I was going to write a song about my brother and sister and I when we were young.

In the song, there are lines about this older woman feeling pain. I was thinking it was just general pains of aging, not necessarily a disease or anything. It's funny, because I'm starting to feel some of these things in my forties already, and I'm thinking, "Why is my knee doing that?"or "Why does my hip feel like that?"

I cut the song and it was put out as a single but didn't do much. I performed it on the CMA Awards, I think, just to get it out there in case somebody else wanted it. It means a lot to me, and it meant a lot that it meant a lot to other people, too. That seems to be the one I get comments on the most.

As far as the unconventional structure, that's what happens when I sit down at the piano; I become a completely different writer. There's no real chorus per se, and the melody is unusual for me. It came very quickly, though. I wasn't really thinking about structure when I wrote it.

Trisha Yearwood cut it, but hasn't put it on an album yet. Garth Fundis, her producer, said it might end up on another one later. I hope so. My own recording of it made it into the movie, *Hope Floats*, so that was pretty exciting!

# Back When We Were Beautiful

"I guess you had to be there," she said, "You had to be."
She handed me a yellowed photograph
And then said, "See,
This was my greatest love, my one and only love
And this is me
Back when we were beautiful."

"I don't feel very different," she said, "I know it's strange
I guess I've gotten used to these little aches and pains
But I still love to dance, you know we used to dance

The night away
Back when we were beautiful, beautiful, yes."

"I hate it when they say
I'm aging gracefully
I fight it every day
I guess they never see
I don't like this at all
What's happening to me
To me."

"But I really love my grandkids," she said, "They're sweet to
        hold
They would have loved their grandpa
Those awful jokes he told
You know sometimes for a laugh, the two of us would act
Like we were old
Back when we were beautiful, beautiful, yes."

# Believe

*Story by Craig Wiseman*
*Song written by Craig Wiseman and Ronnie Dunn*
*Recorded by Ronnie Dunn (Brooks & Dunn)*

After I won a Grammy for "Live Like You Were Dying," back in my hometown of Hattiesburg, Mississippi, somebody from the local TV station wanted to come and interview my mom. They asked her questions like "What is it like being the mother to a Grammy-winning songwriter?" She went and got a couple of laundry baskets full of CDs with songs that I had written. She just dumped them on her dining room table in a pile, and the reporter said, "How does he do that? How does he write so many songs?" And my mom said, "Honestly, I don't know. He's always been interested in music, but I have no idea where all those songs come from."

Later that night, after the piece was on the news, my brother called me and said he got a call from an elderly woman. She said, "Is this the family of the lady who was on the television news tonight?" And my brother told her it was his mother who was on TV, and asked if she would like her phone number. The lady said, "If you could just relay a message for me, I would appreciate it." Then she said, "Tell your mother that all those songs came from God."

My brother said, "I spent about thirty minutes on the phone

with that lady and I was just crying my eyes out. This woman is just amazing. She has the most incredible faith."

I asked my brother to give me her number and he did. Her name was Elma Dennis. I called her one night and I think she thought she was talking to my brother at first. I said, "Ma'am, this is the song-writer up in Nashville that they were talking about on the news. I'm Craig. My brother enjoyed talking to you so much that I wanted to talk to you."

She said, "Gracious, child, what are you doing calling me all the way from Nashville? God is working in your life. I could see it in your mother's eyes on TV. I can hear it in your brother's voice and I can hear it in your voice. God is with you and God loves you and don't you ever doubt it for a minute," and just went on and on. I stood in my kitchen weeping, listening to this lady.

Cut to Ronnie Dunn of the country supergroup, Brooks & Dunn. I had another song that Ronnie's label wanted him to hear and I said, "I drive right past his house on my way home. I'll just go drop it off in his mailbox."

About 5:00 or so, I pulled up to his gate and put it on his mail-box and buzzed on the buzzer and said, "This is Craig Wiseman. I just wanted you to know that I'm dropping off a song for Ronnie Dunn." And his voice came on the speaker box and said, "Hey, come on back to the barn." He has this in-town ranch with a big barn he calls the Star Barn. He refurbished it and has his studio there and it's just gorgeous. Everybody knows that's kind of his lair back there. I went to the barn and gave him the CD with the song. It was actu-ally "Hillbilly Deluxe" and it wound up being a hit for him. Then we started talking and it turns out he has read every book that I've read and more. He collects Russian art. I was ashamed that I had put him in the hillbilly-singer "box." He's a very intelligent, well-read person.

He asked what my wife did and I said she was a minister and has her Master's Degree in Divinity from Vanderbilt. He said, "Really? You know, I almost went to seminary in Oklahoma."

I said, "Are you kidding me?" We started talking about faith and different questions we had. I told him about Elma. I told him, "Faith is like music. There is so much BS out there, but every now and then you come across the real deal. And that's Elma. Her faith and conviction were so real and so contagious. She believes so strongly."

I told Ronnie that during my conversation with her, she said, "You know child, they tell me I'm dying of cancer, but that's okay. I'm with the Lord and it's in His hands and if He wants me to stick around, I will." I told Ronnie that when you run across somebody like that and they're not preaching to you and they're not telling you what to do, they're just telling you where they're at. There's something so powerful about that. It reminded me of another friend of mine who's doing missions work now. He hardly ever even goes to church but his life has changed so drastically. And it's never like he's saying, "Look how cool I am now that I've changed." It's always, "Look how cool *that* is and *that's* where I'm going." It's so inspiring.

So Ronnie and I started trying to write a song. We were trying to run some up-tempo thing and it just wasn't working. After we got to talking about faith that night and I told him about Elma, we started writing what would eventually become "Believe."

We didn't write a word in a notebook. We didn't have a recorder. And I came up with a line or two: "I raise my hand, I bow my head. I'm finding more and more truth in the words written in red." We worked on this long, weird thing until midnight and we called it a day. Then, we both tried to forget about it.

About six months later, after Brooks & Dunn came home from their summer tour, I went back to write with Ronnie. He said, "Hey, remember that thing we were playing around with last time you were here? Let's work on that."

I started strumming and it all came back and the parts we still needed just flowed right out: "Old man Wrigley lived in that white house…." That was a little autobiographical. There was an old guy on our street. But our relationship was more like a "Dennis the Menace-Mr. Wilson" kind of thing. It wasn't quite as lofty as I cast it in the song. I used to go down to his house and I really liked him because he treated me well. There's nothing like an old guy treating a kid cool.

So Elma turned into Mr. Wrigley in the song. When Elma was

talking about her friends she was going to see soon, I wrote, "He said 'I'll see my wife and son in just a little while' / I asked him what he meant / He looked at me and smiled." We started talking about all kinds of spiritual things and we ended up finishing it. The next morning, I went back to my office and sat down with my guitar recorder and put a slow rhythm track and just sang it. I put it on a CD and took it over to his house and dropped it off. Then I was like "Man, that song is done. Now can we please write a song about honky-tonks and trucks?"

A few weeks later, Ronnie called me and said he cut it. It was amazing. Ronnie took that little recording I made and turned it into one of the coolest things that has ever happened to me in this business. It made the album, and then went on to be a single and won the CMA Song of the Year and ACM Song of the Year.

My family got to know Elma after that. My mom loved talking to her. You know, a couple of church ladies. A few months later, Elma went back for a checkup and they couldn't find any cancer. She said, "Well, you know those doctors, they think they know what they're doing, but they don't know everything."

That song is like suicide for a songwriter. The darn thing must be six minutes long and it's mostly recitation, which country music hasn't really done for about 30 years. It's not the typical Brooks & Dunn honky-tonkin' song, for sure. I mean, it had everything working against it from a technical standpoint. But it worked. And it obviously struck a chord with a lot of people who may not be holy-rollers but they just can't believe that this life is all there is.

# Believe

Old man Wrigley lived in that white house
Down the street where I grew up
Momma used to send me over with things
We struck a friendship up
I spent a few long summers out on his old porch swing

Says he was in the war when in the navy
Lost his wife, lost his baby
Broke down and asked him one time
How ya keep from going crazy?
He said "I'll see my wife and son in just a little while"
I asked him what he meant
He looked at me and smiled, said

CHORUS:
"I raise my hands, bow my head
I'm finding more and more truth in the words written in red
They tell me that there's more to life than just what I can see
Oh I believe"

Few years later I was off at college
Talkin' to mom on the phone one night
Getting all caught up on the gossip
The ins and outs of the small town life
She said "Oh by the way son, old man Wrigley's died."

Later on that night, I laid there thinkin' back
Thought about a couple long-lost summers
I didn't know whether to cry or laugh
If there was ever anybody deserved a ticket to the other side
It'd be that sweet old man who looked me in the eye, and said

CHORUS

I can't quote the book
The chapter or the verse
But you can't tell me it all ends
In a slow ride in a hearse
You know I'm more and more convinced
The longer that I live

Yeah, this can't be
No, this can't be, no this can't be all there is

CHORUS

# Bobbie Ann Mason

*Story by Mark D. Sanders*
*Song written by Mark D. Sanders*
*Recorded by Rick Trevino*

I always get a lot of ideas from book titles. That's how I wrote the song, "Bobbie Ann Mason." I loved the books *In Country* and *Shiloh and Other Stories* by Bobbie Ann Mason. After I heard the song, "Norma Jean Riley," I think that name just stuck in my head. Later, I thought, "Bobbie Ann Mason" had a similar ring to it.

I actually wrote the song about a girl who I sat behind in English class when I was a junior in high school. Her name was Sue Struck. But the only words that I could think of that rhymed with Struck I probably couldn't get played on country radio. But there's a line in the chorus that says, "How was I gonna get an education / sitting right in back of Bobbie Ann Mason" that worked pretty well.

Bobbie Ann actually called me one day. It was down at the old Starstruck building on Music Row. The receptionist called me and said, "Mark, Bobbie Ann Mason is on the phone." That shocked me. I didn't know if she would be mad. It turned out that she was a little put off by the fact that I used her name in the song, but I think she got over that. Then she wrote a column about it later on the back page of *The New Yorker*. And then *I* was a little put off because she never credited me as the writer. In her article, she quoted about a third of the lyrics in the song but never credited the songwriter. She talked about Rick Trevino a lot, but I guess she thought it would mix people up a lot if she said that he didn't write it, so she never mentioned my name. So we had an odd relationship there for a while.

The funniest thing about this, though, is that there is a bookstore in Oxford, Mississippi called Square Books. It's a really quaint little place. It's one of the few places that John Grisham has done book signings. They have a "signed first edition" club that I was a member of for about ten years. Every time Bobbie Ann would write a new book, she would participate in this signed first edition club, where the author will actually sign it to you if you want your name in the book. So she signed a couple of books to me and, after that, she started writing little notes to me like, "Okay, Mark, here's another one for you."

I still have those books with her curt little notes to me. But I don't know if she ever put it together: that I was the one who also wrote the song with her name in it.

## Bobbie Ann Mason

It wasn't the books that I didn't read
It wasn't the teach that tried to teach me
It wasn't that varsity baseball coach,
Kept on tellin' them locker room jokes, it was:

CHORUS:
Bobbie Ann Mason, back in high school.
She was way too cute, she was way too cool.
How was I gonna get an education,
Sittin' right in back of Bobbie Ann Mason.

Well, Bobbie knew her history, Bobbie knew her French,
Bobbie knew how to keep the boys in suspense.
She'd tease with a touch, she'd tease with a kiss,
I was three long years being teased by pretty Miss:

CHORUS

Yeah, Bobbie graduated first in her class.
Me, I graduated closer to last.
Bobbie went to college, she got a degree,
I got a guitar so I could sing about me and…

CHORUS

The years have taught me, the basics of math.
Divorce divides; time subtracts; takes away your hair,
Takes away your jump shot,
But it ain't gonna take all the memories I got of…

Bobbie Ann Mason, back in high school
She was way too cute, she was way too cool.
I got most of my education
Sittin' right in back of Bobbie Ann Mason.
Sittin' right in back of Bobbie Ann Mason.

# By the Time I Get to Phoenix

*Story by Jimmy Webb*
*Song written by Jimmy Webb*
*Recorded by Glen Campbell, Johnny Rivers,*
*and others*

I had an old girlfriend and the relationship wasn't going too well. So I just resolved to show her a thing or two and move back home to Oklahoma. That was a pretty stupid thing to do, and didn't do much in the way of punishing her either, of course. But it created a very interesting song. I was a staff writer at a publishing company. It was my first real writing job.

I brought it in for the Motown people to hear. It's a three-verse form. It just has three strophic verses, so it's a ballad in the traditional sense. It tells a story, and when the story is over the song is over. So the Motown guys listened to it and said, "Where is the chorus?"

I said, "There isn't going to be a chorus," and we had a pretty lively discussion over that. They were pretty much into the chorus, the hook, drum breaks, and bridges, and all the ideas they had about how to make hits. And they were right for the most part. They started talking about pitching it to Paul Petersen then, who was an actor on *The Donna Reed Show*.

The first session I went to where I heard it, though, was a Tony

Martin session. It passed into another sphere of influence and I'm not really sure exactly how that happened. It ended up as a Johnny Rivers Music copyright, and it ended up on his album.

Glen Campbell was driving down the road and heard Johnny's version on the radio. This was probably just a few months after Johnny had cut it. For a while, there was a stigma for some producers. They wouldn't listen to any song if it had ever been recorded by anyone. That's just not a very intelligent way to go about doing A&R because there are going to be some great records that get recorded but aren't hits. Some great songs have been just left behind. If you think the producers have gotten them all, you're wrong. Every writer will tell you there are at least a couple that got left by the wayside somewhere.

There are a million reasons why a song does or doesn't become a hit. I've given the matter a lot of thought and I think it's almost supernatural. A hit record is almost a small miracle. There are so many elements. Does the singer sound like he should be singing the song? Is it the right song for him? What about the arrangement? Is it overdone? Is it not big enough? What about the players? Was the drummer too heavy-handed that day? Did he have a hangover? What day of the week was it? What was the temperature in the room? Was it too humid and did it affect the instruments so that it came out sounding flat? Did it have the magic to it that translates to sounding good in a car? What makes a record sound good in a car? It's not going to be a hit if it doesn't sound good in a car. The new album of mine, *Just Across the River*, was mixed to be heard in a car.

Does the song sound like it should come out of this guy's mouth? I wrote something for Willie Nelson one time. I thought it was going to be a hit. I didn't hear him say it, but I heard someone who knew him claim that Willie said, "I just can't hear that coming out of my mouth." So that's another factor.

"By the Time I Get to Phoenix" actually ends on a chord that is out of the key signature. I wrote it in F and it ends on an A chord, a major third higher. That's the way Glen recorded it. He arranged the record. A lot of people don't know it, but Glen Campbell was a great arranger. Most of the songs that he recorded, he contributed to the arrangements, too. He had a flare for arranging and that had something to do with that record's success, too.

The city I chose, Phoenix, is right on Route 66 and it sounded right on the time-space continuum of the singer traveling on the highway, even though it's a little distorted, going from one city to the next. Sometimes as a writer, you come to a decision like that and you just flip a coin. You make decisions based on what sounds real. You want something that sounds authentic. You could try "By the Time I Get to Flagstaff," but does it work as well? Is that one of those tiny little factors that determines whether a song is a hit or not? You bet.

# By the Time I Get to Phoenix

By the time I get to Phoenix she'll be rising
She'll find the note I left hangin' on her door
She'll laugh when she reads the part that says I'm leavin'
'Cause I've left that girl so many times before

By the time I make Albuquerque she'll be working
She'll prob'ly stop at lunch and give me a call
But she'll just hear that phone keep on ringin'
Off the wall, that's all

By the time I make Oklahoma she'll be sleepin'
She'll turn softly and call my name out loud
And she'll cry just to think I'd really leave her
Though time and time I tried to tell her so
She just didn't know I would really go.

# Can't Be Really Gone

*Story by Gary Burr*
*Song written by Gary Burr*
*Recorded by Tim McGraw*

I was reading a newspaper one morning back around 1995. I think it was a local story. It may have been in the *Nashville Banner*. I read this story about a woman who was making lunch for her daughter and they had just sat down to eat it together. Then a friend of her daughter's came by play with her, so the mother let her go out to play. This girl and her mom lived close to the highway and apparently the little girl and her friend were playing too close to the highway, and she was killed by a car.

Her mother went out and found her and, of course, then had to do all of those horrible, horrible things that you have to do when someone close to you dies, especially so unexpectedly. She got home late that afternoon. In the article, it said that the mother looked over to see her daughter's sandwich sitting there still half eaten on the plate, and the first though that went through her mind was, "She can't be really gone. She still hasn't finished her lunch." And that really got to me.

Later, I started to write a song that began with the lines, "Her hat is hanging by the door / the one she bought in Mexico," and goes on to tell the story of a guy whose girl is gone, but he just can't believe it. I like the fact that the lyric is still a little ambiguous, so the listener can decide if she is dead or has left him, or is just out for the time being. Anyone who has lost a loved one, or ever suffered through a divorce, knows what it's like when people leave things behind that remind you of them.

My publisher thought it might be too much of a downer for anyone to record. Then somebody took it to Tim McGraw and played it for him on his bus and he loved it. He recorded it and then put it out as a single. It hit the Top 10 and stayed there for several weeks, and ended up being one of his biggest hits.

It didn't bother Tim that it was too sad. He didn't need someone riding off into the sunset with a happy, upbeat ending. He saw it for what it was: a very tragic, but also very powerful and emotional song.

## Can't Be Really Gone

Her hat is hanging by the door
The one she bought in Mexico
It blocked the wind,
It stopped the rain
She'd never leave that one
So, she can't be really gone

The shoes she bought on Christmas Eve
She laughed and said they called her name
It's like they're waiting in the hall
For her to slip them on
So, she can't be really gone.

I don't when she'll come back
She must intend to come back
And I've seen the error of my ways

Don't waste the tears on me.
What more proof do you need?
Just look around the room
So much of her remains.

Her book is lying on the bed
The two of hearts to mark her page
Now, who could ever walk away
At chapter twenty-one?
So, she can't be really gone.

Just look around this room
So much of her remains.

Her book is lying on the bed
The two of hearts to mark her page
Now, who could ever walk away
With so much left undone?
So, she can't be really gone.

No, she can't be really gone.

# Coward of the County

*Story by Billy Edd Wheeler*
*Song written by Billy Edd Wheeler*
*and Roger Dale Bowling*
*Recorded by Kenny Rogers*

Jerry Leiber and Mike Stoller sold my songwriting contract to United Artists and Murray Deutch at United Artists called me and said, "We want to set up an office in Nashville. Do you have any experience running a business?" I said, "Yes, I was director of alumni at Berea College in Kentucky. I had a staff and had to deal with budgets and hiring, and things like that." They said, "We'd like you to go to Nashville and set up the office." So that's how I ended up in Nashville.

One day, Roger Bowling gave me a call. He used to live in Nashville had moved to Georgia. He wrote story songs, too. He wrote "Lucille" for Kenny Rogers and several other hits. He said, "Let's get together. I'd like to write a story song. Do you have any ideas?" And I said, "Yes, I do. I'd like to write something about an underdog, a guy who comes from behind and wins." For some strange reason, I was thinking of *My Fair Lady*. They took this little cockney girl from the poor part of England and were going to make her over and teach her how to speak and walk and talk and be like a princess. My heart went out to her because they were using her. She was just an experiment for them. So I was rooting for her to show them up.

Roger and I went up to Pine Mountain, Kentucky where they were doing an outdoor drama of mine about the Cumberland Gap. I said, "Let's go up there and see how it's going." So we rented a cabin up there. Roger said, "Why don't you go fix us a drink and I'll get started?" I knew that, for Roger, "fixing a drink" meant pouring some Jack Daniel's in a glass with some ice, so I did that and came back. When I did, he said, "What do you think of this? Everyone considered him the 'coward of the county.'"

I said, "I love it. Everyone thinks he's a coward." I liked the alliteration, too. We didn't know why everyone thought he was a coward, but we had a start. So then we invented the story of how his dad died in prison, and had always told his son, "You don't have to fight to be a man."

We were trying to figure out how Tommy, the son, would have a change of heart. I had him in church praying to his father or getting a vision from him or something. He was saying, "These guys are picking on me and they think I'm a coward. I know I promised you I would never do the things you did, or fight like you did, but I think I need to." I was trying to make it very complicated—somebody would speak behind a curtain and he would think it was his father. It was like a Shakespearean tragedy or something. But it was just too complicated.

Roger said that all he had to do was take his father's picture down from the mantle. Then he wrote, "As his tears fell on his father's face, he heard those words again." Roger was a great songwriter. That really summarized it all.

We chose the name the "Gatlin boys" because we liked the sound of it. They were the ones who violated Tommy's girlfriend, Becky. We tried some other names like the Barlow boys, but they just didn't have the grit of the Gatlin boys. I didn't realize then that Larry Gatlin had dated a girl named Becky, and had written a song about her and he got mad about that later. One time, Kenny Rogers and the Gatlin brothers were on a talk show together and they started picking on him about it and he said, "Don't blame me. I didn't write the song."

We finished the song that weekend. We did a demo later and someone took it to Larry Butler, who was producing Kenny at the time. Larry recorded a lot of Roger's songs.

We liked the drama at the end, where Tommy takes all that he can take, and then goes to the bar where the Gatlin boys are. When one of them gets up to confront him and Tommy turns around, the lines read, "Hey look ol' yellow's leavin'" / But you could've heard a pin drop when Tommy stopped and locked the door."

Of course, he kicks all of their tails one by one and then says, "This one's for Becky," as he watched the last one fall. It was the perfect way to end the song and just the kind of comeback story we were looking for.

# Coward of the County

Everyone considered him the coward of the county.
He never stood one single time to prove the county wrong.
His mama named him Tommy, but folks just called him yellow.
Something always told me they were reading Tommy wrong.

He was only ten years old when his daddy died in prison.
I looked after Tommy 'cause he was my brother's son.
I still recall the final words my brother said to Tommy:
"Son, my life is over, but yours has just begun."

"Promise me, son, not to do the things I've done.
Walk away from trouble if you can.
It won't mean you're weak if you turn the other cheek.
I hope you're old enough to understand.
Son, you don't have to fight to be a man."

There's someone for everyone and Tommy's love was Becky.

In her arms he didn't have to prove he was a man.
One day while he was workin' the Gatlin boys came callin'.
They took turns at Becky. . . (whispers) and there were three of
them.

Tommy opened up the door and saw his Becky cryin'.
The torn dress, the shattered look was more than he could
stand.
He reached above the fireplace and took down his daddy's
picture.
As the tears fell on his daddy's face, he heard these words again.

"Promise me, son, not to do the things I've done.
Walk away from trouble if you can.
Now it won't mean you're weak if you turn the other cheek.
I hope you're old enough to understand.
Son, you don't have to fight to be a man."

The Gatlin boys just laughed at him, when he walked into the
barroom.
One of them got up and met him halfway 'cross the floor.
When Tommy turned around, they said, "Hey look, 'ol yellows
leavin'.
But you could've heard a pin drop when Tommy stopped and
locked the door."

Twenty years of crawlin' was bottled up inside him.
He wasn't holdin' nothin' back; he let 'em have it all.
When Tommy left the barroom, not a Gatlin boy was standin'.
He said, "This one's for Becky," as he watched the last one fall.

And I heard him say,
"I promised you, dad, not to do the things you've done.
I walk away from trouble when I can.
Now please don't think I'm weak, I didn't turn the other cheek,

And papa, I sure hope you understand.
Sometimes you gotta fight when you're a man."

Everyone considered him the coward of the county.

# Delta Dawn

*Story by Alex Harvey*
*Song written by Alex Harvey*
*and Larry Collins*
*Recorded by Tanya Tucker, Helen Reddy,*
*Bette Midler, and others*

For many years, I never really told anyone who this song was about. Some people just thought it was about a crazy woman in Brownsville, Tennessee, where I grew up. But recently, I've started sharing the real story behind this song.

When I was fifteen years old, I was in a band. We had just won a contest and we were going to be on a TV show in Jackson, Tennessee. I just knew, by the next day we would be a household word. My mother said she wanted to go. I told her that I thought she would embarrass me. She drank and sometimes would do things that would make me feel ashamed, so I asked her not to go that night.

We went and taped the TV show and headed back to West Tennessee. When we got home, I was wondering where my mother was. Around dusk, a big, old black Buick came up over the hill. A couple of ladies who I knew got out and I asked them where my mother was. They said, "Son, your momma's gone."

I said, "What do you mean, she's gone?"

They said, "Your momma died."

She had gotten drunk and had run into a tree at a high rate of speed. It looked like a suicide. For the rest of my high school years and into my adulthood, I dealt with the guilt over that event, thinking I had something to do with it. I think that was one of the reasons I started pursuing creative fields. For me, it was a form of therapy. That was the only way I could work it out.

About ten years later, in 1973, I was living in L.A. We had been out partying. We went to the Palomino Club and were listening to Dottie West. I was with a bunch of people, some from Buck Owens' band, some from Merle Haggard's band, Glen Campbell's bass player, and some others. These were some of the friends I hung out with when I wasn't in acting school or hanging out with actors.

After the show, we all decided to go back to Larry Collins' house. Larry and I had just written a song together called "Tulsa Turnaround" that was later cut by Sammy Davis, Jr. and then by Three Dog Night. We started passing the guitar around the room until 4:30 in the morning or so. At one point, I looked around the room and everyone else was asleep. I had the guitar in my hand and was just strumming. And I looked up and I felt as if my mother came into the room. I saw her very clearly. She was in a rocking chair and she was laughing.

My mother had come from the Mississippi Delta and she always lived her life as if she had a suitcase in her hand but nowhere to put it down. She was a hairdresser in Brownsville. She was very free-spirited, and folks in a small town don't always understand people like that. She never really grew up.

The first line that came to me that night was, "She's forty-one and her daddy still calls her 'baby.' All the folks 'round Brownsville say she's crazy." Larry woke up and grabbed the guitar and said, "Let me show you how to play that," and we finished the song. We wrote the song in about 20 minutes, or should I say, the song wrote itself.

I was the first one to record it. I was on Capitol Records at the time. Tracy Nelson sang backup on my record. Bette Midler was a big fan of Tracy's and she came to hear Tracy sing at the Bottom Line in New York one night. Bette loved it and vowed she was going to cut it one day.

In the meantime, someone took a track of it to Barbra Streisand

and she passed on it. Bette put it into her live show and also performed it on *The Tonight Show*. In the meantime, Helen Reddy heard it and decided to cut it.

Eventually, Bette recorded it and was ready to put it out as a single. But a few days before Bette's record was due to come out, Helen Reddy's version came out. So Bette's promoters told the DJs to push the B side instead, which was a song called "Boogie Woogie Bugle Boy." And that became one of Bette's biggest hits.

Tanya Tucker's version came out later that year. So the same song charted on two different charts by two different artists in the same year and was nominated for a Grammy. It was one of the few times that had ever happened. Since then it's been cut 78 times.

I really believe that my mother didn't come into the room that night to scare me, but to tell me "It's okay," and that she had made her choices in life and it had nothing to do with me. I always felt like that song was a gift to my mother and an apology to her. It was also a way to say "thank you" to my mother for all she did.

Until that night in L.A., I harbored a lot of guilt over that. I feel like God allowed my mother's spirit to visit me that night to release me. That night I was finally able to make peace with my mother. Whenever I hear the song on the radio—even today—I feel like my mama is up there saying, "You're welcome."

# Delta Dawn

Delta Dawn, what's that flower you have on?
Could it be a faded rose from days gone by?
And did I hear you say he was a-meeting you here today
To take you to his mansion in the sky

She's forty-one and her daddy still calls her "baby"
All the folks around Brownsville say she's crazy
'Cause she walks around town with a suitcase in her hand
Looking for a mysterious dark-haired man

In her younger days they called her Delta Dawn
Prettiest woman you ever laid eyes on
Then a man of low degree stood by her side
And promised her he'd take her for his bride

Delta Dawn, what's that flower you have on?
Could it be a faded rose from days gone by
And did I hear you say he was a-meeting you here today
To take you to his mansion in the sky

# Desperados
# Waiting for a Train

*Story by Guy Clark*
*Song written by Guy Clark*
*Recorded by Guy Clark, Jerry Jeff Walker,*
*The Highwaymen (Waylon Jennings, Willie*
*Nelson, Kris Kristofferson, and Johnny Cash)*

I was born in a small West Texas town called Monahans, where my grandmother ran a hotel. There was a fellow who stayed at her hotel who was almost like a grandfather to me, except that he was my grandmother's boyfriend.

When he died, I wrote "Desperados Waiting for a Train." He was a wildcatter and worked in the oil fields in West Texas. He drilled the first oil wells in South America and the Middle East, back in the 1920s.

All those things in the song happened. It's as accurate as I can remember it, nearly word for word. I used to play songs for him. I would tag along with him when I was little. As I got older, I would go along with him to a little bar in town where old guys would play cards. Sometimes he'd give me money, and he taught me how to drive. I'd drive his car sometimes if he got too drunk. He was just a crusty old bachelor who lived life on his own terms.

"Desperados" was one of those songs that I knew I had to write. Jerry Jeff Walker was the first one to record it. I recorded it later around 1975, and then Willie and Waylon and Kris and Johnny put it on their *Highwayman* album. It's been covered by a lot of people. Believe it or not, one of my favorite recordings was by Slim Pickens, the old cowboy-actor. He read it as a poem over the music track. That's probably my favorite version of any song of mine that's been recorded.

# Desperados Waiting for a Train

I played the Red River Valley
He'd sit out in the kitchen and cry
Run his fingers through seventy years of livin'
And wonder, "Lord, has every well I've drilled gone dry?"
We were friends, me and this old man
Like desperados waitin' for a train
Desperados waitin' for a train.

He's a drifter, a driller of oil wells
He's an old school man of the world
He'd let me drive his car when he was too drunk to
And he'd wink and give me money for the girls
And our lives were like some old Western movie
Like desperados waitin' for a train
Like desperados waitin' for a train

From the time that I could walk he'd take me with him
To a bar called the Green Frog Café
There were old men with beer guts and dominos
Lying 'bout their lives while they played.
I was just a kid, they called his "Sidekick"
Like desperados waitin' for a train
Desperados waitin' for a train.

One day I looked up and he's pushin' eighty

And there's brown tobacco stains all down his chin
To me he was a hero of this country
So why's he all dressed up like them old men
Drinkin' beer and playin' Moon and Forty-two?
Like desperados waitin' for a train
Desperados waitin' for a train.

The day before he died I went to see him
I was grown and he was almost gone.
So we just closed our eyes and dreamed us up a kitchen
And sang another verse to that old song
Like desperados waitin' for a train
Like desperados waitin' for a train.

# D-I-V-O-R-C-E

*Story by Bobby Braddock*
*Song written by Bobby Braddock*
*and Curly Putman*
*Recorded by Tammy Wynette*

I had written a song called "I-L-O-V-E-Y-O-U, Do I have to spell it out for you?" and I kind of laid it aside. That inspired "D-I-V-O-R-C-E." It's interesting because I eventually did finish the first song and Tammy Wynette recorded it on an album years later.

I finished "D-I-V-O-R-C-E" but there were no takers. I asked Curly Putman one day why he thought nobody had wanted to record it. He said, "Well, there's that one line in the chorus, 'I wish that we could stop this D-I-V-O-R-C-E.' That melody is too happy for such a sad song."

I said, "Well, what would you do?" He grabbed a guitar and started playing it and sang a new melody for that line. He changed the melody around and made it a lot sadder and a lot darker sounding. That's about all Curly did, but it made the difference, I think, between being recorded and not being recorded.

I think that really closed the deal. My melody sounded more like a detergent commercial than a song about divorce. I wanted to give him half the song, but he didn't want any of it. We compromised and he took a fourth of it. When we sat down to do the demo, Curly was playing guitar and I was playing piano, and I came up with that deep piano lick at the beginning of the song—"Bom-bom-bom-bom-dum-da-dum." Billy Sherrill later decided to keep it on the record.

They used to have a local Grammy banquet here in town and I saw Billy Sherrill there and told him about the song. He said, "Well, bring it over tomorrow." So I did. He later told me he was looking for one more song for Tammy and said when he heard it he threw all the other stuff he had for her in the garbage can. He instinctively knew that was going to be a big hit for her and it was. It went to #1 in 1968.

There were other songs of mine that were inspired by divorce, but I don't think this one was. I had a daughter who was about a year old then and I always thought it was cute the way parents spell things out for their children when they don't want them to know what they're talking about, so I just wrote it. There may have been other reasons or inspiration behind it at the time, but if there were, they escape me now. I think I just wrote it for the money. But Tammy had a lot of heartache in her life, so it seemed she really related to the lyrics.

By today's standards, it almost seems like a corny song to me. But Tammy just sang the hell out of it and Billy Sherrill did a great job producing it. They made a great record.

# D-I-V-O-R-C-E

Our little boy is four years old and quite a little man
So we spell out the words we don't want him to understand
Like T-O-Y or maybe S-U-R-P-R-I-S-E
But the words we're hiding from him now
Tear the heart right out of me.

CHORUS:
Our D-I-V-O-R-C-E becomes final today
Me and little J-O-E will be goin' away
I love you both and it will be pure H-E double 'L' for me

Oh, I wish that we could stop this D-I-V-O-R-C-E.

Watch him smile, he thinks it's Christmas
Or his fifth birthday
And he thinks C-U-S-T-O-D-Y spells fun or play
I spell out all the hurting words
And turn my head when I speak
'Cause I can't spell away this hurt
That's dripping down my cheek.

CHORUS

# Everlasting Love

*Story by Buzz Cason*
*Song written by Buzz Cason and Mac Gayden*
*Recorded by Robert Knight, Carl Carlton,*
    *Louise Mandrell, Narvel Felts, Gloria*
    *Estefan, and others*

**M**ac Gayden and I were producing Robert Knight, a young black singer from Franklin, Tennessee, on my label, Rising Sons Records. I owned it with Bobby Russell and it was distributed by Fred Foster on Monument Records. We had cut three songs and we had room for one more. Mac came over with two songs that had real nice riffs and grooves. I asked him, "Could you hook those two songs together in one song somehow?"

He said, "Yeah, I could, but I've got to go right now because my wife's got dinner at home waiting for me."

We were going to finish cutting the next day so I put a lyric to it that night. It was kind of a rush job actually. The original version we cut did not even have a second verse. It just had a bunch of "ooooh's" in the song. The "girls" sang that part, the girls actually being Carol Montgomery and me! Then we added a second verse and Carol and I did all the high background vocals on the Robert Knight version and the Carl Carlton version. Carl's is the version that most people recognize on the oldie stations. He cut his in 1974, and they really upped the tempo for his version.

I got the title from the Old Testament. In the book of Jeremiah, there's a verse that says, "Yea, I've loved you with an everlasting love." That always stuck in my mind, so I thought it would make a good title for a song one day, but that was just the title. The verses talk about a guy who splits up with his girlfriend: "Hearts go astray leaving hurt when they go / I went away just when you needed me so." The singer in the song is obviously not married because there is another verse that says "Need you by my side / girl to be my bride..." I was married at the time, but wasn't thinking of anyone in particular. It wasn't about an old girlfriend or anything like that. It's a pretty simplistic little lyric. Like I said, it was a rush job so we knocked out the lyrics in about 20 minutes. The next day when we were doing the session, we almost ran out of time to put it down.

We cut it at Fred Foster Sound Studio on 7th Avenue downtown in Nashville. It was the first master session for Brent Maher. Ten years later, Brent would be the chief engineer for Creative Workshop, my studio. He also later worked with The Judds and tons of other acts.

It was also a Top 40 song in four consecutive decades: Robert Knight in the 1960s, Carl Carlton in the 1970s, Rachel Sweet and Rex Smith in the 1980s, and Gloria Estefan in the 1990s. In the 2000s, U2 covered it on an album. The biggest single on it was a singer named Sandra who released it in Europe in the late 1980s. Hers was a huge hit in several countries — Germany, Spain, Italy, France, and the Netherlands — and sold three million records. And Jamie Cullum's version was in the movie *Bridget Jones's Diary*. It's been in five or six movies.

Louise Mandrell and Narvel Felts released their country versions of the song at the same time about 1979. Narvel was on ABC/Dot at the time and it was a Top 20 hit for him on the country charts. People didn't think twice about getting in a cover war back then. They would just jump right in.

My favorite is still the Robert Knight one. It was done with a slower, Motown beat. It also had some different sounds on it that, for the time period, were kind of innovative. The string sound is actually an organ and we used a lot of echo. This was before all that crazy dance junk came in during the 1970s and, later, disco. I just think Robert's was the one that had the magic in it.

## Everlasting Love

Hearts go astray, leaving hurt when they go.
I went away just when you needed me so.
Filled with regret, I come back begging you
Forgive, forget, where's the love we once knew?

Open up your eyes, then you'll realize.
Here I stand with my
Everlasting love.
Need you by my side.
Girl to be my bride.
You'll never be denied everlasting love
From the very start, open up your heart, be a lasting part of
Everlasting love.
Ohhh, yeah, yeah, yeah, yeah, yeah….

When life's filled with woes
No one really knows
'Til someone's there to show
The way to lasting love

Like the sun that shines
Endlessly it shines
You always will be my mine
It's eternal love

When other loves are gone
I will be strong
We have our very own
Everlasting love

Open up your eyes, then you'll realize.
Here I stand with my everlasting love
Need you by my side.
Girl to be my bride.
You'll never be denied
Everlasting love.

From the very start
Open up your heart
Be a lasting part of
Everlasting love.

# Everything Is Beautiful

*Story by Ray Stevens*
*Song written by Ray Stevens*
*Recorded by Ray Stevens*

The lyrics to the song really speak for themselves. You have to try to overcome prejudice and be open-minded about people in the world. I think Americans are by and large that way. At least I think they are now more so than they were back in 1970 when I wrote the song.

I had just signed a new recording contract with Barnaby Records, Andy Williams' new label. It was going to be distributed by CBS, so it was basically the same thing as being on Columbia Records. We had all the power of a major label and, at the same time, I was one of just a few artists, so there were a lot of resources to promote us. I was really excited about that, and I really wanted my first record to be a big hit.

I had also been signed to host *The Andy Williams Show* that year, 1970, and I wanted to write a song that would be the theme song for that show. So I sat down at the piano at my house in Nashville and started writing. I would start one song, and think, "No, that's not right," and start another. I was just not going to take "no" for an answer, so I sat there until I hit upon an idea that would work, and this was it.

I also had a little book that summer that I was reading. It was a book of wise little sayings and Chinese or Indian proverbs and things like that. There was one that said, "Everything is beautiful in its own way," or something like that. And I thought, "That's a great idea for the song I'm working on." I wrote it pretty fast once I got the concept, and it sure did fit the bill as far as being a hit as well as the theme for the show.

After I finished the song, I got the idea to record some little kids singing the intro. So I went over to my daughter's school in Nashville—Oak Hill Elementary—and I took a portable recorder with me and recorded her second-grade class singing, "Jesus loves the little children, all the children of the world / red and yellow black and white / they are precious in his sight…"

I won a Grammy that year for the Best Contemporary Vocal Performance, Male. It was released as a pop song and hit #1 on the pop and AC charts, but it got a lot of airplay on country radio and I think a good bit on gospel stations as well.

# Everything Is Beautiful

Jesus loves the little children
All the children of the world
Red and yellow, black and white
They are precious in his sight
Jesus loves the little children of the world

CHORUS:
Everything is beautiful in its own way
Like a starry summer night or a snow covered winter's day
Everybody's beautiful in their own way
Under God's heaven the world's gonna find a way

There is none so blind as he who will not see
We must not close our minds. We must let our thoughts be free
For every hour that passes by, you know the world gets a little
    bit older
It's time to realize that beauty lies in the eyes of the beholder

CHORUS

We shouldn't care about the length of his hair or the color of
    his skin
Don't worry about what shows from without, but the love that
    lives within
We're gonna get it all together now and everything's gonna
    work out fine
Just take a little time to look on the good side, and straighten it
    out in your mind

CHORUS

# Gentle on My Mind

*Story by Betty Harford*
*Song written by John Hartford*
*Recorded by John Hartford, Glen Campbell*
*and others*

In 1966, John and I were living in a little mobile home near Lebanon Pike on the east side of Nashville; our son Jamie was a year old. My mother babysat him one night so we could go see the movie *Dr. Zhivago*. John was very impressed with the movie, as was I. When we came home, he said, "I need to go write down a few things," which was not unusual for him. Our second bedroom was always his music room and he spent much of his time there.

John had been in his room for about thirty minutes while I was putting Jamie to bed. He came out with his guitar and said, "Let me play you this song I just wrote. Tell me what you think about it." He had it completely written. I think it was the romantic relationship between Dr. Zhivago—Omar Sharif—and Julie Christie's character—Lara—that inspired him. It was a movie about wartime Russia and finding love. Maybe it just awakened the wanderer in him. When I heard the song, I liked it, but of course I said, "Wait a minute. You're talking about 'not being shackled by forgotten words and bonds and ink stains that have dried upon some line,' and 'leaving some woman crying to her mother cause she turned and you were gone.' Is that me?"

He said, "No. You're like the Julie Christie character for me." Of course that was the right thing to say. When you listen to the song, it sounds like this guy wants to be out of there, and not entangled with a relationship. But John quickly assured me this was "artistic license" that he was taking. We did divorce, however, a few years later, so I'm not so sure....

He said the song was just a "word movie;" that's what he called it. It doesn't have a chorus, and it's like free verse poetry. He never believed a song had to rhyme or have perfect form to be good.

I worked for the Glaser Brothers' publishing company, John's publisher, as their administrative assistant, and sometimes did vocals for their demos. John was a staff writer for Glaser and moonlighted as a disc jockey at WSIX from 4 p.m. to midnight (he went by John Hart). Every weekday, we would take Jamie to his babysitter and then both of us would go down to Music Row to work at the publishing company. We were quite poor, but those were really good times.

John made a quick demo of "Gentle on My Mind" the day after he wrote it. He always had a little cassette tape recorder with him and would put songs down immediately. He played this tape for Chuck Glaser the same morning. I expect they probably did a little better demo; then Chuck took it right over to Chet Atkins.

Chet was very positive and subsequently signed John with RCA Records based on that song. Chet was also the one who persuaded John to change his stage name from John Harford to John Hartford. John cut this first record with RCA, produced by Felton Jarvis, with "Gentle on My Mind" on the A side and "Washing Machine" on the B side. It had only been out a few weeks when Glen Campbell heard John's version on the radio in California and went into Capitol and covered it. The rest, as they say, is history. It was a little unusual for a song to be covered that quickly, but I think everybody who heard it recognized immediately that the song was really special.

When we first married, in 1963, we lived in St. Louis, where John had a bluegrass band, the Ozark Mountain Trio. Since they didn't work often or get paid very well, we both had to have other jobs. In 1965, we moved to Nashville, which was the best decision he had ever made for his career. That was when John stepped out and performed solo for the first time. He always told interviewers that "Gentle on My Mind" was the song that bought him his freedom. He didn't have to be a disc jockey anymore; he became a full-time songwriter and musician. And I believe he became much more than he ever could have imagined.

# Gentle on My Mind

It's knowin' that your door is always open
And your path is free to walk
That makes me tend to leave my sleepin' bag
Rolled up and stashed behind your couch
And it's knowin' I'm not shackled
By forgotten words and bonds
And the ink stains that have dried upon some line
That keeps you in the back roads
By the rivers of my memory
That keeps you ever gentle on my mind

It's not clingin' to the rocks and ivy
Planted on their columns now that binds me
Or something that somebody said because
They thought we fit together walkin'
It's just knowing that the world
Will not be cursing or forgiving
When I walk along some railroad track and find
That you're wavin' from the back roads
By the rivers of my memory
And for hours you're just gentle on my mind

Though the wheat fields and the clothes lines
And the junkyards and the highways come between us
And some other woman's cryin' to her mother

'cause she turned and I was gone
I still might run in silence
Tears of joy might stain my face
And the summer sun might burn me till I'm blind
But not to where I cannot see
You walkin' on the back roads
By the rivers flowin' gentle on my mind

I dip my cup of soup back from a gurglin' cracklin' cauldron
In some train yard
My beard a roughening coal pile
And a dirty hat pulled low across my face
Through cupped hands 'round a tin can
I pretend to hold you to my breast and find
That you're waving from the back roads
By the rivers of my memory
Ever smilin', ever gentle on my mind

# Ghost in This House

*Story by Hugh Prestwood*
*Song written by Hugh Prestwood*
*Recorded by Shenandoah, Alison Krauss*

I'm from El Paso, but I moved up to New York about 30 years ago to pursue a music career. I lived in Manhattan for about 10 years and then moved out to the end of Long Island. I've never lived in Nashville, although I've spent a lot of time there over the years. If I were more of a co-writer, I probably would have moved there, but I tend to write by myself. I got to the point where I decided I really don't like having the music business right in my face all the time. And if I'm in Nashville for more than a week or so at a time, I start feeling pressure to hurry up and write.

I am a pretty slow, methodical writer. I tend to write about one song a month and I only write one song at a time. The melody comes pretty fast, and then I chew on the lyric for a couple of weeks. There's usually a line or two that I keep thinking I can improve and keep coming back to, and it usually drives me crazy until I get the last couple of pieces of the puzzle.

"Ghost in This House" was like that. I first got the idea for it while I was watching the movie, *The Grapes of Wrath*. There's a scene where the character named Muley has just lost everything he has, and they've run him off this land. At one point, he says, "I'm just an old graveyard ghost. That's all I am." And I thought, "That would be an interesting idea for a song," so I wrote it down in my song idea book.

About a year or so later, it was in the dead of winter. My wife had been in a minor car wreck, so she was in a lot of pain for a month or two. And I began thinking, "What if it had been a really serious accident, and I had lost her?" And it was a really dreary night and I started writing. That's where the song came from, out of that mood that night.

I usually like to visualize a lot when I'm writing lyrics. I started imagining this big house with only one light on upstairs, with this great sense of emptiness and quiet. It came out of a real pure emotion I had, which is where a lot of my best songs come from. I didn't have too much regard for whether it was going to be commercial or not. I kept getting these images of smoke and matches and fire, too, so I put them into the song.

I wrote this song in the 1980s. I really wrote it with Michael Johnson in mind. He had already done a couple of my songs, but he was actually in between deals, so he was not in a position to record it the time I wrote it. Then a little while later, Rick Hall down in Muscle Shoals got it. He was co-producing Shenandoah at the time with Robert Byrne, and he played it for them and they liked it. I really like Marty Raybon's voice, so I was thrilled when I heard what they had done with the song.

I actually had envisioned a version that was a little darker—something a little darker than what they did—much slower and heavier. Then when Alison Krauss recorded it, she took it where I had initially thought I wanted the song to be. It's just two different ways of looking at the same song. Marty's was exactly right for radio.

When the Shenandoah version came out, I was kind of wishing it was less produced, but when *Billboard* reviewed it, they said it was a "numbingly sad song."Alison's version is a little more artistic, but I doubt hers would ever make it as a single. When she played it at the White House last year, she was there with Brad Paisley and both *The New York Times* and *The Washington Post* mentioned the song when they reviewed the show. So that was kind of cool.

# Ghost in This House

I don't pick up the mail
I don't pick up the phone
I don't answer the door
I'd just as soon be alone
I don't keep this place up
I just keep the lights down
I don't live in these rooms
I just rattle around

CHORUS:
I'm just a ghost in this house
I'm just a shadow upon these walls
As quietly as a mouse I haunt these halls
I'm just a whisper of smoke
I'm all that's left of two hearts on fire
That once burned out of control
You took my body and soul
I'm just a ghost in this house

I don't mind if it rains
I don't care if it's clear
I don't mind stayin' in
There's another ghost here
She sits down in your chair
And she shines with your light
And she lays down her head
On your pillow at night

CHORUS

Oh, I'm just a ghost in this house

# Golden Ring

*Story by Bobby Braddock*
*Song written by Bobby Braddock and Rafe*
*Van Hoy*
*Recorded by George Jones and Tammy*
*Wynette*

I got the idea for "Golden Ring" from a made-for-television movie I saw around 1976. It was a biography of a handgun. The gun started off belonging to a police officer. Then someone stole it and committed a murder with it. Then it ended up in a pawnshop. The last scene in the movie showed a little child standing on a bed, finding the gun and looking at it. That's how it ended.

I thought it would be pretty interesting to write a song based on the history of a wedding ring. Normally, when I write a song, I just write it and then figure out later who it would be good for, but in this instance, I knew George and Tammy were recording, and I wanted to write something for them that would sound like a gospel song. There was a band I used to love called the Chuck Wagon Gang, and they did Pentecostal-sounding songs. I wanted to write a song like that that for George and Tammy. I thought it would be a new twist for them. I called up Curly Putman. He was on his farm out near Lebanon and I asked him if he wanted to write a song with me, and he said he wasn't coming in to the office that day.

About that time, Rafe Van Hoy came in the front door of the

publishing house, and I said, "Do you want to get in on this song I just started?" He said, "Sure." His mom worked at a jewelry store and I remember we called her for technical advice about rings. We finished the song together, and Rafe did the demo for me.

Buddy Killen was producing Bill Anderson then, and he couldn't find him for some reason, so he sent the song over to producer Billy Sherrill to play for George and Tammy. It was recorded in a few days and it was playing on the radio within two months of writing it. Today, the trip from the pen to people hearing it is at least a year, but back then, things were different.

There was no reason I set the song in Chicago. I just liked the way "Chicago" sounded. Billy made one small change in the lyric. I wrote the last couple of lines in the second verse as "as they fought their final round / He says 'You won't admit it / but I know you're runnin' 'round." Billy didn't want to rhyme "round" and "'round" even though it's really two different words—"round" and "around"—but he didn't look at it that way, so he added, "I know you're leaving town." Usually when Billy did that, he made it a better song, but in this case, I liked the original lines better. When I do it live, I always sing the original lines. I think "running 'round" has a little more impact than just "leaving town." Even though it's getting to be a pretty old song now, it always gets a good response when I sing it live.

# Golden Ring

In a pawn shop in Chicago
On a sunny summer day
A couple gazes at the wedding rings
There on display

She smiles and nods her head
As he says, "Honey that's for you,
It's not much, but it's the best
That I can do."

CHORUS:
Golden ring, with one tiny little stone
Waiting there, for someone to take it home
By itself, it's just a cold metallic thing
Only love can make a golden wedding ring

In a little wedding chapel later on that afternoon
An old upright piano plays that old familiar tune
Tears roll down her cheeks
And happy thoughts run through her head
As he whispers low, "With this ring, I thee wed."

CHORUS

In a small two-room apartment
As they fought their final round
He says, "You won't admit it,
But I know you're leavin' town."

She says, "One thing's for certain,
I don't love you any more."
And throws down the ring
As she walks out the door

CHORUS

In a pawn shop in Chicago
On a sunny summer day
A couple gazes at the wedding rings
There on display
Golden ring.

# Gone Country

*Story by Bob McDill*
*Song written by Bob McDill*
*Recorded by Alan Jackson*

The people in that song were a composite of real people that I have had lunch or drinks with in Nashville who said the kinds of things that are in the song: all these weak, thinly veiled excuses for moving to Nashville. The only people that said, "That was really neat" were other songwriters.

Some of the other things were made up, and some of it was just obvious cultural bias on my part.

I've met people like the fellow from L.A. in the song who was "schooled in voice and composition," and I've heard over and over that "L.A. is no place for children."

The song was pitched around town and most people were afraid of it. Didn't want to make fun of those Yankees, you know. I've always heard it said that we southerners on Music Row are afraid to make fun of people from New York and L.A. just because nearly everything on Music Row is now owned by people in New York and L.A. But I prefer to think it's just good manners. We love to make fun of ourselves, yet we rarely make fun of people outside of the South.

Dan Hill, my publisher at the time, took the song to Alan Jackson and he loved it. But that's why he's had such an incredible career, because he calls his own shots, and does what he wants to do, and that'll pay off for you in the long run.

Alan introduced the song at the CMA Awards and I think some of the people in the audience were pretty flabbergasted. I'm talking about some of the country singers!

After that, radio stations started playing it off the CD before it was even released. I think it charted before it was ever even released. That almost never happens.

A friend of mine is a dentist and he has Alan as a patient. One time he said to Alan, "That 'Gone Country' was a pretty interesting song. Do you think all those industry people recognized that the song is poking fun at them?"

Alan said, "Nah, all they heard was, 'he's gone country. Look at them boots.'"

# Gone Country

She's been playin' in a room on the strip
For ten years in Vegas
Every night she looks in the mirror
And she only ages
She's been readin' about Nashville and all
The records that everybody's buyin'
Says 'I'm a simple girl myself
Grew up on Long Island'
So she packs her bags to try her hand
Says this might be my last chance

CHORUS:
She' gone country, look at them boots
She's gone country, back to her roots
She's gone country, a new kind of suit
She's gone country, here she comes

Well the folk scene is dead

But he's holdin' out in the village
He's been writin' songs speakin' out
Against wealth and privilege
He says "I don't believe in money
But a man could make him a killin'
'Cause some of that stuff don't sound
Much different than Dylan
I hear down there it's changed you see
They're not as backward as they used to be"

CHORUS

Well, he commutes to LA
But he's got a house in the Valley
But the bills are pilin' up
And the pop scene just ain't on the rally
He says "Honey I'm a serious composer
Schooled in voice and composition
But with the crime and the smog these days
This ain't no place for children
Lord it sounds so easy it shouldn't take long
Be back in the money in no time at all"

Yeah he's gone country, a new kind of walk
He's gone country, a new kind of talk
He's gone country, look at them boots
He's gone country, oh back to his roots

He's gone country
He's gone country
Everybody's gone country
Yeah we've all gone country
The whole world's gone country

# Good Ole Boys Like Me

*Story by Bob McDill*
*Song written by Bob McDill*
*Recorded by Don Williams*

I have a fishing buddy, Tom Connelly, who wrote a bunch of Civil War books, and he reignited my interest in southern literature. He introduced me not only to Robert Penn Warren's literature, but also to the man personally. I read his last novel, *A Place to Come To*, and it inspired the song. That song is just about trying to pack all the standard southern themes into three and a half minutes. There are some lines in there that some people don't understand, but it worked anyway.

I don't think many people knew who John R. and The Wolfman were, unless they grew up in the South listening to R&R music on the radio. Down in Texas on the coast, we got WLAC after 9:00 when all the other radio stations went off the air. We listened to WLAC out of Nashville, which played "race music." The DJs there were John R. and Hoss Allen, and some others. We also got TXLR from Del Rio, which was another 50,000-watt clear channel station and we listened to Wolfman Jack on there.

I later became friends with Hoss Allen in Nashville. One day we were talking and he said, "Some S.O.B. put John R. in a song." I said, "Yeah, I'm that S.O.B." I was at Slick Lawson's one time and was sitting next to Hoss on a bench. There was a girl about my age sitting on the other side of him. She said, "Oh Mr. Allen, I used to listen to you on a transistor radio when I was a little girl, under the covers so my parents couldn't hear." Hoss said, "We had no idea we had that audience. We had all those thousands of kids listening to us."

I played "Good Ole Boys" for Don Williams and he wanted Kenny Rogers to do it. Don was already a big act. This was around 1980. He'd had several #1 records, but he wanted to do me a favor and pitch it to Kenny, who was doing a lot of crossover records then.

But Kenny said, "Nah, it's too literary. It's too esoteric." So Don called me back and said, "I guess you'll have to settle for me cutting it."

I said, "That's fine with me!"

Before I fell in love with country, I was living in Memphis trying to learn to write R&B songs, and we moved up to Nashville to be with Clement Music. I was trying to write all these little pop songs. I was riding around late one night with a bunch of guys and I was in the back of Vince Matthews' Cadillac and George Jones' "A Good Year for the Roses" came on the radio, and I had an epiphany. I got it. There was a real rage bubbling underneath that lyric that I'd never gotten before. There was a real rhythm that I hadn't understood before either, so I decided I wanted to start writing country songs.

## Good Ole Boys Like Me

When I was a kid Uncle Remus would put me to bed
With a picture of Stonewall Jackson above my head
Then daddy came in to kiss his little man
With gin on his breath and a Bible in his hand
He talked about honor and things I should know
Then he'd stagger a little as he went out the door

CHORUS:

I can still hear the soft Southern winds in the live oak trees
And those Williams boys they still mean a lot to me
Hank and Tennessee
I guess we're all gonna be what we're gonna be
So what do you do with good ole boys like me?

Nothing makes a sound in the night like the wind does
But you ain't afraid if you're washed in the blood like I was
The smell of cape jasmine through the window screen
John R. and the Wolfman kept me company
By the light of the radio by my bed
With Thomas Wolfe whispering in my head

CHORUS

When I was in school I ran with kid down the street
But I watched him burn himself up on bourbon and speed
But I was smarter than most and I could choose
Learned to talk like the man on the six o'clock news
When I was eighteen, Lord, I hit the road
But it really doesn't matter how far I go

CHORUS

# Green, Green Grass of Home

*Story by Curly Putman*
*Song written by Curly Putman*
*Recorded by Tom Jones, Jerry Lee Lewis,*
*Johnny Cash, Elvis Presley, and others*

I grew up on a mountain in northern Alabama and left there after high school. In the 1960s, I was working as a shoe sales-man. I worked at several Thom McAn stores around the South, in Memphis and Huntsville, but I came to Nashville every chance I could to be close to the music business. We had grown up around music and I played guitar and tried to write songs every now and then. Somehow I decided that I might be able to make a living from music.

One day I got a chance to meet Buddy Killen, who was the founder of Tree Publishing. He gave me a job as a song plugger, listening to tapes from new writers and pitching them to the singers. So I moved to Nashville. This was in 1964, and I remember seeing the movie *The Asphalt Jungle*, with Sterling Hayden as the lead. He was a country boy just trying to get back to the South. He was a bank robber, but he wasn't really a bad guy; he was the kind of bank robber that you liked. He'd been in jail and then got involved with some bad folks and they robbed a bank and the law was after him. He got within view of his old country home up on a hill, and they caught up with him and killed him. That movie stayed with me for a while. That was the seed, I guess you could call it, for "Green, Green Grass of Home."

I had an office in the Tree building on Music Row, so I went in one day and started thinking about that movie and I started to write the song. It only took a couple of hours to finish it, so it must have been meant to happen. Even in 1964, though, some people thought it sounded dated, like a song that Webb Pierce or Hank Snow might have done 10 or 20 years before that. But once it got recorded the first time, it took off like crazy. So that goes to show you that the music business folks don't always know what people are going to like.

Kelso Herston was a guitar player from Alabama who was living in Nashville. He produced the first record on the song. It was recorded by a fellow named Johnny Darrell, who was running the Holiday Inn over on West End Avenue. Kelso produced Johnny's record for United Artists, and it did okay, but it really took off later. Porter Wagoner covered it and then Jerry Lee Lewis covered it. Then Tom Jones heard Jerry Lee's version and he loved it. A lot of the British singers loved the Memphis rock and roll music. They loved Elvis and Jerry Lee and Carl Perkins. The Beatles were influenced by them, too. So Tom Jones cut it and it went to #1 in the UK and all around the world after that. Tom Jones' version has probably been the biggest yet, in terms of royalties and airplay. It's paid for a lot of dresses and purses for my wife over the years. But since then, it's been cut over and over and over by everyone from Johnny Cash to Elvis to Joan Baez. Gomer Pyle (Jim Nabors) even did it on his television show.

When Porter did his version, we added the recitation at the end. Porter always loved doing recitations and nearly everyone who cut it after that kept that. I've always loved recitations, too. I think it can really make a song memorable if it's done right, like George (Jones) did with "He Stopped Loving Her Today."

Sometimes people ask me what the man in the song was in jail for. You know, mothers who have sons and girlfriends who have boyfriends they haven't seen for a while — they're always going to defend them. They'll stand up for them no matter what. So I don't think he was in there for doing something too terrible. Maybe he just had some bad luck or had been in the wrong place at the wrong time or done something by accident. That was always the thought in my mind when I wrote it but I never really said so in the song.

That was only the second song I ever had recorded and it's been my biggest hit. I had a song recorded by Charlie Walker before that while I was still living in Alabama. Then I wrote "Green, Green Grass" about three or four months after I moved to Nashville. I was really lucky to have written a song like that so soon after coming here. I've been with Sony/Tree for 45 years now. I either didn't have the sense to move on, or maybe "Green, Green Grass of Home" welded me to a spot there, I'm not sure.

Someone at Sony/Tree told me recently that they had done some research on it and found out that it's been recorded by over 700 different artists in every major language in the world. There have even been a couple of TV movie scripts based on it. It's made a lot of money in Japan, too. I don't think they sing it in Japanese. I think they just learn it phonetically and sing it in English. A lot of bar bands play it, too. Maybe it makes a lot of money from the karaoke machines or something.

It's still pretty staggering to me what it's done. I've never had any formal music training, so it's pretty amazing that a simple country kid from the hills in Alabama could have done something that's had such an impact on so many people's lives.

## Green, Green Grass of Home

The old hometown looks the same as I step down from the
    train,
and there to meet me is my Mama and Papa.
Down the road I look and there runs Mary hair of gold and lips
    like cherries.
It's good to touch the green, green grass of home.

Yes, they'll all come to meet me, arms reaching, smiling sweetly.
It's good to touch the green, green grass of home.

The old house is still standing though the paint is cracked and
     dry,
and there's that old oak tree I used to play on.
Down the lane I walk with my sweet Mary, hair of gold and
     lips like cherries.
It's good to touch the green, green grass of home.

(spoken)
Then I awake and look around me, at four grey walls that sur-
     round me
and I realize that I was only dreaming.
For there's a guard and there's a sad old padre
arm in arm we'll walk at daybreak.
Then I'll touch the green, green grass of home.

Yes, they'll all come to see me in the shade of that old oak tree
as they lay me 'neath the green, green grass of home.

# Halfway Home Café

*Story by Ricky Skaggs*
*Song written by Paul Overstreet*
*and Johnny Barranco*
*Recorded by Ricky Skaggs*

aul Overstreet pitched "Halfway Home Café" to me on a demo tape that he had done. I had already done two or three of his songs during my career, so we had a relationship already. When I heard it, I thought, "Wow, what a great story," and I knew it would work as a gospel song on this bluegrass record that I was working on, so it covered a lot of bases for me.

When I heard the song, I knew I wanted to tell that story. I wanted to be the waiter in the restaurant who was sort of eavesdropping on all these different conversations in the café. Paul wrote it from the waiter's point of view. Just imagine the different conversations you hear in a day's time as a waiter: serving coffee, serving breakfast, serving burgers. You're going to hear a hundred stories a day, and these were just three of those stories. There was a man coming home from prison, and another man ending an affair, and then a young girl who was a runaway on her way back home.

It is such a great song about life in general and the bad choices people sometimes make. It's a great story about forgiveness and redemption, too. People sometimes think that forgiveness is a little thing, but it's not. It's really the message of the cross. The world sometimes looks at Christians and they think we have it all together, or that *we think* we have it altogether—but we don't. Jesus had it altogether, but we don't always.

I was listening to a *Focus on the Family* radio show one day. I just happened to turn it on. And they were talking to couples that had either separated or gotten divorced and remarried each other. There was one couple in particular I remember. This man said, "I was in a honky-tonk and I was listening to the radio and this Ricky Skaggs song came on. I was sitting there and I was with someone I shouldn't have been with, and when I heard that song, it broke me so bad. The conviction of God just came over me so strong. I knew I had been found out." Then he said, "I got up from the table and told her, 'I can't do this anymore. I can't see you anymore. This has been wrong from the start,'"—just like it says in the song. He said, "I called my wife and told her, 'I'm so sorry for what I've done. Can I come back home?' And she said, 'I've been praying for you. I was praying for you just now when the phone rang.'"

Just to hear that you were a little piece of this mosaic, this picture that God was painting in this person's life for His purposes, is amazing. To know that God still uses broken people to help put other broken people and broken lives back together again is incredible to me. He loves doing that.

# Halfway Home Café

I was pourin' coffee for table number one
I couldn't help but hearing what was going on
It got my attention when I heard a young man's voice
Saying, "Sheriff, I'll be going now, if it's alright with you boys.
Those years I spent in prison stole too much time from me
I won't waste another minute if I'm really free."

CHORUS:

I'm goin' home my family's waitin' for me, I'm goin' home
I'm amazed that they still love me
They forgive me for the bitter seeds I've sown
Heaven knows I've been away too long
So now I'm going home.

A burger and a special for table number eight
I was bussin' number seven when I heard her young heart
     break
He told her it was over they could never meet again
That he found a taste of courage twisting on his wedding band
Her tears began to fall but they could not touch his heart
I heard him say "I'm sorry, but it was all wrong from the start."

CHORUS

BRIDGE:
There's a million other stories from the Halfway Home Café
It's a never ending saga and they're played out every day

But this one's finally over. The foods all put away
And the coffee pot stands empty at the Halfway Home Café
Over in the corner at table number three
Sits a father and a runaway, well, it looks that way to me
I said "I hate to interrupt you, but it's really getting' late."
The young girl looked up smilin.' She said "Mister that's O.K.
I'm goin' home…"

CHORUS

# Harper Valley PTA

*Story by Tom T. Hall*
*Song written by Tom T. Hall*
*Recorded by Jeannie C. Riley*

When I was a small boy, in the town where I grew up, there was a lady who used to have parties on Saturday nights. Obviously, I changed her name in the song. She would have people over and they would have drinks and talk and listen to records. It wasn't a crack house or anything wild like that. They were all pretty respectable people, and she had a daughter. This is all in the song.

I was on my way from Nashville to Franklin, Tennessee, where I lived, which is about 15 miles from Nashville. I saw a sign that said, "Harpeth Valley Utility District." I changed the "Harpeth" to "Harper" because I thought it would be a good name to use in the song.

I had this song around for a while, but I hadn't finished it. I played what I had for my publisher and he said, "You've got to get off this story-song kick and start writing some regular songs." At the time, the thing in Nashville was what I called "little darling" songs—love songs. I don't say that to denigrate them, because there were some great songs written in that form, but I was not very good at it. I had studied American literature and journalism, so my mind was more bent toward storytelling. I got by for a few years doing that in Nashville. The kind of songs that I liked to write were songs like "Harper Valley PTA." I had been told to write about what I knew and these were people and places that I knew, so I stuck with that. I still write that way. My wife Dixie and I are still in the business of writing songs for bluegrass and acoustic singers and bands. We have a studio at the house with no drums or piano or anything; it's all geared toward acoustic music.

I put that song down on acoustic guitar, and gave it to someone who was thinking of recording it. He took it home and then said, "I don't think I can record that. I played it for my kids and they said nothing like this would ever happen in a school, and no kind of characters like that lived in our neighborhood."

One day a DJ called me and said, "Do you have any songs for girls to sing?" His wife, whose name was Alice Joy, was a singer and she was looking for a new song. So I said, "Yes, I've got a new song called 'Harper Valley PTA' that hasn't been cut yet." So she recorded it. I don't remember what happened after that, but Shelby Singleton of Plantation Records heard the song. He wanted this part-time secretary in Nashville named Jeanie C. Riley to record it.

In those days, they would make up acetates and send them out to all the prominent disc jockeys. They recorded it on a Friday night, and it was a hit record by about Tuesday night. "Harper Valley PTA" was the largest selling single of the time. The single sold about seven million copies even before the album came out. In those days, 100,000 records was a big hit, so you can imagine what a sensation it was. It was #1 on several charts: easy listening, R&B, country, and rock and roll. Then later they made a movie about it, and then a TV series. So from the time of its inception, it just snowballed.

# Harper Valley PTA

I want to tell you all a story 'bout a Harper Valley widowed
    wife
Who had a teenage daughter who attended Harper Valley
    Junior High

Well her daughter came home one afternoon and didn't even stop to play
She said, "Mom, I got a note here from the Harper Valley PTA"

The note said, "Mrs. Johnson, you're wearing your dresses way too high
It's reported you've been drinking and a-runnin' 'round with men and going wild
And we don't believe you ought to be bringing up your little girl this way"
It was signed by the secretary, Harper Valley PTA

Well, it happened that the PTA was gonna meet that very afternoon
They were sure surprised when Mrs. Johnson wore her mini-skirt into the room
And as she walked up to the blackboard, I still recall the words she had to say
She said, "I'd like to address this meeting of the Harper Valley PTA"

Well, there's Bobby Taylor sittin' there and seven times he's asked me for a date
Mrs. Taylor sure seems to use a lot of ice whenever he's away
And Mr. Baker, can you tell us why your secretary had to leave this town?
And shouldn't widow Jones be told to keep her window shades all pulled completely down?

Well, Mr. Harper couldn't be here 'cause he stayed too long at Kelly's Bar again
And if you smell Shirley Thompson's breath, you'll find she's had a little nip of gin
Then you have the nerve to tell me you think that as a mother I'm not fit

Well, this is just a little Peyton Place and you're all Harper
Valley hypocrites

No I wouldn't put you on because it really did, it happened
just this way
The day my Mama socked it to the Harper Valley PTA
The day my Mama socked it to the Harper Valley PTA

# Have You Forgotten?

*Story by Darryl Worley*
*Song written by Darryl Worley and Wynn*
*Varble*
*Recorded by Darryl Worley*

In 2002, Jack Tilley invited us to be a part of the Hope and Freedom Tour. We started in Kuwait and then went on to Afghanistan, but we spent most our time in Afghanistan.

When you go to a place like that with someone like him, you see things that most entertainers are not going to see. It's his job to go into the toughest places and talk to the troops. He's their liaison and takes the word back to Washington and says, "This is what the boys and girls need out there." So we went not just to the big airbases and places where there was a lot of security, but also to all the forward operating bases and the small outposts. We were able to take our flat-tops and go out there with him. It was a very surreal and eye-opening experience for me.

When we started flying home, I told my manager at the time, "When I get home, I want to do something for these troops. I'm not sure what form it's going to take, but I want to do something." I grew up in a military family and I grew up thinking I knew all about these things, but I came back from there with a new saying: "You don't really know until you go." I never had really written anything about 9/11. I hadn't digested the whole experience yet, and I started thinking, "What could I write that would pull all of this together?"

While I was there, I was amazed at how many soldiers had re-upped as a result of 9/11. The level of patriotism and commitment was really inspiring. I got to thinking about how I felt on 9/11, jumping in my vehicle and heading home to West Tennessee from Nashville. I drove mostly on the back roads and there were flags flying and bumper stickers everywhere. It was like driving down a parade route. I thought, "What a shame that it takes something of this magnitude and something this horrendous to make us pull together and display our colors and shout from the mountaintops that we are Americans." I don't know that I'll ever see anything like that again.

When I got home from my trip to Afghanistan, I got my stuff together and headed back here to West Tennessee so I could be home for Christmas. It was Christmas Eve 2002 and I drove that same route and I remember only seeing a flag or two. It just ripped my heart out, and I thought, "Here we are just a year after this tragedy and people are already starting to forget." I thought, "We have to write a song to remind people what happened."

Right after 9/11, I had gone to a gym near where I live and I saw a guy there who I've known most of my life. He was just about in tears because his daughter had been trapped in New York City when this happened. They couldn't reach her for a day or two and they didn't know if she was okay or what had happened. They were basket cases. I wanted to help them, but there was really nothing anybody could do. She ended up being fine and she got out of there.

Then, after I got back from Afghanistan, I saw the same guy at the same gym and he made a comment that floored me. He said, "I think this country's just looking for a fight." It caught me off guard. First of all, anybody who thinks that we could've taken that lick on the chin and not done anything about it, as far as I'm concerned, is a nut. I looked at him and said, "Are you the same guy who was a basket case when his daughter was missing for two days? Maybe I misunderstood your story or something because I don't think you're even the same guy."

At that moment, I thought, "Somebody needs to just give people a good slap across the noggin and wake them up." I came back to Nashville and sat down with Wynn Varble and we started talking about it and he said, "I had the exact same conversation the other day with someone and I just wanted to grab him around the throat and say, 'Have you forgotten?'"

When he said that, I told him, "That's our song title. That's not just about 9/11. It's about all of our history. It's about all the soldiers who went out and laid their lives down over the years. This could be huge. It could be almost like an anthem." We wrote it in an hour and a half. It just fell out. We went to lunch and then came back to see if we had it all tweaked. We played it two or three times and decided we weren't going to change anything.

It just floors me how, if our soldiers make a mistake out there in the field somewhere and we botch something, the media will take that and turn it into a huge fiasco. But when somebody comes against us, it's always downplayed and excused. What that does is it breeds complacency and people start thinking, "I guess we're just supposed to forget about that. And our wonderful government will take care of us." And it's just not always like that.

The most frustrating thing about this song is that a lot of people thought I was trying to make a comparison between 9/11 and Saddam Hussein, which I wasn't. I wrote it after going to Afghanistan and I mention bin Laden in the song, but because it came out about the time we were going into Iraq, people thought I was talking about that.

I don't want people constantly walking around in a state of anger or fear, but we've got to make ourselves aware. We have the greatest country and enjoy the greatest amount of freedom of any nation, and there is a big part of the world that despises us just for that. They are very envious of that. Since the beginning of this country, we have had enemies and we've had to fight and fight and fight, just like other countries have had to do, to preserve what we have. And the memory of that should stand for something and we need to be aware of where our freedom comes from. I think of myself as a patriot. I want people to know that I love this country and our way of life and that there are a lot of other men and women out there who have proved that by their sacrifices.

I think this song is going to be around for a while, and it will always stand on its own. I feel blessed that we got to be the vehicle to deliver it.

# Have You Forgotten?

I hear people saying we don't need this war
But I say there's some things worth fighting for
What about our freedom and this piece of ground?
We didn't get to keep 'em by backing down
They say we don't realize the mess we're getting in
Before you start your preaching, let me ask you this my friend

Have you forgotten how it felt that day?
To see your homeland under fire
And her people blown away?
Have you forgotten when those towers fell?
We had neighbors still inside going through a living hell
And you say we shouldn't worry about bin Laden
Have you forgotten?

They took all the footage off my T.V.
Said it's too disturbing for you and me
It'll just breed anger, that's what the experts say
If it was up to me I'd show it every day
Some say this country's just out looking for a fight
Well, after 9/11, man, I'd have to say that's right

Have you forgotten how it felt that day?
To see your homeland under fire
And her people blown away?
Have you forgotten when those towers fell?

We had neighbors still inside going through a living hell
And we vowed to get the ones behind bin Laden
Have you forgotten?

I've been there with the soldiers
Who've gone away to war
And you can bet that they remember
Just what they're fighting for

Have you forgotten all the people killed?
Yeah, some went down like heroes in that Pennsylvania field
Have you forgotten about our Pentagon?
All the loved ones that we lost and those left to carry on
Don't you tell me not to worry about bin Laden
Have you forgotten?

Have you forgotten?
Have you forgotten?

# He Didn't Have to Be

*Story by Kelley Lovelace*
*Song written by Kelley Lovelace and*
*Brad Paisley*
*Recorded by Brad Paisley*

I met Brad Paisley while we were both students at Belmont University in Nashville. We became friends before we ever started collaborating and had written several songs before we wrote "He Didn't Have to Be." Then Brad got his record deal with Arista Records around 1999. On his first album, *Who Needs Pictures?*, he recorded another song that I had written called, "It Never Would've Worked Out Anyway," which was a funny song about a guy being rejected time after time.

Brad came over to our apartment in Bellevue, just west of Nashville, and had dinner my wife Karen and me one night. I remember we had pot roast and mashed potatoes. After dinner, we went out on the screened-in porch to write something. While we were sitting there, my stepson McCain came and hugged me and Brad said, "You really love that little guy, don't you?" Then he said, "Let's write a song about him. Let's write a song that will make Karen cry."

I started thinking about what I would like my stepson to say about me when he's grown. So then we decided to write the song from his point of view. Since there are a lot of blended families in our nation right now, we thought that a lot of people would be able to relate to the song, at least the ones that had good stepfathers. And I was thinking about my wife when I wrote "When a single mom goes out on a date with somebody new / It always winds up feeling more like a job interview." We pretty much wrote the song in one sitting that night.

The rest of the song is pretty autobiographical. When I started dating my wife, McCain usually came along with us. He was five when we got married and the kid in the song is five, too.

The next night, Karen heard it all the way through for the first time when Brad played it at producer Frank Rogers' house. She got pretty teary.

The publisher wanted to pitch it to George Strait, who was in the process of cutting a new album, but he passed on it because he didn't want to record anything sad. At this point, Brad was all set to release *Who Needs Pictures?* But then we were somewhere in town, it may have been the Country Radio Seminar in Nashville, and Brad played the song live. There were a lot of tears in the room that night and Arista President Tim DuBois came up to him later and said, "Mister, you need to cut that song." They actually held up the album so they could add this song to it. It would have been a strong debut either way, but it's nice that this song really broke Brad's career open. It was his first #1 as an artist and my first #1 as a writer.

I remember watching it inch up the charts every week, first to the Top 40 and then 30 and then 20 and then 10. And by that time, you start thinking, okay if it can get this far, maybe it can hit #1. And it did.

McCain was a little out of control for a few weeks when the song became a hit, of course. Then he accompanied Brad to the 2000 Academy of Country Music Awards, where it was nominated for Song of the Year.

We heard reports from DJs all over the country saying that people were pulling off the road and crying when they heard it on the radio.

We got a lot of letters from fans. Almost everyone who wrote either had a story about themselves, or knew of a person who was affected by the song. That was really great, and very validating to see that something that was so close and personal to me and my wife was able to move so many people emotionally.

# He Didn't Have to Be

When a single mom goes out on a date with somebody new
It always winds up feeling more like a job interview
My momma used to wonder if she'd ever meet someone
Who wouldn't find out about me and then turn around and
    run

I met the man I call my dad when I was five years old
He took my mom out to a movie and for once I got to go
A few months later I remember lying there in bed
I overheard him pop the question and I prayed that she'd say
    yes

And then all of a sudden
Oh, it seemed so strange to me
How we went from something's missing
To a family
Lookin' back all I can say about
All the things he did for me
Is I hope I'm at least half the dad
That he didn't have to be

I met the girl that's now my wife about three years ago
We had the perfect marriage but we wanted somethin' more
Now here I stand surrounded by our family and friends
Crowded 'round the nursery window as they bring the baby in

And now all of a sudden
It seems so strange to me

How we've gone from something's missing
To a family
Lookin' through the glass I think about the man
That's standin' next to me
And I hope I'm at least half the dad
That he didn't have to be

Lookin' back all I can say about
All the things he did for me
Is I hope I'm at least half the dad
That he didn't have to be

Yeah, I hope I'm at least half the dad
That he didn't have to be
Because he didn't have to be
You know he didn't have to be

# He Stopped Loving Her Today

*Story by Curly Putman*
*Song written by Curly Putman*
*and Bobby Braddock*
*Recorded by George Jones*

**B**obby Braddock and I had been writing for a while and we just couldn't get anything cut. Some of the lyrics we were writing at the time were kind of silly and nothing seemed to be working for us.

Bobby initially brought the idea to me for "He Stopped Loving Her Today" back in 1979. We sat down in my office at Tree Publishing and we worked on it off and on. When it was mostly written we got hung up trying to figure out how to get the woman back to see him before he died. Finally, Bobby and I got back together and finished it.

Johnny Russell was the first one to record it, but I don't think he even released it. Then we pitched it to producer Billy Sherrill and he played it for George Jones. George passed on it at first because he said it was too sad. That's pretty bad when a song is too sad even for George Jones!

Later, Billy wanted us to change it a little for George. We would work on it and send it and Billy would say "Well, that's not exactly what we wanted," so we'd work on it some more. It is a little morbid, you know. Finally, we added the recitation at the end where she shows up at his funeral. Billy called us over to listen to what he had just produced with George and we were blown away. His voice was perfect for that song and nobody could do the recitation like him.

One of the interesting things about this song is that George released it as a single in 1980, but then it was still on the charts during the eligibility period for 1981, so it was nominated again in 1981. I never thought it could happen. I've only heard of that occurring once before. Freddie Hart won Song of the Year for "Easy Loving" in 1971 and 1972. So when "He Stopped Loving Her" was nominated twice, I thought, "There's no way." But darned if it didn't win again the next year.

There are so few real story songs anymore in music, the kind that make you listen all the way to the end and have some sort of plot to them, or maybe a twist at the end. Pop music doesn't really do much of that and a lot of modern country doesn't really either. It's rare to hear those kinds of story songs now, but listeners really love them.

It hit #1 for George in 1980 and revived his career at the time, but the number of awards that it's won since then has been really amazing. Johnny Cash and others have covered it and I've heard Alan Jackson and Vince Gill say it's their favorite song.

The Library of Congress just recently honored it as one of the top 25 country songs of all time or something like that. *Country America* magazine rated it as one of the top country songs of all time, and so did CMT, which is sometimes puzzling to me. We really didn't think that much of it, Bobby and I, when we wrote it. We thought it was okay, but never dreamed it would get honored like that.

# He Stopped Loving Her Today

He said "I'll love you 'til I die"
She told him "You'll forget in time"
As the years went slowly by
She still preyed upon his mind

He kept her picture on his wall
Went half crazy now and then
He still loved her through it all
Hoping she'd come back again

Kept some letters by his bed
Dated 1962
He had underlined in red
Every single "I love you"

I went to see him just today
Oh but I didn't see no tears
All dressed up to go away
First time I'd seen him smile in years

CHORUS:
He stopped loving her today
They placed a wreath upon his door
And soon they'll carry him away
He stopped loving her today

(Spoken)
You know she came to see him one last time
Oh and we all wondered if she would
And it kept running through my mind
This time he's over her for good

CHORUS

# Here in the Real World

*Story by Mark Irwin*
*Song written by Alan Jackson and Mark Irwin*
*Recorded by Alan Jackson*

When I came to Nashville, I got a job at The Bluebird Café as a "bar back," which means that I would clean glasses, stock beer for the bartender, clean tables, and do all the other grunt work. I did that for two years and eventually graduated to bartender. That's what I was doing when I met Alan Jackson.

While I was tending bar there, I got a chance to meet a lot of people. That was one of the best things about working at The Bluebird. I met a lot of other songwriters and publishers. In that environment, everybody was always networking and giving everyone else advice and letting them know who was looking for songs and which publishers were looking for writers and that kind of thing. Then someone told me, "You should check out this company called Ten Ten Music." It was a fairly new publishing company. It was run by Barry and Jewel Coburn, who were from Australia and had been in business for a couple of years. Barry was also managing several new acts and one of them was Alan Jackson.

I started taking songs to them and they liked what they heard. They didn't hire me as a staff writer, but they did allow me to bring in material on a song-by-song basis. If they liked the song, they would go ahead and write up a contract and pay for the demo and start pitching it. One night we were having dinner at Barry and Jewel's house and they introduced me to Alan and said we should try to write together. Alan had a songwriting deal with a publishing company owned by Glen Campbell then. He and I got together the next day.

I've always been a big movie buff, particularly when it comes to movie trivia. I can remember who played what in a movie I saw ten years ago, but I can't remember something I read ten minutes ago. So we were sitting around trying to come up with some ideas and Alan had the first lines, but didn't know where to go with it. He was sitting there and just hit a D chord and started singing, "Cowboys don't cry and heroes don't die…" and I don't know what happened, but the idea of movies popped out. Once that happened, the song came together in about 45 minutes. Alan and I have written together only two times and that day we wrote "Here in the Real World" and another time we wrote a song that was later recorded by Chely Wright.

I've discovered that when I'm writing with someone, the thing that takes up most of the time is coming up with the song ideas. Once you figure out the theme—what you want to write about—the song comes out pretty fast after that.

Barry had taken Alan around to several labels in town, but couldn't get a deal for him. Then when he found out Tim DuBois was going to be running the Arista Record label in town, he took him over there and Alan got his record deal with Arista. When Alan sat down with Tim, he played him nearly everything he had written, and Tim loved "Here in the Real World" and said, "That's going to be your next single."

When the song hit #1 for Alan, I was still bartending at The Bluebird. I hadn't seen any royalty checks yet because they take several months to come in. A lot of people gave me grief over that. They didn't think I needed any tips since I had a #1 record on the radio, but I did!

After Alan started selling millions of records, he bought a

vacation house on Center Hill Lake near Nashville and named it "The Real World" since that was his first really big hit. He had that written in big letters on the brick entrance to his home there. When I heard he did that, I bought some paint and took it home to my house in Nashville and painted "The Real World" on my mailbox!

## Here in the Real World

Cowboys don't cry and heroes don't die.
Good always wins, again and again.
And love is a sweet dream that always comes true
Oh, if life were like the movies, I'd never be blue.

CHORUS:
But here in the real world,
It's not that easy at all,
'Cause when hearts get broken,
It's real tears that fall.
And darling, it's sad but true,
But the one thing I've learned from you,
Is how the boy don't always get the girl,
Here in the real world.

I gave you my love, but that wasn't enough,
To hold your heart when times got tough.
And tonight on that silver screen, it'll end like it should,
Two lovers will make it through, like I hoped we would.

CHORUS

# Hey Cinderella

*Story by Suzy Bogguss*
*Song written by Suzy Bogguss, Matraca Berg,*
*and Gary Harrison*
*Recorded by Suzy Bogguss*

Matraca Berg and I had never written a song together before we wrote this song. So we sat down to have a chat about where we came from and our backgrounds and that kind of thing, just to get to know each other better. We were talking about how Matraca's mom and my mom had grown up in the same time period. They had both gotten married in the late 1950s and we were talking about what a different time that was for women.

We started getting a little catty talking about how, if you had the right coffee pot and got all the right things on the gift register when you got married, then everything was going to work out fine for you. And a lot of times, of course, it didn't. We were thinking about that bright-eyed, 1950s mentality, and how a lot of women bought it and then got clobbered, because they weren't expecting what life eventually had in store for them. We all take different turns in life and you never know if you are going to take the same turns as your partner or not.

My big sister was a hero to me when I was little. I wanted to do everything she did. She played the drums; I wanted to play the drums. She left her guitar at home and I picked it up and began playing it. I also really admired my mom. She and her friends were a lot different from the typical Donna Reed type. They were kind of salty. In a lot of ways, my mom didn't really buy into the things that a lot of women her age believed, that all your happiness is going to come from a man or staying home or whatever. She was a working mother and she had her own friends outside of her relationship with my dad. I used to go bowling with her on Wednesday nights. She really encouraged me, just as a human being. She would have been as big a supporter of me if I had chosen to be a nurse or an engineer or whatever. She really gave us that "you can do anything if you work hard enough" attitude. That's the problem with today's young people. You can't just build up their self-esteem without finding a way to get them motivated and driven to show what they can do. If you heap praise on them and they haven't really done anything, then you're really taking something away from them.

So Matraca and I were discussing these things, and we started needling the whole "Cinderella" thing more and more as we wrote the song. We were like, "Okay, come on, chick, now give us the *real* story here. What *really* happened?"

We were at Pat Higdon's office and we went out to get a cup of coffee and Gary Harrison was there in the hallway, so we asked him to come in and give his perspective. We were told we might be getting a little too catty, so we said, "What are you doing? Come on in and help us write this song." He's a great lyricist. Matraca and I thought maybe this would help us write something that would be better than just a novelty song, and maybe help us edit out some of the nasty digs we were getting in, too.

We finished it that day and I took it home and played it for my husband. I've never been the type of person who wants to cut only what I write. This town is full of incredible writers and you have to find the best songs. But as soon as Doug heard it, he said, "Well, that's a no-brainer. You have to cut that song." So I did.

It's funny how many of the lines are starting to come true in my life now, especially the line that says, "Sometimes we still curse gravity when no one is around." I've been happily married for 24 years now, but I've seen a few of my friend's marriages explode. It's not an easy thing to watch, especially if you've been friends with both of them and now you have to pick one. It's really difficult to stay friends with both.

I love a good story. I tend to be a hopeless romantic and a cock-eyed realist at the same time. So when I look for a song, I look for something that has a good story and redeemable characters in it and has a message, but I try not to be too bitter when I'm writing it. I think this song accomplished both.

# Hey Cinderella

We believed in fairy tales that day
I watched your father give you away
Your aim was true when the pink bouquet
Fell right into my hands

We danced for hours and we drank champagne
You screamed and laughed when I got up and sang
And then you rode away in a white Mustang
To your castle in the sand

Through the years and the kids and the jobs
And the dreams that lost their way
Do you ever stop and wonder
Do you ever just wanna say

Hey hey, Cinderella, what's the story all about?
I got a funny feeling we missed a page or two somehow
Oh-oh, Cinderella, maybe you could help us out
Does that shoe fit you now?

We're older but no more the wise
We've learned the art of compromise

Sometimes we laugh, sometimes we cry
And sometimes we just break down

We're good now 'cause we have to be
Come to terms with our vanity
Sometimes we still curse gravity
When no one is around

Yeah, our dolls gather dust in the corner of the attic
And bicycles rust in the rain
Still we walk in that fabled shadow
Sometimes we call her name

Hey hey, Cinderella, what's the story all about?
I got a funny feeling we missed a page or two somehow
Oh-oh, Cinderella, maybe you could help us out
Does that shoe fit you now?

Hey! Cinderella, maybe you could help us out
Does the shoe fit you now?

# Highway 40 Blues

*Story by Larry Cordle*
*Song written by Larry Cordle*
*Recorded by Ricky Skaggs*

In the 1980s, I was living and working in Kentucky. I was a CPA by day in Paintsville. Three nights a week I worked in a little club band in Hazard, Kentucky, about 60 or 70 miles away. I came home late one night after a gig. When I passed the road sign where I turned off Route 40 to go to my house, the title "Highway 40 Blues," popped into my head. I pulled over and wrote the first verse right there.

Of course, a lot of people who hear it think it's about Interstate 40, which runs right through Nashville, but I actually wrote it about that little state highway in Kentucky. The next day, I sat down and wrote the other two verses. I had the melody in my head for about a week before that and I actually finished writing the whole song without even picking up a guitar.

I knew Ricky Skaggs and Keith Whitley. The whole reason I started thinking I could do this music thing was because I saw how successful Ricky was getting and I decided maybe I could give it a shot, too.

We started playing around, first at people's houses, and then playing some clubs. To be honest, I probably wasn't good enough at the time. I was a decent guitar player, sang some and did a little writing, but when you are raised around people like Ricky, it can be pretty intimidating. Ricky was playing with Emmylou Harris at the time and hadn't really come into his own as an artist quite yet. The original recorded version of "Highway 40 Blues" was a thing that Ricky produced in 1980. That version actually had a young kid named Béla Fleck playing on it and some other real killer players. We had the same instrumental breaks and everything. I don't think mine had steel slide on it like Ricky's eventually did, but it had some great licks. I think we had Dobro, and banjo and lead guitar. Ricky told me, "If I ever get a record deal, I'm going to record some of your songs." I just laughed about it. I knew it was probably a long shot for either of us.

Then one day, after he had moved on to Nashville, he called me and said he was coming through Kentucky and said, "I've got something I want you to hear." When he got here, he played me the rough mix of "Highway 40 Blues" that he was going to include on his album.

He asked if I wanted to move to Nashville and I said, "You mean try to write music for a living?" I didn't know if it could even be done. I had no idea how the business worked or anything else. He said, "Well, yes." So eventually I moved to Nashville, and Ricky got his deal with Columbia. The song was released as a single from his *Country Gentleman* album and became a big hit.

It's been recorded by several other people since then and all the artists and musicians still think it's about I-40 because that's the road they all take when they go out on the road from Nashville. It runs east to west all the way to both coasts so it's a major road for touring busses.

"Highway 40 Blues" was actually the first cut I ever had as a writer and it went to #1, which is almost unheard of. It also helped boost Ricky's career as an artist and it's still a favorite song for his band to play live today. It's a great jamming song.

# Highway 40 Blues

Well, these Highway 40 blues,
I've walked holes in both my shoes.
Counted the days since I've been gone,
And I'd love to see the lights of home.
Wasted time and money too;
Squandered youth in search of truth.
But in the end I had to lose,
Lord above, I've paid my dues.
Got the Highway 40 blues.

The highway called when I was young,
Told me lies of things to come.
Fame and fortune lies ahead
That's what the billboard lights had said.
Shattered dreams, my mind is numb,
My money's gone, stick out my thumb.
My eyes are filled with bitter tears,
Lord, I ain't been home in years.
Got the Highway 40 blues.

INSTRUMENTAL BREAK

You know, I've rambled all around,
Like a rolling stone, from town to town.
Met pretty girls I have to say,
But none of them could make me stay.
Well, I've played the music halls and bars,
Had fancy clothes and big fine cars:
Things a country boy can't use,
Dixieland I sure miss you.
Got the Highway 40 blues.

# Holes in the Floor of Heaven

*Story by Billy Kirsch*
*Song written by Steve Wariner and Billy Kirsch*
*Recorded by Steve Wariner*

I got the title for "Holes in the Floor of Heaven" from my wife Julie. She came across that line in a novel she was reading and it really resonated with her. I remember we were in the kitchen doing dishes after dinner and I said, "That sounds like a great title for a song." I wrote it down on a pad while I was sitting at my piano and tried writing to it several times. I would get excited, but then I would wake up the next morning and come in and look at it and think, "Nah, it's not real enough."

Several months after that, my grandmother passed away. This was back around 1997. I was living in Nashville and my daughter was maybe six or seven, and my son was about a year old. I took my daughter to the funeral with me in New York. It was a Friday night and American Airlines had a direct flight from Nashville to New York about 6:00 p.m. As we began the flight from Nashville, we were seated on the left side of the plane so we were looking west. It was a beautiful night. There were what my kids call "mashed potato clouds" and a bright orange sunset. And out of the mouths of babes, my daughter said, "I think I see God on his throne and I think I see

Nanna Molly sitting next to Him." Of course, I just lost it. I still get a catch in my throat when I tell that story years later. It was very real and very impactful, just the kind of thing that a six-year-old imagination would see.

As soon as she said that, I was starting to process it. I began to scribble that first verse. I wrote, "one day shy of six years old... grandma passed away... I was a broken hearted little girl." By the time Steve recorded it, it became "eight years old" and a "little boy."

When I got home from New York, I had finished the first verse. When you get an idea like that, you don't share it with just anybody. We, as songwriters, start to get protective of those ideas when we're still in the process of creating. I had been working on it for several months already and those kinds of ideas don't come along every day.

Steve Wariner and I had already written several songs together and I went over to Steve's one night to write. His wife and manager, Caryn, was standing in the kitchen making coffee when, out of the blue, she said, "You guys ought to write a story song today." I smiled and reached for my bag and said, 'Well, as a matter of fact..."

So Steve and I went up to the studio and I played him that first verse. I didn't have a melody yet, but Steve picked up his guitar, like a great co-writer does, and launched into the chorus, singing "and there's holes in the floor of heaven...." We were off and running.

Then, like a lot of writers, we started to go from inspiration to craft and we were at the "Okay, what do we do next?" stage. We were trying to follow that "problem, evolution, and resolution" format, and realized we needed more. We knew that in the second verse, in order to move the story forward, somebody else might have to die or something. At the time, my wife was recovering from being treated for thyroid cancer, so it was a pretty emotional time in my life. I don't know whether subconsciously that was on my mind, but we came up with the idea for the mother to pass away. Then it was Steve's idea for the daughter to get married later and have her mom's tears falling on her during the wedding. It was a great collaboration.

We played it for Caryn and she said, "That song is for Steve," because we had written for other artists together before. He was at the end of his deal with his record label and was starting to shop himself again. Caryn would say, "Yeah, Steve met with so-and-so, but they don't hear 'Holes' as the first single." She was very passionate about that song. She just knew it was going to be his comeback song and she wanted it out as soon as possible. And, of course, we said "Oh, just sign the deal already! It will come out sooner or later." But she has a great business sense, and she was right.

A few months later, Steve was on a plane coming back from L.A. Garth Brooks and Pat Quigley, who was the head of Capitol Records then, were also on the plane. Steve played the demo for Garth. As soon as he heard it, he put the headphones on Pat Quigley. Pat just flipped and said, "Let's go. Let's put this out. We want to do a record deal with you." So Garth helped Steve get his deal with Capitol. Garth is very selfless that way. He is always willing to help out other artists.

Two or three weeks later, we were in the studio recording the song, and Steve was doing the vocal and we were adding the strings and parts. It was on the radio within weeks. In 1998, it was named Song of the Year at the Country Music Association and at the Academy of Country Music Awards.

# Holes in the Floor of Heaven

One day shy of eight years old
Grandma passed away
I was a broken hearted little boy,
blowing out that birthday cake
Oh, how I cried when the sky let go
with a cold and lonesome rain.
Momma smiled, said "Don't be sad, child
Grandma's watchin' you today"

CHORUS:
'Cause there's holes in the floor of heaven
and her tears are pourin' down

That's how you know she's watchin'
wishin' she could be here now
And sometimes if you're lonely
just remember she can see
There's holes in the floor of heaven
and she's watchin' over you and me

Seasons come and seasons go
Nothin' stays the same
I grew up fell in love
met a girl who took my name
Year by year we made a life
in this sleepy little town
I thought we'd grow old together
Lord, I sure do miss her now.

CHORUS

Well my little girl is 23
I walk her down the aisle
it's a shame her mom can't be here now
to see her lovely smile

They throw the rice
I catch her eye
as the rain starts comin' down
She takes my hand says, "Daddy don't be sad 'cause
I know momma's watchin' now"

CHORUS

# How Do You Get That Lonely?

*Story by Rory Feek*
*Song written by Rory Feek and Jamie Teachenor*
*Recorded by Blaine Larsen*

I was writing one morning with Jamie Teachenor. It was the first time we had written together, and I met him at a building where he writes. We were just talking about ideas, our fathers, our backgrounds and different things, when my phone rang. It was the office at my daughter Heidi's school, Zion Christian Academy, in Columbia, Tennessee. Heidi was 16 or 17 at the time. The lady said that a boy had committed suicide the night before. He was actually the boyfriend of Heidi's best friend. The secretary wanted to know if Heidi could take the day off to be with the family. We had just seen this boy at a football game and he seemed like he was fine, so we were shocked.

I hung up the phone and told Jamie and we started talking about it. Then we started writing about it. We didn't start with the title; we just started with the story. That boy went to Mt. Pleasant and their football team is called the "Tigers." The Lawrence Funeral Home is the name of a funeral home close to where we live in Chapel Hill, Tennessee, and Mooresville Highway is the highway out where we live, too. So all of these elements came from close to home.

I tend to write songs from the very first line. We started with "It was just another story, printed on the second page underneath the Tigers' football score...." and it unfolded from there. We really didn't know what was going to happen. When we got to the end of the chorus, the lines "How do you get that lonely, and nobody know?" just came out. It really floored us because it fit perfectly. It all just happened. We didn't plan it at all.

We tried to get it recorded by several other people but my publisher said nobody wanted to record it because it was too sad. They even asked us if we would consider rewriting it so that it had a different ending and we said, "No. This is just a moment in time we were trying to capture, and that's the way life is sometimes." You can't always end a song like that with "so if you're feeling bad, then call someone" or something like that.

Later, a friend of mine and I ended up producing a young artist named Blaine Larsen. He was still in high school. We were referred to him through someone else and I heard his demo and liked it. We brought him down to Nashville and cut some sides with him and he ended up getting a record deal. Like a lot of people, Blaine had also been touched by suicide. A friend of his in high school had committed suicide. All we did was change the line from "a boy about my daughter's age" to "a boy about my age" for Blaine, and he ended up having a hit.

It's great to see people using that song on YouTube to memorialize people they have known. You never really get over losing someone like that. They still love that person and that's why they want to keep their memory alive.

We live in a world that is moving so fast. It's filled with things that are distracting us and none of it really fills us up. It's easy to be empty inside even though your life is cluttered. I've had relatives who have committed suicide, too. It's a terrible thing and it's easy for me to ask those questions, too.

It's really special for me as a songwriter to write something that touches people in their own way. It's not our story or the one we wrote that moves them, but it helps them relate to their own stories. That's what's really great. I believe when you start writing, you should just start from the blank page and then write as a reader. You're just turning pages and you don't know what's going to happen next. By the time you get to the end of the story, sometimes you're in tears. Even though they are usually fictional characters, they really move you in what they do and what they say in the song. I'm a big believer in the magic of songwriting and so not only do they touch other people, they also touch me and cause me to stop and think and reflect.

One of my favorite memories is when Blaine sang this at the Opry. We were backstage with him and Lorrie Morgan was there with her son, Jesse, who was Keith Whitley's son. They were both big fans of that song. As many people know, Keith died from excessive alcohol use and Jesse said he knew someone who had committed suicide. I remember listening to Lorrie talking to her son while Blaine was walking off the stage and she was having a real heart-to-heart talk with him. She was saying, "I want you to listen to the words of this song. Never, ever let yourself get that far down. You can always talk to someone or call me. You can always find help." It was really a beautiful moment.

I can only hope that song has prompted other people to have those kinds of conversations.

## How Do You Get That Lonely?

It was just another story printed on the second page
Underneath the Tigers' football score
It said he was only eighteen, a boy about my age
They found him face down on the bedroom floor
There'll be services on Friday at the Lawrence Funeral Home
Then out on Mooresville highway, they'll lay him 'neath a stone

CHORUS:
How do you get that lonely? How do you hurt that bad?
To make you make the call, that havin' no life at all

Is better than the life that you had
How do you feel so empty, you want to let it all go?
How do you get that lonely... and nobody know?

Did his girlfriend break up with him? Did he buy or steal that gun?
Did he lose a fight with drugs or alcohol?
Did his mom and daddy forget to say "I love you son"?
Did no one see the writing on the wall?
I'm not blamin' anybody, we all do the best we can
I know hindsight's 20/20, but I still don't understand...

CHORUS

It was just another story printed on the second page
Underneath the Tigers' football score...

# I Believe

*Story by Skip Ewing*
*Song written by Skip Ewing and Donny Kees*
*Recorded by Diamond Rio*

I always wanted a piano. When I first started out as a songwriter and artist, things were tight until I had a few hits. When I finally bought a house, the first thing I bought for it was an acoustic piano. The house was basically empty except for a few things in the living room and my piano.

The first night after I bought it, I played every note on that piano. I played every chord on it. I ran my fingers across the keys without playing anything. I was just in love with it. Then I played a few chords and hit the sustain pedal, then let go very quickly and then put it back on again. When you do that with an acoustic piano, you can still hear the ringing of the notes even though you aren't playing anything.

This made me think of the energy that people put forth into the world and the effect they have. I thought to myself, when we sing a note or play a note, or write a note, it doesn't really stop. Where does it go? Those waves, that energy — they keep going somewhere. Those notes keep ringing. In fact, they can keep ringing in people's awareness and the choices they make down the road in their lives.

I realized there had been so many people who had an effect on me. I was able to remember their kindnesses, or I was able to gain some wisdom from what they did. I had been really touched and moved by a lot of people over the years. My grandmother and grandfather, for instance, both passed years ago, but there is still a resonance from them, just like from this piano, that rings on in me from the notes they played in my life.

I'm not talking about ghosts or anything like that, but there is a resonance of their existence that is still there. Our ancestors are still a part of us, whether we want them to be or not. They are indelibly a part of us. There's a wonderful man whose teachings I've become familiar with. He often encourages us to look at our hands. He says, "If you look at your own hand closely enough, you can't help but see your mother and your father's hands. And if you look deeply enough, you'll see the entire depth and breadth of your ancestry. It's impossible to separate us from them."

I began playing a classical melody that I knew. It had this descending movement. I played it up in the high register on the piano and it felt as if I were bringing this melody down from heaven. It just sounded very angelic to me. That stayed in the record for "I Believe." You can hear Dan Truman play it on piano in the song.

My friend Donny Kees came over the next day. I stayed up all night and was working on this melody and I played it for him. His mother was not doing well at the time so it was really moving for him. He and I worked on it and almost finished it that day.

That song was also one that my daughter loved. For a long time, she made me play it for her so she could sleep. She said she thought it was a little sad, but wanted to hear it before she went to sleep each night.

"I Believe" was another song that sat around for several years until Diamond Rio finally cut it in 2002. Someone from Acuff-Rose Music, who I was writing for back then, eventually played it for Diamond Rio and they decided they wanted it.

The video is very interesting. There is a lady who is lying on the ground after a violent car crash and it seems like her spirit starts to leave her. But that's the beautiful thing about sharing songs with people. Someone who hears a song often will project their own life experience into what they are hearing in order to be able to connect with it. And a director will often do the same thing. I know when I play that song live, when I sing those lines, "Every now and then, soft as breath upon my skin, I feel you come back again," everyone responds to that. And that could mean something metaphysical, it could mean something emotional, or it could mean something even physiological. Everybody's experience is going to be different. But I believe everyone on the planet has someone from their past that has a resonance like that.

# I Believe

Every now and then
Soft as breath upon my skin
I feel you, come back again
And it's like, you haven't been

Gone a moment from my side
Like the tears were never cried
Like the hands of time
Were pulling you and me

And with all my heart, I'm sure
We're closer than we ever were
I don't have to hear or see
I've got all the proof I need

There are more than angels watching
Over me. I believe...oh, I believe.

Now when you die, your life goes on
It doesn't end here, when you're gone
Every soul is filled with light
It never ends, if I'm right

Our love can even reach, across-
Eternity. I believe…oh, I believe.

Forever, you're a part of me
Forever in the heart of me
I will hold you even longer
If I can.

Oh, the people who don't see the most
See that I, believe in ghosts
If that makes me crazy, then I am
'Cause I believe…oh, I believe.

There are more than angels watching
Over me…I believe…oh, I believe.

Every now and then
Soft as breath upon my skin
I feel you, come back again.
And I believe.

# I Can't Make You Love Me

*Story by Mike Reid*
*Song written by Mike Reid and Allen Shamblin*
*Recorded by Bonnie Raitt and others*

I was at home reading the *Nashville Banner* one morning and there was a story in there about a relative of a local politician—sort of the "black sheep of the family" type—who got all tanked up on moonshine and shot up his girlfriend's car tires. I seem to remember the article quoting the judge, who, I think, was about to send him to jail. The judge said something along the lines of "I hope you learned something from this experience." And the guy said, "Yeah, I learned that I can't make her love me if she don't."

That's where the idea for this song came from. Seeing as how we had a guy tanked up on moonshine, angry at his girlfriend and shooting at inanimate objects with high-powered weaponry—I thought that's a country song if I've ever heard one! Ricky Skaggs was having a lot of hits then, and I thought we should write this for him, as a country song with a touch of bluegrass to it. So Allen Shamblin and I got together and banged around on it for probably six months. But something was stopping us. We couldn't get any further than those first two lines.

A few years before that, I had a hit with a song by Alabama called

"Forever's As Far As I'll Go." I had always loved Irish music and I had in my mind doing something similar. My kids were little then and, one morning, I drove them to school and came home and sat down at the piano and the whole first verse just popped out. At that time, I was at the best place a writer can be, and that's "out of my head." It's always to my advantage to lose myself in whatever idea I have at the time. How you do that is the trick.

One of my faults is I tend to be an over-analyzer, but I wasn't thinking of anything when I started writing those lines, except when I wrote the line, "Don't patronize me." Then I came out of it and said, "Can I say 'don't patronize me' in a song? Can I use that word?" The minute I said that to myself, I knew that I was brought out of the moment. I still wasn't aware that it was going to be related to the other idea we had for the bluegrass song. So I thought of the title that Allen and I had been banging around for six months and I wondered if they could be related. I called Allen and said, "Are you doing anything right now? Why don't you come over?" I played for him what I had, and we probably took another two days to finish the song.

When we finished it, I didn't sit back and say, "That's a great song." But I did think, "That's finished. That's exactly what I mean. There's really nothing more we can do with this." I've never been good at making judgments about whether a song is good or not, but I know when it's done. I had a little four-track Fostex mixer that a friend had given me, because he didn't know how to work it. I started pushing buttons. Actually, the first two song demos I did on that were "Forever's As Far As I'll Go," and "I Can't Make You Love Me."

When I used to teach musical theater to the kids at NYU, I was constantly asking them, "Is this what you mean? Is that what you mean?" And that's all a writer can do as a songwriter—spend enough time with a piece of work to know it's what you meant to say. Everyone knows what it's like to want someone who doesn't want you, and that's what we were trying to get at with this song.

I had a song on Bonnie Raitt's album *Nick of Time* called "Too Soon to Tell." And as soon as Allen and I finished this song, we both agreed there were only a few places we could go with this. I recall thinking of Linda Ronstadt, Bette Midler, or Bonnie Raitt. Bonnie loved it.

The piano lick at the beginning of the song was mine but Bruce Hornsby played on her session and he did a lot of those leads in the middle. That was all his. He really made that song his own. There are probably about 40 or 50 covers of this. Prince recorded it. It's been on a George Michael album. There are probably 15 or 20 jazz versions of it. The great jazz singer Nancy Wilson did a splendid version and so did Will Downing, the R&B singer. Boyz II Men released it as a single a while ago.

It's been recorded in every single format *but* country. Considering it started out as a potential bluegrass song, that's pretty interesting. A number of artists have come up to me and said, "Write me another 'I Can't Make You Love Me,'" and I never say what I'm really thinking, which is "If I do, you probably won't record it!"

# I Can't Make You Love Me

Turn down the lights
Turn down the bed
Turn down these voices
Inside my head
Lay down with me
Tell me no lies
Just hold me close
Don't patronize
Don't patronize me

CHORUS:
I can't make you love me if you don't
You can't make your heart feel
Something it won't
Here in the dark, in these final hours
I will lay down my heart

And I'll feel the power if you won't
No you won't
'cause I can't make you love me
If you don't

I'll close my eyes
Then I won't see
The love you don't feel
When you're holdin' me
Morning will come
and I'll do what's right
Just give me till then
To give up this fight
Then I will give up this fight

CHORUS

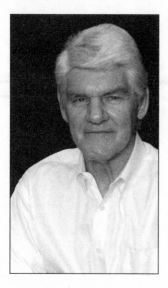

# I Fall to Pieces

*Story by Harlan Howard (as told to Country
    Music Foundation historian John Rumble)*
*Song written by Harlan Howard and Hank Cochran*
*Recorded by Patsy Cline*
*Story reprinted with permission and edited for continuity*

I think I met Patsy at the Grand Ole Opry. It was either at the Opry
or over at Tootsie's, across the alley from the Opry, where we'd
go and have a beer. These singers would do a couple of songs on
a Saturday night, except they'd be about two hours apart. So, they'd
come over there and have a beer or a Coke or something while they
were waiting to do their next show. It was customary back then for
all of us songwriters to hang out there with all these Grand Ole Opry
stars or at a couple of little restaurants around there. I'm sure it was
one of those times. Probably Hank Cochran introduced me to her.
Hank and I were writing for the same publishing company; Hank was
a songplugger. Patsy's husband Charlie and I were good buddies.

Somewhere along the way, it was my custom to go out to
Goodlettsville, where this little publishing company was, just about
every day. Willie Nelson had just come to town, and he was getting a
lot of good records by different people. I was out there one day sitting
with Hank in the office, and Owen Bradley called. He would check
with Hank to see if we had anything new. Hank and I were pretty hot
right at the moment. The day before, Hank had come to my house

and had a new song started called, "I Fall to Pieces." And so we went out into a little garage setup I had at my house and wrote that song.

Hank told Owen that we had a ballad called "I Fall to Pieces," which a guy or a girl could do without changing a word. They're the best songs to write.

Owen said, "Well, I kind of like that title. Why don't you bring me a copy of it?"

So, Hank did. Then, I remember Owen telling me he played it for, I think, Roy Drusky, and two or three other singers that were doing pretty good—you know, they were pretty hot at the time. They all turned it down. Then Patsy was coming out to do a session. I think Owen, more or less, insisted that she do that song. But I don't remember Patsy being flipped out over it.

Back then, we went to all the sessions. In fact, that's where we spent our evenings. It was either at RCA or the Quonset Hut, which was a studio owned by Owen Bradley. Of course, if we had a song in the session, we'd be there. That was quite common back then. There'd be four or five hungry songwriters sitting around hoping their song turned out best. We were caught up in the fever—I mean, I'd write three or four songs a day, and we'd go in and do a demo session of fifteen, sixteen, seventeen songs every couple of weeks. So, yes, I went to the session. We used the No.1 band, of course, which was Grady Martin, Ray Edenton, Harold Bradley, Bob Moore, Floyd Cramer, and the lead player on that record happened to be the lead guitar player, Hank "Sugarfoot" Garland.

I liked the record, but I had no idea, truthfully, that the song would do what it's done all these years later.

Two things were unique to that particular recording with Patsy: For one, it was the first time I'd ever had a record that had this little echo/tremolo thing on the guitar. That sound that's on her record, at that time, was very unusual; kind of a little delay. I'm sure that wasn't the first session in the world where that sound was included, but it was the first time it was used on a song I'd written.

Second, the musicians used a few tricks. There was a beat going around in country music at the time. It was kind of like the "Ray Price shuffle," which was a "walking" bass. It was just kind of like a slow, country/rock and roll beat, but it makes the music very danceable. So these guys had snuck a shuffle in on this record, and Owen Bradley did not like shuffle. He used to have a pop band. One of the reasons he didn't like, was it was being used so much—and not only by Ray Price, but by Buck Owens and everybody—all using the same tempo, slow or fast. Owen normally wouldn't let any of the records he produced be a shuffle, but they snuck it in there, and he didn't say nothing. Well, for one thing, it sounded good, and Owen was a smart man. If something sounded good, he was going to leave it alone. But to this day, they're still delighted that they snuck a shuffle by him!

When the record came out, it didn't take too long before it was a #1 country hit. And then, doggone it, it just stayed there and it stayed there. It stayed in the Top Ten for I don't know how long.

I remember Pamper Music had a couple of promotion men, and I remember Hal Smith, the publisher, talking to Hank Cochran one time, and they had been trying to make Patsy's recording go into the "pop" field and really hadn't had too much success. Hal told Hank, "We're spending a lot of money on this thing." I remember we were standing outside of this little studio out in Goodlettsville, and I just happened to overhear the conversation. He said, "I'm about to take these boys off of Patsy's record. We're not making it."

Hank said, "Doggone, Hal. We're almost there. All we need is one little break." There was a promotion man who took Patsy to Ohio. They used to have these showcases for young kids, like a Dick Clark-type thing. She did several of these in Ohio.

So, this record consumed about a year of promo time. I mean, it was a long time, but it was a hit for a long time. When it started to subside, Owen Bradley rounded up Hank and I and Willie Nelson, and a bunch of other writers, and got all the best songs from us. Patsy cut three or four more songs. At this particular time, Willie's song, "Crazy," won, you know. I believe that was a follow up to "I Fall to Pieces," some months later, when she needed a follow-up.

I think one of the interesting things about that, which has to do with success, is Patsy always was a real good singer throughout her career, from "Walking After Midnight" on, which is when I first heard of her. But I can detect a lot more confidence in the way she sings "Crazy" than the way she sings "I Fall to Pieces," which is pretty much on the beat, not much room for playing around, just the way it's written. And with "Crazy" she took a lot of bluesy liberties. Patsy just had her way with "Crazy" and, for about three hours, just sang it over and over. Owen kind of felt like she'd already sang it good enough on the regular session—good enough to be a hit. But she was just getting started, and she said, "Well, if you think that's something, watch this."That was her attitude. You could see her confidence had risen so much. She hadn't had a hit for a long time. I don't know how long it was from "Walking After Midnight" to "I Fall to Pieces," but it was a lot of records.

From then on, it's just been an interesting thing for me here in Nashville to watch friends of mine as they get their careers going—writers, singers, whoever—watch their confidence factor rise. That's when they really usually take the ball and run with it.

# I Fall to Pieces

I fall to pieces,
Each time I see you again.
I fall to pieces.
How can I be just your friend?

You want me to act like we've never kissed.
You want me to forget, pretend we've never met.
And I've tried and I've tried, but I haven't yet.
You walk by and I fall to pieces.

I fall to pieces,
Each time someone speaks your name.
I fall to pieces.
Time only adds to the flame.

You tell me to find someone else to love,
Someone who'll love me too, the way you used to do.
But each time I go out with someone new,
You walk by and I fall to pieces.

You walk by and I fall to pieces.

# I Hope You Dance

*Story by Tia Sillers*
*Song written by Tia Sillers and Mark D. Sanders*
*Recorded by Lee Ann Womack*

I didn't move to Nashville until I was in junior high school. When I was a teenager, I babysat for some musicians and recording artists, but growing up, I didn't have any real inclination to work in the music business.

As far as how I got interested in songwriting, it's easier to romanticize about it now than to remember it accurately. I would go to The Bluebird Café a lot when I was in high school and college. You didn't have to be 21. You could listen to live music seven nights a week and they had early and late shows, so it was a great place to feel grown up. Amy (Kurland) would let me enter from the back door and walk through the kitchen. She even let me sit at the rear corner of the bar sometimes.

All the songwriters there would tell these fabulous stories and these "blue" jokes and puns. They were incredibly witty. That was almost as attractive to me as hearing them perform. I still didn't think about writing songs. I just studied them as "creatures." I was drawn to them as "personalities." Songwriters, as an ilk of people, are just kind of odd. I liken them to pirates. Pirates are not at all like sailors. Even though they're all out at sea, being a pirate is a far cry from joining the Navy.

Later in college, I decided I wanted to be a novelist or a journalist or something of that sort, and that's when I first began contemplating writing songs. One summer I went to see Don Schlitz and Rodney Crowell and they just devastated me. I thought, *How do they do that?* And I remember at that point getting CDs of theirs and beginning to study them.

One of the first things I discovered is that poetry and lyrics are not the same thing. Poetry works perfectly well without music. You can read a poem and feel something without the help of melody or instrumentation. But lyrics really need music to cradle them. That's something I was drawn to. With a song it isn't just the music or just the lyrics; it's the synergy between the two.

I was about twenty when I got serious about writing and I signed my first publishing deal not long after. I was fortunate to have songs on the charts at a fairly young age, so for a long time I don't think I appreciated how really hard it was to do this.

A few years after I started writing professionally, I was going through a nasty break-up and I went down to the beach in Florida to figure out how to reinvent my life. My mom, who was this crazy, fabulous woman, kept calling me on the phone while I was there. She would say things that were reminiscent of future lines in "I Hope You Dance," but they were all bad things about my ex, like "I hope he stays miserable," and "I hope he knows he's an idiot"—not exactly words of inspiration you would put in a song. But occasionally she would say something more positive like, "I hope you get that light in your eye back" or "I hope you get to travel around the world."

One night, I was sitting on the beach at St. George Island near Apalachicola and it was just so unbelievably beautiful. There I was, absorbing the deepness of the sea and the vastness of the sand and thinking how I was going to be ashes soon enough and how so little of our life really matters in the big picture. There were seagulls and pelicans flying above me, and a dolphin was coasting in the distance, and I remember feeling so small.

Then all of a sudden, straight out of *CSI: Miami*, came this huge black Humvee racing across the empty beach—this is a nature preserve, mind you—all the windows were down and loud music was pouring out. The car screeched to a halt about 50 feet away from me and this man got out and he even looked like the guy on *CSI*, with dark sunglasses and a silk shirt. He got out and he was screaming into his cell phone, cussing up a storm. It was so strange. I remember thinking, "Wow, this guy definitely does not feel small when he stands beside the ocean, and it's his loss."

On my way back to Nashville, I got a call from a music publisher who happens to be one of my best friends—Diana Maher. She was calling from Estes Park, Colorado. She said, "I've got some of my writers, including Mark Selby, and we're all up here in the Rocky Mountains. Why don't you come out and work with us?"

I explained that I wasn't in Nashville at the moment and she asked, "Where are you?"

I said, "I'm about 50 miles south of Atlanta."

She said, "Great, park your car at the Atlanta airport and catch a flight to Denver."

I bought a ticket, arrived that night and spent a few days collaborating with writers, including Mark, who is now my husband, and we had a great writing retreat. We climbed an 11,000-foot mountain and I was scared to death. So the line, "I hope you never fear those mountains in the distance," came from that experience. The song was slowly coming together in bits and pieces during both of my trips.

I got back to Nashville and had a writing appointment with Mark D. Sanders that next week. Mark D. is the most wonderful man; he's like a shrink in that he wheedles things out of you that you have no intention of telling. And before I knew it, I was sitting there crying and mumbling and singing this thing I had in my head. I still remember Mark D. saying, "Oh, I think we should write that."

We went to lunch at a Mexican restaurant when he came up with the refrain at the end, "Time is a wheel in constant motion always rolling us along."

I said, "This is another song, right?"

He said, "No, it's for this song. Trust me."

It probably took us another couple of sessions to finish it and then we did the demo. We hired Karen Rochelle to sing, as well as a group of background singers, men and women. The finished product had some flaws. The guitar part wasn't really working and we had it arranged in a less than inspired fashion. But Mark Wright, the producer, did what a great producer should do—he took it to another level. He didn't just expect the demo to be handed to him and then try to copy it. He came up with the whole lush arrangement, and it was his idea to add the Sons of the Desert on the background vocals. They are like a chorus in a Greek tragedy, like when Cicero is about to give a speech and all of a sudden the Greek chorus comes out and says, "Cicero must give a speech that is very important to convince the public that he is in his right mind." That's essentially what the Sons of the Desert were doing on this record. The texture of their voices was great. Anyway, Mark Wright came up with all of that.

We found out that Lee Ann was going to cut it and it was going to be released as a single, so we were thrilled, but we never dreamed it would win a CMA, let alone a Grammy, and then later be performed at the Nobel Prize Awards ceremonies.

The night we won the Grammy for Best Country Song, the funniest thing happened. Mark and I went up on stage and accepted our award. After our speech, an escort came and ushered us backstage where we got in line for media questions. In front of us were Eminem and Madonna and a bunch of other big stars. One by one, they brought them in front of the reporters and announced their awards and the flash bulbs popped and people started firing questions. When our turn came, they said, "Here are Tia Sillers and Mark D. Sanders, writers of 'I Hope You Dance,' which won Best Country Song. Any questions?"

Silence. Not a single question, no flash bulbs, nothing—we just walked off. It was hysterical. So any inflated ego that I might have had while I was on stage was immediately squashed backstage!

I'm intrigued when people come up to me and say, "This song is really for children, right?" because that shows there is more than one way for the song to be interpreted. That's something that Lee Ann chose to do. She put her children in the video, and that made it magical. But truthfully, while writing it, we were trying to create a list of hopes for all of humanity. It's for everybody at every age.

A lot of us, when we get to a certain point in our lives, we think that we don't need to have hopes anymore. And the truth is, we need to have even more hope as adults than as children, because kids already live in a fantasy world. Most kids have the luxury of wishes and hopes. But so many times we adults sacrifice our own dreams and hopes for our children.

The thing that I wanted to impart to someone else with the song is: Even I had to figure out how to have those hopes and dreams for myself again—because I was ending a terrible relationship. Many of the lyrics are very mature. The line, "When you come close to selling out, reconsider," that's an adult hope. "Don't let some hell-bent heart leave you bitter"—that's not a line you're going to say to a child. "Loving might be a mistake but it's worth making"—that's a realization that only comes from experience. It's great when younger people say how much they love the song, but I think it's mostly adults who have really grabbed on to bigger concepts in "I Hope You Dance."

One of the loveliest things about "I Hope You Dance" was that it was written the way I always imagined writing a song should be. It's the first lines that move me the most, "I hope you never lose your sense of wonder / you get your fill to eat but always keep that hunger." So many people lose that hunger as they get older. They lose that curiosity, that drive, that desire, particularly because the vicissitudes of life are hard and can beat you down, but I think it's imperative in our journey as humans to keep that sense of wonder and hunger at all costs.

# I Hope You Dance

I hope you never lose your sense of wonder
You get your fill to eat
But always keep that hunger
May you never take one single breath for granted

God forbid love ever leave you empty handed
I hope you still feel small
When you stand beside the ocean
Whenever one door closes, I hope one more opens
Promise me that you'll give faith a fighting chance

And when you get the choice to sit it out or dance
I hope you dance
I hope you dance

I hope you never fear those mountains in the distance
Never settle for the path of least resistance
Living might mean taking chances
But they're worth taking
Lovin' might be a mistake
But it's worth making
Don't let some hell-bent heart
Leave you bitter
When you come close to selling out
Reconsider
Give the heavens above
More than just a passing glance

And when you get the choice to sit it out or dance
I hope you dance
(Time is a wheel in constant motion always)
I hope you dance
(Rolling us along)
I hope you dance
(Tell me who wants to look back on their years and wonder
where those years have gone)

I hope you still feel small
When you stand beside the ocean
Whenever one door closes, I hope one more opens

Promise me that you'll give faith a fighting chance

And when you get the choice to sit it out or dance
Dance. I hope you dance.

# I Love the Way You Love Me

*Story by Victoria Shaw*
*Song written by Victoria Shaw and Chuck Cannon*
*Recorded by John Michael Montgomery and*
*Boyzone*

I started "I Love the Way You Love Me" while driving to a gig in Pennsylvania from New York City. The first six lines, with music, popped into my head, which was pretty unusual. Then I was down in Nashville and wrote with Chuck Cannon for the first time. But writing it with him was what made this whole song explode. I brought it out to him and he totally got it and we just clicked. We both were in love (with other people), so we could draw from our own lives. That song was one that took under four hours to finish.

Gary Morris, who was my publisher at the time and also a successful artist, really liked it and was interested in recording it, but he wanted us to change something—I can't remember now what it was. Even though I had no success as a writer, there was something inside me that knew it was right just the way it was. I told him I'd like to leave it as is, and he did.

A little while later it was pitched to John Michael Montgomery and it was his first #1 and Chuck and I won the ACM award for Song of the Year for it.

I always have people tell me that it was their wedding song and I say to them "It was mine too!" Somehow the song got pitched to Boyzone, who are huge in the UK, and it became an international pop hit, too.

# I Love the Way You Love Me

I like the feel of your name on my lips
And I like the sound of your sweet gentle kiss
The way that your fingers run through my hair
And how your scent lingers even when you're not there

And I like the way your eyes dance when you laugh
And how you enjoy your two-hour bath
And how you convinced me to dance in the rain
With everyone watching like we were insane

CHORUS:
But I love the way you love me
Strong and wild
Slow and easy
Heart and soul
So completely
I love the way you love me

I like to imitate old Jerry Lee
And watch you roll your eyes when I'm slightly off key
And I like the innocent way that you cry
At sappy old movies you've seen hundreds of times

CHORUS

BRIDGE:
And I could list a million things

I love to like about you
But they all come down to one reason
I could never live without you

CHORUS

# I Run to You

*Story by Tom Douglas*
*Song written by Tom Douglas, Charles Kelley,*
*David Wesley Haywood, Hillary Scott*
*Recorded by Lady Antebellum*

When we wrote "I Run to You" I had just run a road race in Nashville and I saw a guy wearing a shirt that said, "I Run This Town." I really love words and playing with words and I thought that was a pretty creative play on words, so it stayed with me. Then later I started hearing about this talented new trio called Lady Antebellum. I eventually got a chance to sit down and write with the members of the band—Hillary Scott, Dave Haywood, and Charles Kelley—and we started kicking around ideas and this topic came up, so we finished it together.

There are a lot of words in that song that some singers might be afraid to use in a pop song, such as "pessimists" and "prejudice," but it didn't bother them. Paul Worley and Victoria Shaw ended up producing their first album and I wasn't sure if this was going to be on their album or not. Then I found out that they were cutting it and I heard what the producers had done with the song and I was just blown away. We had done a pretty darn good demo on the song, but it couldn't compare with what Paul and Victoria did when they produced it. The production and the harmonies and the vocal mix are just fantastic in that song. But Hillary and Dave and Charles are so darn talented anyway, they could sing the phone book and it would be a hit. They also did a remix of the song as more of a pop version and released it to adult contemporary and easy listening radio stations as well.

As far as the theme, we do seem to be living in a day and time when there is a "new disaster" every day in the news and we all need something to run to in times of trouble. We need something to run to for security in the midst of all the chaos that is going on in the world around us.

We wrote the song a couple of years before the economic meltdown and the Haiti earthquake and the Gulf Oil spill and things like that, so the lyric seems even more relevant now than it did then. Of course, people can read this as a song about a relationship and turning to someone in your life to help you deal with all the insecurity around us, but it can also be interpreted as something bigger.

For me, I am at a point right now in my life where it seems like God is running towards me in a good way. God seems to be passionately pursuing me, and that's kind of a new concept for me, and I'm trying to embrace that. As a result, the song has taken on a new meaning for me as well.

# I Run to You

I run from hate
I run from prejudice
I run from pessimists
But I run too late
I run my life
Or is it running me?
Run from my past
I run too fast
Or too slow it seems
When lies become the truth
That's when I run to you

CHORUS:
This world keeps spinning faster
Into a new disaster so I run to you
I run to you baby
And when it all starts coming undone
Baby you're the only one I run to
I run to you

We run on fumes
Your life and mine
Like the sands of time
Slippin' right on through
And our love's the only truth
That's why I run to you

CHORUS

# I Was Country When Country Wasn't Cool

*Story by Dennis Morgan*
*Song written by Dennis Morgan and Kye Fleming*
*Recorded by Barbara Mandrell*

We were writing in a building that was owned by Charley Pride. I lived and breathed music and my writing partner, Kye Fleming, and I worked all the time, morning and night. We were always looking for ideas, and Kye had the idea for this song written down in a book of hers.

Even though we wrote the song with Barbara Mandrell in mind and thought it would be a perfect song for her, every line in the song is locked into our backgrounds. When it says, "I was listening to the Opry when all my friends were diggin' rock 'n roll and rhythm and blues," that was certainly my life. There is a line in the song about "putting peanuts in my Coke," and it's funny because I remember talking to Kye about putting peanuts in my Coke when I used to hang out at Craig's Pool Hall in Tracy, Minnesota. She grew up in Fort Smith, Arkansas, but she said she used to do it, too. I'm not sure why. Maybe it made the Coke fizz or made it taste saltier or whatever, but we both did it.

This was around 1980, about the time of the *Urban Cowboy* craze. Country was getting more exposure. We went to play the song for Barbara while she was in L.A. taping her weekly television show. She fell in love with it, and she cut it there, too. A lot of people don't know this, since the record sounds like it was recorded in front of a live audience, but it wasn't. That was all overdubbed later.

There is the line in the song about "circling the drive-in and turning down George Jones," so George came in and sang the last verse on the record. I think he did one take and he nailed his part perfectly.

Another funny thing happened. When we were recording it, the bass player didn't show up. I think he was working with Ray Charles or another artist and was held over at that session. So the song was recorded without a bass player, and we overdubbed that part back in Nashville, too, at Woodland Studios.

It won the ACM Song of the Year for Barbara in 1982. Since then, Reba McEntire cut it with Kenny Chesney, and Martina McBride has covered it, too. It's a song that has had some pretty good legs over the years, which is nice.

# I Was Country When Country Wasn't Cool

I remember wearin' straight leg Levis
and flannel shirts, even when they weren't in style
I remember singin' with Roy Rogers
at the movies, when the West was really wild
And I was listenin' to the Opry when all of my friends
were diggin' rock 'n roll and rhythm & blues
I was country when country wasn't cool

I remember circlin' the drive-in
Pullin' up and turnin' down George Jones
I remember when no one was lookin'
I was puttin' peanuts in my Coke

I took a lot of kiddin', 'cause I never did fit in
now look at everybody tryin' to be what I was then
I was country when country wasn't cool

CHORUS:
I was country, when country wasn't cool
I was country, from my hat down to my boots
I still act, and look the same
what you see ain't nothin' new
I was country when country wasn't cool

They call us country bumpkins, for stickin' to our roots
I'm just glad we're in a country, where we're all free to choose
I was country when country wasn't cool

CHORUS (George Jones part)

Yeah, I was country when country wasn't cool

# It Matters to Me

*Story by Mark D. Sanders*
*Song written by Mark D. Sanders and Ed Hill*
*Recorded by Faith Hill*

One of the first times I heard one of my songs on the radio, I was driving a van for Stardust Tours in Nashville. It was a Sunday morning and the radio was tuned to the Top 40 Country Countdown. The song was "Oh Carolina" by Vince Gill. It had apparently broken into the Top 40 that week and I turned the radio up and started yelling to everyone on the bus, "Hey listen, that's my song on the radio. I wrote that!" And they all just stared at me. Then I realized that they didn't believe me! It was like they were thinking, "If you really wrote that, you wouldn't be driving this bus." They didn't realize that just because you have a Top 40 hit as a writer doesn't mean you can retire.

I grew up in California and played basketball in high school. Then I went to college, where I majored in literature and then taught high school for a few years. I knew I loved poetry, but I also knew poets didn't make any money, so I started thinking about writing songs. I moved to Nashville in 1980 when I was 29 and started working odd jobs. Then I started getting a few hits and was finally able to leave the tour bus company.

"It Matters to Me" is one of the more personal songs I've ever written. We wrote the song on a Friday, and it had been a bad week for me at home. My wife and I had been fighting about something.

My approach to anger back then was just to shut up, which is probably the most maddening thing you can do.

When Ed Hill, my co-writer, and I went in to write on that Friday, I didn't really want to write. The funny thing about the brain is if I'm upset about something else, I have trouble getting to that songwriting part of the brain. So I told that to Ed and he started whining and complaining. He would do that sometimes. He said, "Come on, let's just try to write."

He said, "I've got this title—'It Matters to Me,'" and I thought, *Oh, no. I know where this is going.*

We ended up writing the song from my wife's point of view. I didn't tell Ed that at the time. I do that a lot. I don't always tell my co-writers who or what I'm writing about. But that one was definitely from her point of view, looking at me. I came up with the lines, "When we don't talk, when we don't touch, when it doesn't feel like we're even in love." She didn't really say that, but I know that's what she was thinking, so I said it for her. Because we weren't talking to each other!

Even the first lines, "Baby tell me where did you ever learn / to fight without saying a word"—I usually try to use pure rhymes instead of slant rhymes, but in a song like that, when it says exactly what I need it to say, I just go along with it. I didn't mind rhyming "word" and "learn."

If I remember correctly, Faith didn't want to record it at first. I'm not sure why. Scott Hendricks was her producer and her husband then and he had to talk her into it. The first time I talked to Faith about it, I told her I knew her voice was just perfect for it. The first time I heard her sing it on the radio, I was turning off Franklin Road onto Tyne Boulevard (in south Nashville), and I got tears in my eyes because I knew what it was really about. That was back before I discovered anti-depressants.

# It Matters to Me

Baby, tell me where'd you ever learn

To fight without sayin' a word?
Waltz back into my life
Like it's all gonna be alright
Don't you know how much it hurts

CHORUS:
When we don't talk
When we don't touch
When it doesn't feel like we're even in love
It matters to me
When I don't know what to say
Don't know what to do
Don't know if it really even matters to you
How can I make you see?
It matters to me

Baby I still don't understand
The distance between a woman and a man
So tell me how far it is
And how you can love like this
'Cause I'm not sure I can

CHORUS

I don't know what to say
Don't know what to do
Don't know if it really even matters to you
How can I make you see
Oh it matters to me
Oh it matters to me

# Jackson

*Story by Billy Edd Wheeler*
*Song written by Billy Edd Wheeler and Jerry Leiber*
*Recorded by Johnny and June Cash*

"Jackson" was actually inspired by *Who's Afraid of Virginia Woolf?* I was in my early thirties and was studying playwriting at Yale University as a graduate student in their school of drama. I couldn't afford to go see the Broadway play by Edward Albee, but I somehow managed to get a copy of the script. The two main characters were so nasty in their arguments with each other. They just went at each other all the time. It made me think how men and women, couples, just seem to do that naturally. Usually it's fairly good-natured, but in *Virginia Woolf* it was subterranean and evil. So with that thought in mind, I sat down to write "Jackson."

When I left Yale, I drifted down to New York, and by a great stroke of fortune, got a chance to meet Norman Gimbel, who wrote "Killing Me Softly with His Song" and tons of other hits. He also won an Oscar for his song "It Goes Like It Goes" that was in the movie *Norma Rae*. He introduced me to Jerry Leiber and Mike Stoller on Broadway and Jerry helped me a little with "Jackson." Most of it was editorial. I already had the melody and the lyric. But Jerry is a great lyricist, and he said, "Billy Edd, your first four verses suck. You've gotta throw them away. Just start the song with "We got married in a fever / hotter than a pepper sprout."

I said, "Jerry, that's the climax of the song. I can't start with that," and he said, "Sure you can. Just write some stronger verses to go with it and then you can end with that, too." So I did.

When I was searching for a town to use for the title, I tried a lot of different cities. I tried "going to Nashville," but it was just too soft, so I came up with Jackson. Jackson is in Mississippi, but there's also a fairly large town in Tennessee named Jackson, too. I just liked the sound of it; it had a nice snap to it.

A little while later, I had an album out on Kapp Records, and I recorded "Jackson." Jerry and Mike produced the album. I had a lot of songs on that album that were eventually covered by bigger artists, which was wonderful, because I would have starved if I had to live on my royalties.

Johnny's brother-in-law took it to Johnny Cash and said, "I think this is something you and June could do," so they started playing the song in their live shows. This was really unusual. Most of the time, an artist records a song and then starts playing it on tour, but in his case, it was just the opposite. It was like he was testing it out before he decided to record it. There are many circuitous routes to how artists get songs and how they get recorded.

I met Johnny Cash at Carnegie Hall in the 1960s. They were having a New York folk festival, and I was invited to be a part of it. I was not a headliner, of course. Johnny was. Because I was in the show, I got to hang out backstage and I met Johnny and June. This was before they were even married. They were just performing together. Johnny said, "You know, Billy Edd, whenever I'm doing a show and I think the audience is getting sleepy, or they are drifting away from me, I whistle for June. She comes out and we do 'Jackson,' and it brings them right back. We're going to record that one of these days."

They did record it and Johnny and June won a Grammy for that song. It's been covered a lot since then, too. Later, Nancy Sinatra recorded "Jackson" with Lee Hazlewood. They were doing an album of covers of some big country songs. She did a little echo thing at the end where she says, "Jackson, Jackson..." so that's an example of how well the name worked.

The most recent version was Gretchen Wilson and Charlie Daniels. They do some really great bantering together at the end of their version. Charlie says, "You know where Jackson is? I'm not talking about Jackson, Mississippi. I'm talking about Tennessee." Then he says, "Will you lend me the car keys, give me a few bucks for gas?" and she says, "If you take me with you," and Charlie says, just as the song is fading out, "Ohhh, I guess so...." They did a wonderful job with it. It really cooks. But I guess Johnny's version will always be my favorite because Johnny and June were the ones who made it a valuable copyright.

# Jackson

We got married in a fever
Hotter than a pepper sprout
We've been talkin' 'bout Jackson
Ever since the fire went out
I'm goin' to Jackson, I'm gonna mess around
Yeah, I'm goin' to Jackson, look out Jackson town

Well, go on down to Jackson
Go ahead and wreck your health
Go play your hand you big-talkin' man
Make a big fool of yourself
Yeah, go to Jackson, go comb your hair
Honey, I'm gonna snowball Jackson, see if I care

When I breeze into that city
People gonna stoop and bow
All them women gonna make me
Teach 'em what they don't know how
I'm goin' to Jackson, you turn loosen my coat

'Cause I'm goin' to Jackson
"Goodbye," that's a-all she wrote

But they'll laugh at you in Jackson
And I'll be dancin' on a pony keg
They'll lead you 'round town like a scalded hound
With your tail tucked between your legs
Yeah, go to Jackson, you big-talkin' man
And I'll be waitin' in Jackson, behind my Jaypan fan

Well now, we got married in a fever
Hotter than a pepper sprout
We've been talkin' 'bou-out Jackson
Ever since the fire went out
I'm goin' to Jackson, and that's a fact
Yeah, we're goin' to Jackson, ain't never comin' back

Well, we got married in a fever
Hotter than a pepper sprout
And we've been talkin' 'bout Jackson
Ever since the fire went out (fade out)

# Jesus
# Take the Wheel

*Story by Hillary Lindsey*
*Song written by Hillary Lindsey, Brett James*
*and Gordie Sampson*
*Recorded by Carrie Underwood*

I wrote this song with Gordie Sampson and Brett James at my house near West End Avenue. Gordie actually came in with the title "When Jesus Takes the Wheel." He told us that he had an aunt who always said, "Oh Jesus, take the wheel," whenever she was frustrated or in a bind. Then Brett told us about a time when his wife Sandy actually was in an accident on the interstate. Her car went under a tractor-trailer, and she pretty much walked away without a scratch.

We started talking about the idea. Words just started flowing from all of us. I said, "She was driving last Friday on her way to Cincinnati." I have no idea why I said Cincinnati because I've never even been to Cincinnati. It just fell out. Brett and Gordie kept adding lines and the song came together pretty quickly. That was one song that definitely came from the spirit in the corner of the room. I'm not quite sure it actually came from us.

Not long after that, Carrie Underwood won *American Idol*, and of course won a record deal, and started looking for material for her first album. She heard "Jesus Take the Wheel" and it became one of her first singles and then won the Grammy for Country Song of the Year in 2006.

I knew it was a special song with a good message, but it's kind of funny how art imitates life. I was driving home to Georgia, oddly enough, at Christmas time—I say "oddly enough" because it's Christmas in the song. I was going through some tough things emotionally right then. As I was driving, the song came on the radio, and the song started speaking to me, even though I was one of the writers! I cranked it up and I just started bawling. It was like the song was saying, "You can let go of this. You can let somebody else take over for you if you just let it go."

I've never had a song do that before. It was like it was saying, "Hey! Hey you! Listen to me!" It was pretty weird—being a part of giving birth to something and actually writing the words and the message, and then it not hitting me until a while later on a random night driving to Georgia.

There were so many letters that came to us about the song. There is a man we know who works in the publishing field. His wife found out she had breast cancer when she was about five months pregnant. She had to deliver early and then go in for surgery about two days after she delivered. The baby was in the I.C.U. We sang the song at the ASCAP Country Music Awards because we won the ASCAP Song of the Year Award for "Jesus Take the Wheel." That husband came up to us after the song that night with great big tears in his eyes saying that this was the song that got him and his wife through that difficult time together. I've known him for a while and he's never been a particularly emotional man. This is a guy who hears a thousand songs a day because of his work, so the fact that this song spoke to him and meant so much to him was really special.

# Jesus Take the Wheel

She was driving last Friday on her way to Cincinnati
On a snow white Christmas Eve
Going home to see her Mama and her Daddy with the baby in
the backseat
Fifty miles to go and she was running low on faith and
gasoline
It'd been a long hard year

She had a lot on her mind and she didn't pay attention
she was going way too fast
Before she knew it she was spinning on a thin black sheet of
glass
She saw both their lives flash before her eyes
She didn't even have time to cry
She was so scared
She threw her hands up in the air

CHORUS:
Jesus take the wheel
Take it from my hands
Cause I can't do this on my own
I'm letting go
So give me one more chance
Save me from this road I'm on
Jesus take the wheel

It was still getting colder when she made it to the shoulder
And the car came to a stop
She cried when she saw that baby in the backseat sleeping like
a rock
And for the first time in a long time
She bowed her head to pray
She said "I'm sorry for the way
I've been living my life
I know I've got to change

So from now on, tonight"

CHORUS

# Johnny Cash Is Dead and His House Burned Down

*Story by Larry Gatlin*
*Song written by Larry Gatlin and John Cash*
*Recorded by Larry Gatlin & The Gatlin Brothers*

One time we were all backstage at a show somewhere, me and Johnny Cash, Kris Kristofferson, Willie Nelson, and Roger Miller and a bunch of people. And it got quiet back there for a minute—if you can believe that—and all a sudden John burst out with one of his mystical sayings. He would do that every now and then. He said, "Boys, if you get a good idea for a song, well, just go ahead and write it. It doesn't matter if it's a hit or not. Just do the best you can and everything else will take care of itself."

A while back, I was in Austin, Texas. I was in the car with my son, Joshua Cash Gatlin. Josh was driving us to a restaurant with my wife, Janice, and his fiancée, who is now his wife. And he said, "Daddy, country music's different. What's the deal? It just doesn't sound like it did when you and Uncle Rudy and Uncle Steve were making music. What's wrong with it?"

I said, "There's nothing wrong with it son. It's just different. They're doing it their way. We did it our way. Johnny Cash did it his way." I said, "We need to root for them and cheer for them. Those kids are living out their dreams and getting to do what's in their heart. You've got to realize the world will never be the same. Nashville will never be the same. Country music will never be the same. After all, Johnny Cash is dead and his house burned down."

We got to the restaurant and I turned that placemat over and borrowed a pen from the waitress and started writing the song. I wrote the idea and part of the song and went home and wrote the rest of it. It wasn't until a week later that I woke up at two o'clock in the morning and realized I had stolen one of John's old melodies.

I got up the next day and called John Carter Cash and explained to him what I had done. I called Lou Robin, who helps with John's publishing and the estate, and told Lou what I had done and said I didn't do it on purpose. I told him it was just as if J.R. himself were singing it in my ear. So I said, "I'll split the royalties and split the credit. He's the one that wrote it and it's about him. It's a tribute to him."

And it's also just a little gentle nudge to the country music people of today. It's got the line in it: "I got nothing against the young country stars, but I could use more fiddles and steel guitars." In other words: Do it your way. Do what you feel in your heart, but let's not forget upon whose broad and tall shoulders we all stand: the Johnny Cashes, the Marty Robins, and the Patsy Clines.

## Johnny Cash is Dead (and His House Burned Down)

Well, Johnny Cash is dead and his house burned down, down, down.
There's a whole lotta weepin' and wailin' in Nashville town, Nashville town.
Well the man in black ain't comin' back and Waylon ain't a gonna come around.
Johnny Cash is dead and his house burned down.

Chet Atkins & Marty Robbins ain't here to play, sing and play.

Miss Patsy Cline was one of a kind lord knows, oh by the way,

I got nothin' against the young country stars, but I could use
more fiddles and steel guitars,

Johnny Cash is dead and his house burned.

Who's gonna strap on that black guitar, walk out and sing
about the way things are,

Like the man in black singin' "Folsom Prison Blues"? Lord have
mercy, what are we gonna do?

Johnny Cash is dead and his house burned down.

Well, Johnny Cash is dead and his house burned down, down,
down.

There's a whole lotta weepin' and wailin' in Nashville town,
Nashville town.

Well the man in black ain't comin' back and Waylon ain't a
gonna come around.

Johnny Cash is dead and his house burned down.

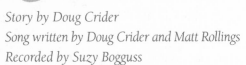

# Letting Go

*Story by Doug Crider*
*Song written by Doug Crider and Matt Rollings*
*Recorded by Suzy Bogguss*

I was probably thinking about two different people when I wrote "Letting Go." I was thinking of how my own parents must have felt when I went off to college, but I was also thinking about my mother-in-law. My wife, Suzy Bogguss, and I were married in 1986, and I wrote this maybe a year later, so I was definitely thinking of Suzy's mom letting go of her at that point also.

I grew up in Tampa and went off to Belmont College in Nashville. I was one of those guys who wanted to be gone. I wanted to be out of the house and on my own. I was ready but my mother wasn't. I remember going to Nashville and my mom helping me move in and her being really emotional and having a tough time with it.

This is one of those themes that make people sad, but it feels right to be sad about it. Somehow the singer in the song became a female. I'm not really sure how that happened. There's a line that says, "She's had eighteen years to get ready for this day," which could apply to either the mother or the daughter. I hadn't written the song to pitch to Suzy at all.

There's another line in the song about "the painting in the hallway that she did in junior high." That was definitely about my wife. She was an art student and we still have the paintings that she did in junior high and high school up in our attic. They were the paintings that went with her to college and then came to Nashville when she moved here. There's another line about "the lamp up in the attic, so she'll have a light to study by." A good friend of my family's here in Nashville had a chair in her attic, and she gave it to me when I came to Belmont so I could have some place to sit and study. So the chair became a lamp, but that was based on my experience.

I was a staff songwriter for Warner Bros. at the time, and the song got pitched around town a little, but frankly it was pretty pop for what was going on in country music at the time. The demo was pretty darn pop, too, so it got pitched some in L.A. but not very much in Nashville. This was in the middle of the "New Traditionalist" movement when Randy Travis and people like that were really hot, so the labels all wanted pure country.

People knew it was a great song, but nobody knew what to do with it. So it sat around for a few years until Suzy did her *Aces* album in 1991. She said she wanted to do this, and everybody was surprised. She said, "Well, just let me do it and we'll see what happens." The timing was a little better then so it turned out to be a hit. It went all the way to #6.

Oprah Winfrey did a show using the song as a theme, and then there is a radio talk show in Chicago on WGN that does an annual special using the song each fall. When it's back-to-school time, a couple of women up there do a show where people call in and talk about their kids going off to college. The song also sells a lot of sheet music because it gets sung at a lot of commencements.

Over the years, the song has completely turned around for Suzy. Now we have a sixteen-year-old son, so she is getting ready to be the mom in the song. Ever since Ben was born, we've had this song around, so we've always talked about it happening to us one day. It's easy to talk about it now, but it will be a lot harder when it actually happens.

# Letting Go

She'll take the painting in the hallway,

The one she did in jr. high
And that old lamp up in the attic,
She'll need some light to study by.

She's had 18 years to get ready for this day
She should be past the tears, she cries some anyway

Oh, oh letting go
There's nothing in the way now,
Oh letting go, there's room enough to fly
And even though, she's spent her whole life waiting,
It's never easy letting go.

Mother sits down at the table
So many things she'd like to do
Spend more time out in the garden
Now she can get those books read too.

She's had 18 years to get ready for this day
She should be past the tears, she cries some anyway.

Oh, oh letting go
There's nothing in the way now,
Oh letting go, there's room enough to fly
And even though, she's spent her whole life waiting,
It's never easy letting go.

Oh, oh letting go
There's nothing in the way now,
Oh letting go, there's room enough to fly
And even though, she's spent her whole life waiting,
It's never easy letting go.

# Little Rock

*Story by Tom Douglas*
*Song written by Tom Douglas*
*Recorded by Collin Raye*

W hen I wrote "Little Rock," I had just left Nashville, never to
return—or so I thought. I had come to Nashville to make
it in the music business in the early 1980s, but hadn't had
much success. So I gave it all up and went to sell real estate in Dallas.
It seemed like I was reinventing myself every few years back then, so
this was another chance to do so. It turned out, though, the changes
in the real estate laws in 1986 made it almost as tough to make it
in real estate as it was to make it in the music business in Nashville,
so it was pretty frustrating. It was a terrible time to be in real estate,
and Texas had a lot of its own challenges with the oil boom dying off
overnight.

   In the song, the guy is writing to his old girlfriend after he leaves
town to try to sober up. I was never really an alcoholic myself, but I
have had times in my life when I overindulged in a lot of things, so I
could relate to the singer in the song. I never sold VCRs at a Walmart
either, but I felt like I was when I was selling real estate. I never lived
in Little Rock either, but this was in the early 1990s, and Bill Clinton
was running for president, so Little Rock was in the news every time
you picked up the paper. I also liked the play on words with: "I'm

on a roll here in Little Rock." That obviously wouldn't have worked with Dallas.

When I got to Dallas, I kept writing songs, but I gave up trying to achieve commercial success as a songwriter, and that's when my writing got a lot better. While I was living in Dallas, I went to a song-writer's seminar in Austin one weekend. A Nashville producer, Paul Worley, was there, and he heard the song and a verse and a chorus from another song and said he really liked them. I gave him a cassette tape to take with him, and never thought much more about it.

When Paul got back to Nashville, I got a call from him. He said that he was going to play it for Collin Raye, who was also from Texas, and he later recorded it. It ended up being a pretty big hit for him.

What was really rewarding for me about this song was that, at the end of the video, the label and the people who produced the video decided to put up a phone number with an 800 number for Al-Anon. I heard later that whenever that video aired, they would have thousands of calls from all over the country from people who wanted to find out more about Alcoholics Anonymous. It was really gratifying as a songwriter to know that the song had such a positive impact on so many lives.

# Little Rock

I know I disappeared a time or two
And along the way I lost me and you
I needed a new town for my new start
I'm selling VCR's in Arkansas at a Wal-Mart

I haven't had a drink in 19 days
My eyes are clear a bright without that haze
I like the preacher from the Church of Christ
Sorry that I cried when I talked to you last night

CHORUS:

I think I'm on a roll here in Little Rock
I'm solid as a stone baby wait and see
I got just one small problem here in Little Rock
Without you, baby I'm not me

I don't why I held it all inside
You must have thought I never even tried
You know your daddy told me when I left
Jesus would forgive, but your Daddy won't forget

CHORUS

Right here upon this motel bed
My thoughts of you explode inside my head
and like a castle build upon the sand
I let love crumble in my hands

CHORUS

# Live Like
# You Were Dying

*Story by Craig Wiseman*
*Song written by Craig Wiseman and Tim Nichols*
*Recorded by Tim McGraw*

Tim Nichols and I got together one morning to write. We had
a friend who had one of those misdiagnoses. The doctor had
looked at an X-ray and said "Uh-oh" and our friend freaked out.
It turned out to be nothing. But that led to other conversations about
how people react to those events, whether they are a misdiagnosis or
the real thing. We started talking about people who responded very
positively. And we thought, "There's got to be a song in that." I started
rattling off titles and I finally said, "Live Like You Were Dying," and
Tim said, "Yeah, that's it."

As soon as he stopped me on that, I picked up my guitar and
scatted out pieces of the first verse and the chorus. We ended up
writing the second verse over the phone at midnight.

We could tell the chorus was getting a little Hallmark-y, so we
said, "We need a random weird thing in the middle just to break it
up." So Tim said, "What about horse riding or something? Horses
have interesting names." So I said, "No *bulls* have interesting names."
So that's how we got to the line, "I went 2.7 seconds on a bull named
Fu Man Chu."

We knew that Tim McGraw was cutting so we got it over to him right away. We were doing a demo on Monday and finished it later that week. We bumped it up and put it on the demo session and even the session players, who can be a cynical bunch, said they loved it.

So we sent it over to his label and somebody there said, "Did you know that Tim rode bulls?"

We said "No." Then she said, "Did you know Tim's father, Tug, is probably within weeks of dying?" And we said, "No." So later I talked to Tim and said, "Hey if this is too personal, and you want to pass on it, I completely understand."

He said, "I realized this is right where I am with my dad, but then I asked myself, 'Would I cut this anyway just on the strength of the song?'" And the answer was yes, he would. So he did it.

It's really odd that most of the conversations I've had about this song were things that happened after the song came out. This story should be called "the story *after* the song." It went on to win ASCAP, BMI, NSAI, CMA and ACM Song of the Year as well as the Grammy for Best Country Song and was nominated for best overall song.

Somebody forwarded an e-mail to me that was sent to Tim's label. And there was a picture of this couple, late thirties, maybe 40, standing on the deck of their house. And it was just a very simple, short letter, but it brought me to tears. It said, "My wife has been battling cancer for a few years. It's been tough and I just want you to know that it's meant a lot to us."

I'd like to think that that's my philosophy of life. I'd like to think that I try to live life with some balls, play with some house money, you know. I mean here I am buying buildings and signing new songwriters when the music industry is shrinking. It's just about having some passion in life. So many people just make so many *safe* decisions. You start making decisions to ensure nothing happens. And then, the first thing you know, you're sitting around bitching about how nothing is happening in your life. But you've made a lot of decisions to bring about those circumstances. You've locked yourself in to "repeat steps two through five."

I do a lot of songwriter showcases and that kind of thing. The most amazing thing about this song is that I've had 300-pound bulldozer drivers—guys who aren't used to talking about their emotions—come up to me with tears in their eyes and give me bear hugs. Sometimes they aren't even sure what to say. They just stand there and look at me and say something like, "Man, that song, you know, it's... it's..."

I just share a few seconds of silence with them. Then I say, "I understand, man. And I appreciate it."

# Live Like You Were Dying

He said "I was in my early forties,
With a lot of life before me,
And a moment came that stopped me on a dime.
I spent most of the next days,
Looking at the x-rays,
And talking 'bout the options and talkin' 'bout sweet time."
I asked him when it sank in,
That this might really be the real end?
How's it hit you when you get that kind of news?
Man, what'd ya do?

And he said, "I went sky-diving, I went Rocky Mountain-
     climbing,
I went 2.7 seconds on a bull named Fu Man Chu.
And I loved deeper and I spoke sweeter,
And I gave forgiveness I'd been denying."
And he said: "Someday, I hope you get the chance,
To live like you were dyin'."

He said "I was finally the husband,
That most the time I wasn't.
And I became a friend a friend would like to have.
And all of a sudden goin' fishin'

Wasn't such an imposition,
And I went three times that year I lost my dad.
Well, I finally read the Good Book,
And I took a good long hard look,
At what I'd do if I could do it all again,

Then, I went sky-diving, I went Rocky Mountain-climbing,
I went 2.7 seven seconds on a bull named Fu Man Chu.
And I loved deeper and I spoke sweeter,
And I gave forgiveness I'd been denying."
And he said: "Someday, I hope you get the chance,
To live like you were dyin'."

Like tomorrow was a gift,
And you got eternity,
To think about what you'd do with it.
And what did you do with it?
And what did I do with it?
And what would I do with it?

Sky-diving, I went Rocky Mountain-climbing,
I went 2.7 seconds on a bull named Fu Man Chu.
And then I loved deeper and I spoke sweeter,
And I watched an eagle as it was flyin'
And he said, "Someday, I hope you get the chance,
To live like you were dyin'."

# 48

# Long Black Train

*Story by Josh Turner*
*Song written by Josh Turner*
*Recorded by Josh Turner*

ometime back in 2000, I went over to the music library at Belmont University, where I was a student. I got into this little cubbyhole and was listening to the complete boxed set of Hank Williams songs that Mercury had just released. Being the poor college student that I was, I didn't have the money to buy it, so I was excited when I saw the library had it on file.

It was kind of late, and I was sitting there with my headphones on, just immersed in the music. It was as if I had entered another world. Several of the songs were just Hank and his guitar. He was doing radio ads and work mix demo and those kinds of things. A lot of it had never been released before, and it really inspired me. It made me want to break the music down to its rawest form.

As I was walking back to my apartment, which was on the other side of campus, I had a vision of a wide open place in the plains with a train track running straight down the middle of the fields. It was completely dark, but you could see everything around. There was a harvest moon that was lighting up the sky. I noticed a bunch of people standing around this track. A long, beautiful, shiny black train came down the track and the people were trying to decide whether to get on it. Somehow they knew that this train led to nowhere, but they were wondering what it would be like to ride on it. They were struggling with the decision. As I was seeing all of this in my mind while I was walking, I was wondering what it all meant. It finally dawned on me that this train was a symbol for temptation.

When I got back to my apartment, I picked up my guitar and strummed a B flat chord. I just strummed for what seemed like an eternity, but once the words finally started pouring out, they didn't seem to want to quit. I wrote three straight verses and a chorus that night and then went to bed. The next morning, I got up and a feeling came over me that this song was not finished, so about 11:00 that morning, I wrote the fourth and final verse. Then I knew it was done. The ironic thing was that I thought to myself, "Nobody is ever going to want to hear this song. It's too old fashioned. It's too old-timey. Nobody is really going to get the metaphor."

I was sitting there playing that song and a friend of mine walked in and said, "What is that?" I told him it was something I had just finished, but I wasn't sure how good it was. He said, "That's incredible. You need to play it for so-and-so." So I went and played it for this person and he said, "You need to put that in your senior recital." Then it started snowballing. I started playing it at showcases and writers' nights.

Before long, I did a demo of it there at Belmont and played it in one of my classes. One of my classmates was doing her internship at a publishing company owned by Jody Williams. This girl asked me if she could take it to Jody and, of course, I said "yes." She came back later and said, "Jody wants to sit down and talk with you." I called him up and he wanted to sign me to a publishing deal. He signed me to a production deal, he took me to MCA, and we played them a few songs, and the next thing you know I had a record deal, too. And it all happened because of "Long Black Train."

I was going through a lot personally during that time. It was my first time away from home, I was chasing this dream, and I was in a long distance relationship, so I was going through a lot of different emotions. "Long Black Train" ended up becoming the title track on my first album and I started playing it on the road. The song really related to what I was going through. But when I started coming into contact with fans, I found out that many of them were looking at the song in different ways. They would say, "My brother is going through alcoholism," or "My sister is going through a drug addiction," or whatever. So, it dawned on me, "This song is not just for me. This song is for everybody, because everybody has their own weaknesses and their own struggles. Everybody has their own long, black train."

I went down to Alabama to do a promotional thing for a radio station after the song was released, just an acoustic thing, and a lady pulled me aside after the show. She said, "Josh, I want you to know that I've struggled with depression. Just the other day I had a whole bottle of painkillers and I was going to take the whole bottle and end it all. And the radio in my bedroom started playing 'Long, Black Train.' When it came on, it distracted me for a moment, and then I started listening to the words, and I realized how selfish I was being." She said, "That song changed my life. I threw the pills down the toilet and walked away a different person." She said she was pretty much over her depression. Here I was, this young kid straight out of college, thinking that nobody would even want to hear this song, and here this woman was telling me how it saved her life. It was at that moment that I realized how powerful this song could be.

In November of 2001, I signed my record deal and I played the song on the Opry the Friday before Christmas that year. That time of year, the show moves to the Ryman Auditorium downtown for a few months. I had been signed for about a month. I didn't have a website; I didn't have a record out; I didn't have a video. Nobody had ever heard of me when I walked onto that stage. I was scared to death. I was playing with the Opry staff band because I didn't even have a band at that time. That was the only song I had learned. Pete Fisher of the Opry agreed to let me go out and sing this one song late in the show. When I sang the song, the crowd just erupted. People were standing up and cheering before I could even finish the song. I was completely overwhelmed.

Then Bill Anderson, who was hosting that segment, said to the crowd, "Do you want to hear some more?" And they got even louder.

I made it all the way down the stairs toward my dressing room when I heard Bill say, "Hey Josh, let's make that train a little bit longer."

I came back onstage and told him I couldn't do an encore, because we had only rehearsed one song. So he asked if I would sing it again. I did, but I was really emotional the whole time. What really choked me up, though, was when I looked up into that balcony and it hit me that this was the same balcony that Hank looked up and saw when he played here. I barely got through the song after that.

## Long Black Train

There's a long black train, comin' down the line,
Feeding off the souls that are lost and cryin'
Rails of sin, only evil remains
Watch out brother for that long black train

Look to the heavens you can look to the sky
You can find redemption starin' back into your eyes,
There is protection and there's peace the same
Burn in your ticket for that long black train

CHORUS:
Cause there's victory in the Lord I say,
Victory in the Lord
Cling to the father and his holy name,
And don't go ridin' on that long black train,

There's an engineer on that long black train,
Makin' you wonder if your ride is worth the pain,
He's just a waitin' on your heart to say
Let me ride on that long black train

CHORUS

Well, I can hear the whistle from a mile away,
It sounds so good but I must stay away,
That train is a beauty, makin' everybody stare
But its only destination is the middle of nowhere,

CHORUS

Yea watch out brother for that long black train,
That devil's drivin' that long black train

# Long Black Veil

*Story by Buck Wilkin*
*Song written by Danny Dill*
*and Marijohn Wilkin*
*Recorded by Lefty Frizzell, Johnny Cash,*
*Rosanne Cash, Joan Baez, and others*

49

[Editor's note: In the 1970s, songwriter Danny Dill told author Dorothy Horstman, "So I said, 'I'll write me a folksong'—an instant folksong if you will. I worked on it for months and then it all came to me. There was a Catholic priest killed in New Jersey many years ago under a town hall light, and there were no less than 50 witnesses. They never found a motive. They never found the man. Until this day, it's an unsolved murder. Then the Rudoloh Valentino story's always impressed me—about the woman that always used to visit his grave. She always wore a long, black veil. The third component was Red Foley's 'God Walks These Hills With Me.' I always thought that was a great song, so I got that in there, too. I just scrambled it all up, and that's what came out."]

D anny Dill walked into the office with a poem. This was at Cedarwood Publishing, downtown on 7th Avenue, before there really was a Music Row. The staff writers down there were my mom, Mel Tillis, Wayne Walker, John D. Loudermilk, Fred Burch, and Danny Dill. Danny walked in and gave that poem to my mom and she tweaked the lyric a little bit, put a melody to it, and then they did a demo.

The publishers then were almost like the old Hollywood Studios. They were strong and they romanced people for cuts and things like that. This was when the publisher was king.

I saw Rosanne Cash recently on the Don Imus show and she was talking about how this song was on 'the list' of classic songs that her dad had given her and, of course, she just released a collection of those. She said it was a love story, a murder mystery, and a ghost story all in one.

A lot of people think it is an old folk song, but it's not. It was written in 1958. My mom wrote for Cedarwood from about 1958 until 1962 or 1963. She started Buckhorn in 1964. In that one year or two—around 1958 or 1959—she won several BMI Awards. She had "Long Black Veil," "P.T. 109," "Waterloo," "Cut Across Shorty"—just a whole bunch of songs. The first song that was in the Buckhorn catalog was a song I wrote and sang called "GTO (The Hot Rod Song)." Kristofferson came to town in 1965, and he wrote for Buckhorn.

"Long Black Veil" has probably been recorded 700 or 800 times. Right now, Rosanne Cash's version is my favorite. She put in a few extra chords and added a nice rock beat to it. That was a nice Christmas present, to hear her sing that song. And times have been a little slow in the music publishing business, too, so when that came out in the fall of 2009, I thought, "This is great. My mom's alive and well," and it made me very happy to hear Rosanne's version. My second favorite version of it is probably the one by Joan Baez. I've heard Dave Matthews' version and I didn't really get it. But I'm 63, so he is like a punk rocker to me. But I thought, "Well, this is cool. Congratulations, Mom."

I think it was the biggest song my mom wrote, maybe second to "One Day at A Time." She had two distinct periods in her life. She went through a period of alcoholism and then she quit drinking and she quit writing secular music after that. She only wrote gospel music after that.

Her dream was to come to Nashville and write music. She was an elementary school teacher in Tulsa, Oklahoma. It's one of those dream-come-true success stories. There were very few women pioneers in that industry and in that era, especially ones like my mom, who was a successful writer and then became a successful publisher, too.

# Long Black Veil

Ten years ago on a cold dark night
There was someone killed 'neath the town hall light
There were few at the scene and they all did agree
That the slayer who ran looked a lot like me

The judge said "Son, what is your alibi?
If you were somewhere else, then you won't have to die"
I spoke not a word, though it meant my life
I had been in the arms of my best friend's wife

CHORUS:
She walks these hills in a long black veil
She visits my grave when the night winds wail
Nobody knows, nobody sees
Nobody knows but me

The scaffold is high, and eternity's near
She stood in the crowd and shed not a tear
But sometimes at night when the cold wind moans
In a long black veil she cries over my bones

CHORUS

# Love, Me

*Story by Skip Ewing*
*Song written by Skip Ewing and Max T. Barnes*
*Recorded by Collin Raye*

I was getting ready to go out on tour one year, back in the early 1990s. This was when I had a record deal and was performing quite a bit. I had a girlfriend and she wasn't able to travel with me, so she wrote me a letter before I left. At the end of the note, she just signed it, "Love, Me."

I got on the bus and I said to my guitar player at the time, Max T. Barnes, "There is something very intimate about that little act. You can't sign something to someone as simply, 'Love, Me' unless you are really close to that person. I love that. Is there any way we could work this into a song? I think that is something a lot of people could relate to."

I am someone who looks deeply at relationships and do my best to try to understand the different kinds of energies of love and the feelings between two people in relationships, especially the ones that last a long time. We talked about how certain kinds of love traverse those boundaries that we, as human beings, seem limited to. But love doesn't recognize any of those limits. It's as big and wide and deep as it's able to be.

So Max and I started talking about my grandmother and grand-father. We talked about the brother that he had lost, and other people we had known. We were on our way to Utah to open for the Judds, and we talked all night long.

There are elements of the song that are based on true events. I was very much affected by my grandfather. He was a thoroughbred horse rancher in California—kind of a John Wayne type. He treated my grandmother very well. He always called her "mother." There was no note left in a tree or anything like that, but there were elements of that kind of love and connectedness in their relationship in the song. The line about "I'll meet you when my chores are through" is really reflective of their relationship when you consider he lived on a ranch.

When we first wrote it, I was so excited and wanted to record it myself, but I had a producer who told me that it was basically junk. He said, "Nobody wants to hear that. Give me something that will play on the radio and sell records." For years and years, nobody wanted to record that song. So we just put it away.

Then one day, we got a call and someone told us there was this new artist named Bubba Wray (that was actually the name he was going to record under) and he was interested in "Love, Me." I said, "Well, does he sing pretty well?" And they said "yes." So I said, "Well, go ahead and let him cut it." Bubba turned out to be Collin Raye, of course, and it ended up being a big hit for him. It was the last single released from the first album that he did and they almost didn't release it. But it hit #1 and stayed there for several weeks and was nominated for Song of the Year.

## Love, Me

I read a note my grandma wrote back in nineteen twenty-three.
Grandpa kept it in his coat, and he showed it once to me.
He said, "Boy, you might not understand, but a long, long time ago,
Grandma's daddy didn't like me none, but I loved your grandma so."

We had this crazy plan to meet and run away together.
Get married in the first town we came to, and live forever.
But nailed to the tree where we were supposed to meet, instead
I found this letter, and this is what it said:

"If you get there before I do, don't give up on me.
I'll meet you when my chores are through;
I don't know how long I'll be.
But I'm not gonna let you down, darling wait and see.
And between now and then, till I see you again,
I'll be loving you.
Love, me."

I read those words just hours before my grandma passed away,
In the doorway of a church where me and grandpa stopped to
        pray.
I know I'd never seen him cry in all my fifteen years
But as he said these words to her, his eyes filled up with tears.

If you get there before I do, don't give up on me.
I'll meet you when my chores are through;
I don't know how long I'll be.
But I'm not gonna let you down, darling wait and see.
And between now and then, till I see you again,
I'll be loving you.
Love, me.
Between now and then, till I see you again,
I'll be loving you.
Love, me.

# Mamas Don't Let Your Babies Grow Up to Be Cowboys

*Story by Patsy Bruce*
*Song written by Ed and Patsy Bruce*
*Recorded by Ed Bruce, Willie Nelson and*
*Waylon Jennings, and others*

I wrote "Mamas Don't Let Your Babies Grow Up to Be Cowboys" with my husband, Ed Bruce. Ed started it on the way home from a recording session in Nashville in 1975. It actually started out to be "Mamas Don't Let Your Babies Grow Up to Be Guitar Players," which didn't sound very commercial. By the time he got home, he had a verse and part of a chorus, but it lay around for a while and he could never finish it. So, one night we sat down together to work on it and we finished it that night.

If you listen to the lyrics closely, you can tell it's really about being a musician. Ed recorded it, and then later it got pitched to Waylon while he was recording in Nashville. Willie just happened to be there, as he was on lots of things with Waylon. I was at lunch and I got a phone call from someone who I knew in the studio who said, "Waylon is cutting a song of yours." I asked them which song, and this person said, "It's 'Mamas Don't Let Your Babies Grow Up to Be

Cowboys.'" And the next thing I knew, Waylon had added Willie to the track. They made it sound live, but it was in the studio.

Ed saw them perform it in Memphis for the first time and I went to see them perform it in Fort Smith, Arkansas, at a retail convention, I believe. Since then, I've seen them sing it hundreds of times. These days, it's always interesting to me to see the reaction to that song, because the song is older than most of the fans in the audience.

That was one of the first collaborations that Ed and I wrote together and we went on to write a few hundred songs after that. After a while, people forget that you wrote any other song, because you become so closely identified with one like that. You almost seem like a one-song wonder, even though you have this huge catalog.

It's still one of my favorite songs, though, and it's definitely one of my banker's favorites! It's been cut over 300 times, and there are tons of different parodies on it: "Mamas Don't Let Your Babies Grow Up to Be Ad Agency Men," and "Don't Let Your Babies Grow Up to Be Programmers." We get requests like that all the time.

One of the most amazing things is that when the song turned 20 years old, I got calls from people wishing me and the song a happy birthday. Now that tells you something about the impact it had. A dean of one of the major law schools told me once that he was painting a building in Philadelphia the first time he heard it. He told me what day it was and what color he was painting the building. Tom Brokaw always said it was his favorite song, too.

One day, a lady stopped me in a Kroger store and asked me for an autograph. She had a pen but nothing to write on. She said, "My husband Leroy is just never going to believe I ran into you unless I take him an autograph," Then she reached into her buggy and picked up a box of Kotex and asked me to sign it for her, and I did. Now that was a first.

# Mamas Don't Let Your Babies Grow Up to Be Cowboys

Cowboys ain't easy to love and they're harder to hold.

They'd rather give you a song than diamonds or gold.
Lone Star belt buckles and old faded Levis,
And each night begins a new day.
If you don't understand him, and he don't die young,
He'll prob'ly just ride away.

CHORUS:
Mamas, don't let your babies grow up to be cowboys.
Don't let 'em pick guitars or drive them old trucks.
Let 'em be doctors and lawyers and such.
Mamas don't let your babies grow up to be cowboys.
'Cause they'll never stay home and they're always alone.
Even with someone they love.

Cowboys like smoky old pool rooms and clear mountain
    mornings,
Little warm puppies and children and girls of the night.
Them that don't know him won't like him and them that do,
Sometimes won't know how to take him.
He ain't wrong, he's just different, but his pride won't let him
Do things to make you think he's right.

CHORUS

# Man of Constant Sorrow

*Story by Dan Tyminski*
*Song originally attributed to Dick Burnett*
*    (Soggy Bottom Boys arrangement by*
*    Carter Stanley)*
*Recorded by Ralph Stanley, The Grateful*
*    Dead, Bob Dylan, Dan Tyminski (for O*
*    Brother Where Art Thou?), and various*
*    other artists*

"**M**an of Constant Sorrow" is a song that I've heard for years. I grew up with bluegrass music and I've heard Ralph Stanley do it in person many times and, of course, knew about his recordings of it. I was somewhat surprised to hear that it was going to be used in a Coen brothers movie, and that George Clooney would be singing it. I just couldn't imagine it, but then I don't make movies, so that's no shocker. But I got a big grin when I found out they were going to make that happen.

The Coen brothers had been in contact with our manager, Denise Stiff, and had slotted us in for an audition to play some of the soundtrack music. We did that at a studio in Nashville. At that point, they still had to cast a few of the parts, Clooney's voice on the song being one of them. They said they were still looking, and my manager mentioned that I might be a candidate. I was asked to come back the following day to audition separately for the Clooney role, and I got it.

It was the first time I ever had to record anything that way. Part of the deal was that there could be no overdubs and no studio magic. It had to be one take, start to finish, and that scared me. I'm used to being able to listen to tracks over and over and, if there is something that you don't feel you did your best performance on, you can go back and play it over or sing a certain part again. So it was a little intimidating to do this kind of live version with one microphone in front of me and no headphones and no monitor.

We did it as if we were back in the 1930s, with an old microphone and old instruments. They (the Coen brothers and producer T Bone Burnett) were very particular that it be authentic and pure. The whole point of the soundtrack was to make it as organic as possible. That's one record where you don't hear any overdubs or people who have fixed anything. That was completely raw, untouched music.

It was definitely a surprise to see the level of enormous popularity that it attained. It was amazing to watch all the heads from outside that genre turn to look at some new music—at least new music to them. For us, of course, it's been here forever.

We had the Ralph Stanley version of the song that we drew on, but through the process of working it up for the movie, it was changed and it morphed into something completely different. They were giving visuals and trying to explain where in the movie this was taking place. They said, "You just escaped from prison. Your fingers are flying and you're trying to play rock and roll, but it hasn't been invented yet. You know if you knock it out of the park singing into this can, you're going to get a big payday."

That was the first time I had ever cut anything where they were so insistent upon what we were thinking about and what the visual was to go along with it. Then they said, "You just stole a chicken, too." I'm not sure how that makes you want to play or sing, other than the fact that you are so hungry that you're really reaching for it hard, but

I think they were able to capture what they were looking for in our recording.

T Bone Burnett produced the soundtrack but I was really surprised at how much involvement the Coens had with the soundtrack. When we walked into that first audition, T Bone and Joel and Ethan Coen had every recorded piece of music they could find from the 1930s: boxed sets from the most obscure artists you would ever imagine. Literally, if it was recorded during that time, they had researched it and heard it. They did some pretty extensive work to come up with the feel of that soundtrack, and there was definitely a continuity to it.

A lot of the cuts on the soundtrack were original recordings from the 1930s, but I guess they decided to do a few new versions like this one because they wanted to keep to the premise that it was George Clooney singing, so his vocal would have to be someone who is a little younger than some of the older recordings.

I remember the initial talks we had at Mercury with Luke Lewis and T Bone. I think we went to play golf and T Bone was still trying to shop this project. It was really neat to see the level of confidence he had even then. He foresaw that it was going to be a huge record and he kept saying over and over how big it was going to be. Luke and I were listening and I think we were both thinking, "I know you think this is going to be big, but we all know the type of music this is and what the ceiling is on those kinds of records." He was predicting millions in sales, which is insane for that type of music, but sure enough, he was right.

There was a lot of publicity as far as that record being tied to the movie and the Coens and the actors, so radio stations started picking it up. I'm not sure it was even released as a single initially, but when it started getting some action, the label started pushing it. It's just rare to see something of that genre break into the field it was in and get that much attention, whether it be from the awards shows or country radio or pop radio. It was phenomenal to watch that unfold.

It took a lot of stars to line up for this to happen. It was more than just a movie, or just the music, or just the actors. More people than not were fooled into thinking that George Clooney was singing, and it got a lot of attention just for that. That's hard for me to imagine, but you believe what you see. When you see someone open their mouth and you hear something come out, you don't ever question whether it's them or not. You just believe it. And he did a fantastic job in the way that he performed it, too.

The song was also an amazing thing for me personally. It brought a spotlight to me that I had never seen before. The press factor went up a thousand times after the movie came out. When you play the type of music that I do, and you're able to obtain a song of that magnitude, you're just very grateful.

## Man of Constant Sorrow

I am a man of constant sorrow
I've seen trouble all my day.
I bid farewell to old Kentucky
The place where I was born and raised.
(The place where he was born and raised)

For six long years I've been in trouble
No pleasures here on earth I found
For in this world I'm bound to ramble
I have no friends to help me now.
(He has no friends to help him now)

It's fare thee well my old true lover
I never expect to see you again
For I'm bound to ride that northern railroad
Perhaps I'll die upon this train.
(Perhaps he'll die upon this train.)

You can bury me in some deep valley
For many years where I may lay
Then you may learn to love another

While I am sleeping in my grave.
(While he is sleeping in his grave.)

Maybe your friends think I'm just a stranger
My face you'll never see no more.
But there is one promise that is given
I'll meet you on God's golden shore.
(He'll meet you on God's golden shore.)

# Marie Laveau

*Story by Bobby Bare*
*Song written by Shel Silverstein*
*and Baxter Taylor*
*Recorded by Bobby Bare*

The first time I met Shel Silverstein was at a party at Harlan Howard's house in the late 1960s. I thought he was brilliant. The following week, he came in from Chicago and he brought me a whole bunch of songs. A couple of years later, we put them on an album called *Legends, Lullabies, and Lies* and "Marie Laveau" was part of that album. It also had "Daddy, What If?" and a bunch of other great songs.

"Marie Laveau" was about a voodoo witch in Louisiana and a suitor who tries to get her to use her powers for his gain. I thought it was a great song, but I wasn't sure how big a hit it would be. Chet Atkins knew, though. He produced *Legends, Lullabies, and Lies* and he said it would be the biggest song on the album and it was. Chet always knew what he was talking about. It hit #1 and stayed there for about thirteen weeks.

When we went to record "Marie Laveau," there is a part where Marie screams this god-awful witch's scream, and Shel was the one that did that scream. That was about the extent of his singing ability. He was an incredible songwriter, but he couldn't sing worth anything.

# Marie Laveau

Down in Louisana, where the black trees grow
Lives a voodoo lady named Marie Laveau
Got a black cat's tooth and a Mojo bone
And anyone who wouldn't leave her alone
She'd go (scream) another man done gone.

She lives in a swamp in a hollow log
With a one-eyed snake and a three-legged dog
She's got a bent, bony body and stringy hair
If she ever seen y'all messin' 'round there
She'd go (scream) another man done gone.

And then one night when the moon was black
Into the swamp come handsome Jack
A no-good man like you all know
He was lookin' around for Marie Laveau.

He said "Marie Laveau, you lovely witch
Gimme a little charm that'll make me rich
Gimme a million dollars and I tell you what I'll do
This very night, I'm gonna marry you
Then it'll be (scream) another man done gone."

So Marie done some magic, and she shook a little sand
Made a million dollars and she put it in his hand
Then she giggled and she wiggled, and she said "Hey, Hey
I'm getting' ready for my weddin' day."

But old handsome Jack he said, "Goodbye Marie
You're too damned ugly for a rich man like me."
Then Marie started mumblin', her fangs started gnashin'
Her body started tremblin' and her eyes started flashin'

And she went (scream) another man done gone.

So if you ever get down where the black trees grow
And meet a voodoo lady named Marie Laveau
If she ever asks you to make her your wife
Man, you better stay with her for the rest of your life
Or it'll be (scream) another man done gone.

# 54

# Maybe It Was Memphis

*Story by Michael Anderson*
*Song written by Michael Anderson*
*Recorded by Pam Tillis*

I grew up in Michigan and moved to Los Angeles in the late 1970s and played in a lot of rock and roll bands. Then, in 1983, I signed a publishing deal with a company, Criterion Publishing, which had an office in Nashville. There was a secretary who worked there, and we got to be friends. While I was there one time, she went out of town for a few days, and she let me stay at her apartment and drive her car while she was gone. She also introduced me to her aunt and her cousin. After having lived in Michigan and L.A., I realized that these women were different from anyone I'd ever met. They were very genteel and gracious.

I would go and visit her cousin, and she and I would sit and talk on the front porch for hours at a time. It was late summer—very hot days and warm, humid nights. The katydids—cicadas—were also out that year and they would make the loudest noises while we were sitting on the front porch having sweet tea and her mother's key lime pie. All of that detail in the song—the porch swing, the katydids, the willow tree—was true to life, and I used it in the song.

I finished the first verse and originally thought of the title,

"Maybe It Was Nashville." But I knew that was never going to work. First of all, back then there was an unwritten songwriter rule that you didn't write songs about Nashville. Second of all, it just didn't sound right, so I came up with "Maybe It Was Memphis." Sounded much more atmospheric and romantic. I had never been to Memphis at that time, but I liked the feel.

I wrote the first verse, last verse, and the chorus, but had a hard time coming up with a second verse. When we were going to make a demo of it I needed to put something down, thinking I could always go back and change the vocal later if I needed to. I had written the song in Nashville, so I wanted to demo it in Nashville, even though it would cost the publisher more, because they would have to pay for Nashville players instead of using the ones we had in L.A. I talked them into doing it in Nashville. And the first thing that came to mind when I tried to finish the second verse was "I read about you in a Faulkner novel, met you once in a Williams play." The interesting thing was, I don't think I had read any Faulkner, and was only familiar with a couple of Tennessee Williams plays, but it just sounded so right and so southern. Since then, I've become more familiar with both of them, but at the time, I wasn't thinking of any specific character in any of the novels or plays. The key phrase for me was "country love song." I didn't think anyone would know what I was talking about with "Faulkner novel" and "Williams play."

When I got back to L.A., the song was pitched for several years, but everyone passed on it. Then Pam Tillis heard it and she put it on her album, *Put Yourself in My Place*, in 1991. Later, I found out that she had actually recorded the song while she was still on Warner Bros. It was released as a single on that label but nothing ever came of it. Then she signed with Arista and she re-cut it, with Paul Worley producing it. It was the fourth single off her album, and made it to #2 and stayed there for a long time right behind a Garth Brooks hit at the time.

I've heard a couple of different stories about how Pam first heard the song. The folks at Criterion said she just heard it in a pitch session. But there was another secretary at Criterion—a different one from the one who lent me her car and all—who saw me once in a restaurant in Nashville. She was eating there with her boyfriend (an original member of the Eagles). She said that while she was working at Criterion she fell in love with the song and made a cassette for herself that she gave to Pam Tillis with the song on it when Pam was at the publishing office one day. I asked Pam once and I didn't get the feeling she knew exactly either. A publisher and good friend of mine, Michael Puryear, says he pitched the song to Paul Worley directly around that time also. Sometimes you never really know in Nashville. I'm just happy she decided to cut it.

After it became a hit, life changed for me. I was at the Bound'ry Restaurant in Nashville one day and was introduced to Tanya Tucker. She dramatically got down on her knees and started begging me, "Please write me song like 'Maybe It Was Memphis.' Please!" She said she had passed on it earlier and was acting like she was crying. It was pretty funny.

I had another interesting encounter while the song was still on the charts. I was at Sunset Grill in Nashville. It was early afternoon and there was hardly anyone there. I walked through the bar area on my way to the restroom and there, all by himself in the bar, drinking a whiskey and smoking a cigarette, was Harlan Howard. I really wanted to meet him, but I also try to respect people's privacy and don't usually interrupt them at restaurants. Since there was no one else there, I thought, what the heck, so I went over and said, "Mr. Howard, my name is Michael Anderson and I just wanted to say hello."

He cocked his head to one side and said, "Maybe It Was Memphis?" and I said "Yes."

He started telling me where the song was on the charts and how many weeks it had been there and how many albums had been sold. He knew more about my song than I did. Then he said something I'll never forget. He said, "Do you know why that song was such a big hit?" Of course, I wanted to say it was because I'm such a great songwriter, but I said, "No, why?"

He said, "It's the only song in country music where a nice girl gets laid and you still like her at the end of the song." I had never thought about it that way. Then he said, "Every great songwriter has a least one song written in a waltz beat, too." He said, "Now you've had yours, so don't ever do that again."

I moved to Nashville from about 1992 to 1997 and then moved back to L.A., but I still spend a lot of time in the South. Every time I go to Memphis or Atlanta or Nashville, or any city like that, and I meet people and they find out I wrote that song, they nearly always say the same thing. They say they are very appreciative that I wrote that because it's one of those songs (because of the second verse) that make southerners and the South sound romantic, literate and sophisticated, instead of just a bunch of hicks, like so many songs do.

## Maybe It Was Memphis

Lookin' at you through a misty moonlight
Katydids sing like a symphony
Porch swing swayin' like a Tennessee lullaby
Melody blowing through the willow tree

What was I supposed to do
Standin' there lookin' at you
A lonely boy far from home?

CHORUS:
Maybe it was Memphis
Maybe it was southern summer nights
Maybe it was you, maybe it was me
But it sure felt right

Read about you in a Faulkner novel
Met you once in a Williams play
Heard about you in a country love song
Summer nights beauty took my breath away

What was I supposed to do

Standin' there lookin' at you
A lonely boy far from home?

CHORUS

Every night now once I've been back home
I lie awake at night drifting in my memory
I think about you on your momma's front porch swing
Talking that way so soft to me

What was I supposed to do
Standin' there lookin' at you
A lonely boy far from home?

CHORUS

55

# Mississippi Squirrel Revival

*Story by Buddy Kalb*
*Song written by Buddy and Carlene Kalb*
*Recorded by Ray Stevens*

Wendy Bagwell and the Sunliters was a gospel group that I used to listen to. They played churches a lot and did comedy, too. Wendy used to tell a story about a blind man who came to church with a seeing-eye dog. One day, the dog got after a cat in the church and it caused a lot of mayhem. I first heard Wendy tell that story one night on the radio when I was driving to Florida with my family. It was early in the morning, and they were all asleep, and I just thought it was hilarious. It's a funny concept—something gets loose in church and it's happening on the left side and the people on the right side of the church don't know what it is, and they misinterpret it. So that's where the idea for "Mississippi Squirrel Revival" got started.

I kept that in my mind for a while, and later I began working on the song. Back in those days, I had a habit of putting in references to people and places I knew in a song. I actually had a friend named Harv Newlin, who lived in Kansas City. And I had some friends who lived in Pascagoula, too, so that—and the fact that it was the only word I could find that rhymed with hallelujah—made me put them in the song. My wife is down as a co-writer, because I used to bounce ideas off her all the time and she would give me feedback on the songs I was writing.

I did have a background in things charismatic, so I sort of knew of what I spoke. I've never really belonged to many mainline denominations. Everybody always thinks the song says "the First Baptist Church" of Pascagoula, but it's "the First Self-Righteous Church."

I was writing for Ray's publishing company and some others as well when I came up with this idea and I thought I would write this for him. He was doing some Barry Manilow-ish stuff and I kept telling him he needed to give the people what they wanted, which was more comedy. So one day, he got frustrated with me and said, 'Well, then why don't you write me some comedy?" So I decided I would give the squirrel song a shot, and it worked out pretty well for us. Since then, Ray has recorded over 100 of my songs.

# Mississippi Squirrel Revival

Well, when I was a kid I'd take a trip every summer down to
    Mississippi
To visit my granny in her ante-bellum world
I'd run barefooted all day long, climbin' trees, free as a song
And one day I happened to catch myself a squirrel.
I stuffed him down in an old shoe box, punched a couple of
    holes in the top
And when Sunday came I snuck him into church
I was sittin' way back in the very last pew showin' him to my
    good buddy Hugh
When that squirrel got loose and went totally berserk
What happened next is hard to tell
Some thought it was heaven others thought it was hell
But the fact that something was among us was plain to see
As the choir sang "I Surrender All" the squirrel ran up Harv
    Newlan's coveralls

Harv leaped to his feet and said, "Somethin's got a hold on me!
Yeow!"

CHORUS:
The day the squirrel went berserk
In the First Self-Righteous Church
In the sleepy little town of Pascagoula
It was a fight for survival that broke out in revival
They were jumpin' pews and shoutin' Hallelujah!

Harv hit the aisles dancin' and screamin'
Some thought he had religion others thought he had a demon
And Harv thought he had a weed eater loose in his Fruit-Of-
The-Looms
He fell to his knees to plead and beg and the squirrel ran out of
his britches leg
Unobserved to the other side of the room
All the way down to the amen pew where sat Sister Bertha
better-than-you
Who'd been watchin' all the commotion with sadistic glee
But you should've seen the look in her eyes
When that squirrel jumped her garters and crossed her thighs
She jumped to her feet and said "Lord have mercy on me"
As the squirrel made laps inside her dress
She began to cry and then to confess to sins that would make a
sailor blush with shame
She told of gossip and church dissension but the thing that got
the most attention
Was when she talked about her love life, and then she started
naming names

CHORUS

Well seven deacons and the pastor got saved,
Twenty-five thousand dollars was raised and fifty volunteered

For missions in the Congo on the spot
Even without an invitation there were at least five hundred
   rededications
And we all got baptized, whether we needed it or not
Now you've heard the Bible story I guess
How he parted the waters for Moses to pass
Oh the miracles God has wrought in this old world
But the one I'll remember 'til my dyin' day
Is how he put that church back on the narrow way
With a half-crazed, Mississippi squirrel

CHORUS

# Mr. Bojangles

*Story by Jerry Jeff Walker*
*Song written by Jerry Jeff Walker*
*Recorded by Nitty Gritty Dirt Band and others*

The song "Mr. Bojangles" is a true story. It happened almost exactly the way I wrote it. I was in the first precinct city jail in New Orleans. The building's not there anymore. There was a murder in the French Quarter one weekend. Somebody had been stabbed to death. The police wanted to prove that they were really looking for their man and show a better arrest record, so they rounded up all the street people—all the dancers, painters, singers, jugglers, and bums. It resulted in a 60% increase from their normal arrest record.

I was one of the street characters and we all were thrown in, which made the jail cells quite crowded. It happened to be a holiday weekend, so it was about four days before we could see a judge and then we were either bailed out or let go.

I was just a young kid, 19 or 20, so I was nervous. This old guy came in and sat down near me. He said, "I'll just sit over here, kid. I won't bother you." He was white, because the jails were segregated then. This was around 1964. He seemed like a nice enough fellow, so I said, "Sure, have a seat."

As you can imagine, we got pretty bored over the course of those three or four days and we needed to pass the time. We started singing and telling stories. And this fellow started telling us about his life.

It turns out he was an old Vaudeville-style entertainer. He had done a lot of dancing and singing for different shows over the years. He said his name was just Bojangles, not "Mr. Bojangles"—just Bojangles. There was a famous black dancer named Bill "Bojangles" Robinson, and some people think this was a story about him, but this was someone entirely different.

He started telling us stories about his life and all of his travels and other things. He told us he had a dog that traveled with him for about twenty years and was his best friend. I changed that to fifteen years in the song because the line, "he spoke in tears of fifteen years how his dog and him, traveled about" just flowed a little better than "twenty years." He stopped to get gas one day and his dog saw a female dog and started to run after her, maybe because she was in heat. When he did, he ran across the street and was hit by a car. Bojangles really got choked up when he talked about his dog, just like it says in the song.

When he was done telling his stories, one of the other guys in the cell yelled, "Hey Bojangles, dance!" I remember he hiked up his trousers and started dancing a soft shoe for us. That's when he told us how he used to dance at minstrel shows and now he danced on the street corners and in honky-tonks for tips, but said he spent a lot of time in the jail when he drank too much.

When Monday finally rolled around, we got a chance to see a judge and he saw that we were harmless, so he let us go. I don't know if they solved the murder that week or not, but I didn't stick around to find out. I got back on the highway, stuck my thumb out and started hitchhiking. I lived like that for several years, just playing my guitar on street corners or in coffee shops or wherever I could. This was at the beginning of the hippie era, so in every major city, there was a coffee shop on just about every corner, where people sang and read poetry or played music and you could make enough money to pay for your meals, and maybe a room and a shower before you got back on the road to the next city.

Sometimes, if I was having a hard time getting a ride, I would make up a sign that said, "Veteran" or "need ride back to college" or something that would make people trust me more, and then I could get a ride easier. I would often head up north during the summer months, where it wasn't quite as hot.

Over the next few days after I got out of jail, I started writing the song. I actually added another verse about his several marriages, but the song was getting too long, so I cut that one verse. I've always loved stories and characters and this was one character who had a lot of living to share in his stories. I finished it within a few days and then put it away.

That vagabond life was a pretty interesting way to live for a few years. I wouldn't trade those experiences for anything. I got a lot of material for songs during those years.

# Mr. Bojangles

I knew a man Bojangles and he'd dance for you
In worn out shoes
With silver hair, a ragged shirt, and baggy pants
The old soft shoe
He jumped so high, jumped so high
Then he lightly touched down

I met him in a cell in New Orleans I was
down and out
He looked to me to be the eyes of age
as he spoke right out
He talked of life, talked of life.
He laughed, clicked his heels and stepped
He said his name "Bojangles" and he danced a lick
across the cell
He grabbed his pants and spread his stance,
Oh he jumped so high and then he clicked his heels
He let go a laugh, let go a laugh
and shook back his clothes all around

Mr. Bojangles, Mr. Bojangles
Mr. Bojangles, dance

He danced for those at minstrel shows and county fairs
throughout the south
He spoke through tears of 15 years how his dog and him
traveled about
The dog up and died, he up and died
And after 20 years he still grieves

He said "I dance now at every chance in honky-tonks
for drinks and tips
But most the time I spend behind these county bars
'cause I drinks a bit"
He shook his head, and as he shook his head
I heard someone ask him please, please...

Mr. Bojangles, Mr. Bojangles
Mr. Bojangles, dance.

# Murder on Music Row

*Story by Larry Cordle*
*Song written by Larry Cordle and Larry Shell*
*Recorded by George Strait and Alan Jackson*

L arry Shell, one of my longtime friends and co-writers, called me up one day back in early 1999 and said he had an idea for a song. I had just come off the road and was in the middle of recording a new album, so I really wasn't in the mood to write anything. He told me he had a title. It was "Murder on Music Row." And no sooner did he get that out of his mouth than I said, "Oh, man, is it about killing country music?" And he started laughing and said yes. He knew that I got it right away.

Since we were already on the same wavelength, I said, "Let's get together sometime over the next few days and write this thing." It only took us a few hours to finish it. I was making a bluegrass album at the time and I didn't think it was a bluegrass song. I thought it was a traditional country song, so I had no intention of recording it. But I got out and played it a couple of places. I played it first at The Bluebird Café. I did a show there with Rebecca Lynn Howard and some other folks, and it got such a response. The Bluebird is a listening room. You usually get good responses there, but it was really over the top, even for The Bluebird. Then I played it at The Station Inn in Nashville one night, and it was the same way—just over the top.

So the last night of the session, I told the guys, "Let's record this." It was about midnight. I said, "At the least, I still need a demo to pitch." Well, that became the record. I took a disc and put a yellow crime scene tape around it and took it over to the disc jockey Carl P. Mayfield. He made a website and did this whole thing. For about a month, it was his whole show, his mantra. He told me the first day he played the song on his show, he played it eight times. And his show was only four hours long. It was just a CD with no label printed on it or anything. I think the song title was just handwritten. Apparently, the station manager, Herb Woolsey, heard Carl play it on the radio and then called George Strait and said, "I've got a song for you."

Renee White at MCA called my cell phone. I was in Louisville at the IBMA Convention when it was still being held up there, and she asked if we would hold the song. I said, "Sure, Renee, I wasn't planning on playing it for anybody anyway. I was just planning on releasing it myself." She said, "Well, George Strait is thinking about doing it and he'd like Alan Jackson to record it with him." And I said, "Well, lord yes!"

After we wrote it, we stood back and looked at it, and I knew that some people on Music Row might not like it. I can't say we never got any negative reactions. But it won the CMA Song of the Year in 2001 and neither Larry nor I could even vote for it. We weren't even CMA members at the time. We had no lobbying strength. The song won on its own merit. And it was not even released as a single. It was never promoted. It got up into the 30's I think, on the charts, just from people playing it straight from the CD.

George Jones cut it with Dierks Bentley a few years later. There are things about their version that I love, and there are things about my version that I love, too. Gene Wooten played Dobro on mine and that was the last real record that he played on before he died. But I guess Alan and George's version will always be the definitive version. I mean how can you not love Alan Jackson and George Strait together on the same record?

It may have been the first time something has won Song of the Year without ever being released as a single. I think the song came through us for a reason and it just needed to be written, so we wrote it.

# Murder on Music Row

Nobody saw them running
From 16th Avenue
They never found the fingerprints
Or the weapon that was used
But someone killed country music
Cut out its heart and soul
They got away with murder
Down on Music Row

The almighty dollar
And the lust for worldwide fame
Slowly killed tradition
And for that, someone should hang
They all say "Not Guilty!"
But the evidence will show
That murder was committed
Down on Music Row

For the steel guitars no longer cry
And the fiddles barely play
But drums and rock 'n' roll guitars
Are mixed up in your face
Ol' Hank wouldn't stand a chance
On today's radio
Since they committed murder
Down on Music Row

They thought no one would miss it

Once it was dead and gone
They thought no one would buy them ol'
Drinkin' and cheatin' songs
Well there ain't no justice in it
And the hard facts are cold
Murder's been committed
Down on Music Row

For the steel guitars no longer cry
And you can't hear fiddles play
With drums and rock 'n' roll guitars
Mixed right up in your face
Why the Hag wouldn't have a chance
On today's radio
Since they've committed murder
Down on Music Row

Why they even tell the Possum
To pack up and go back home
There's been an awful murder
Down on Music Row

# My List

*Story by Rand Bishop*
*Song written by Rand Bishop and Tim James*
*Recorded by Toby Keith*

"**M**y List" was the idea of my writing partner, Tim James. Tim and I had been collaborating for several years and were good friends. He came in one day and said, "You know I always make a list of things to do every day. Let's write a song about that." And I thought, "That's good enough for me," so I started picking on my guitar and the first line just fell out: "Under an old brass paperweight / is my list of things to do today." We wrote it in one session basically. We changed one line the next day and then did the demo.

This was in 1999, and both Tim and I had been dropped by our publishers. I started working for the Census Bureau. Tim was painting houses, so we got together on rare occasions when we had the time to write. We wrote this at my house, which was a rental on Natchez Trace Avenue, near Vanderbilt. It was a little Tudor and I had a studio in the attic.

After we wrote it, Tim said, "So are you going to start changing your priorities now that we've written this song?" And I said, "Are you kidding? I'm trying to make it in show business. I don't have time for that stuff!" Really, though, this was a message that I needed to hear myself, even as I was writing it. I didn't think it was a particularly original or fresh idea. I thought it was a well-written and well-constructed song, but I didn't know if the world really needed another song like that.

When we finished it, it just sat around for about two years. No publishers really took note of it. The only artist that showed any interest was Dan Seals. He had recorded a couple of my other songs, but then he decided against it.

Tim called me one day and said, "Did Dan Seals ever cut that song, 'My List?'" I said he hadn't and then asked him why. He said, "Because there's a good chance that Toby Keith is going to cut it today." Toby Keith had started his own publishing company and the first writer he signed was Tim.

By then, I had basically retired from the music business. I was very grateful for the opportunities that I had. I had about 200 of my songs recorded. One was a Grammy nominee and one was a BMI award-winner. But I felt like I had put my family through so many ups and downs. So I started another business selling legal representation plans for small businesses and families. But Tim just kept knocking on doors. Thank God for him because Toby cut the song. It's been the kind of gift that keeps on giving. It got released on three different CDs: once on the original album, then he did a greatest hits album, and later a boxed set.

When the record came out, it was right after 9/11. It was the perfect time for people to hear a song like this, because Americans were really beginning to reevaluate their priorities. It's an incredible experience having a big hit song, but it's even more gratifying when it's a song that has affected so many people's lives in a positive way. One time I played it live and the audience applauded the song after the first chorus. They actually interrupted the song with their applause. It was the only time that had ever happened to me. It was like being on one of those TV shows where the audience is instructed with the neon signs that say, "Applause, Applause!"

We got so many e-mails and letters from people whose lives had been affected by the song that Tim and I later decided to write a book based on it, and we got it published by McGraw-Hill. It's called, *My*

*List: 24 Reflections on Life's Priorities.* The letters came from people who were having financial problems, or had lost jobs, or had family or health challenges, and they wrote us to tell us how that song helped them cope with those challenges and reminded them of their real priorities. In the book we expounded on every line in the song, with an essay or short story and then a prayer or affirmation. A lot of the other books like this are more like an extended greeting card, but this one was a little more substantial; it was kind of a self-help book.

That success of this also got me really passionate about working outside the three-minute song genre. I wrote three screenplays and a stage play that was produced here in Nashville and I've written three more books since. And it was all because of the experience of writing the book based on "My List."

# My List

Under an old brass paperweight
Is my list of things to do today
Go to the bank and the hardware store
Put a new lock on the cellar door
I cross 'em off as I get 'em done
but when the sun is set
There's still more than a few things left
I haven't got to yet

Like go for a walk, say a little prayer
Take a deep breath of mountain air
Put on my glove and play some catch
It's time that I make time for that
Wade the shore, cast a line
Look up a long lost friend of mine
Sit on the porch and give my girl a kiss
Start livin', that's the next thing on my list

It wouldn't change the course of fate
If cuttin' the grass just had to wait
'Cause I've got more important things
Like pushin' my kid on a backyard swing
I won't break my back for a million bucks
I can't take to my grave
So why put off for tomorrow
what I could get done today? Like…

Go for a walk, say a little prayer
Take a deep breath of mountain air
Put on my glove and play some catch
It's time that I make time for that
Wade the shore, cast a line
Look up a long lost friend of mine
Sit on the porch and give my girl a kiss
Start livin', that's the next thing on my list

Raise a little hell, laugh 'til it hurts
Put an extra five in the plate at church
Call up my folks just to chat
It's time that I make time for that
Stay up late, then oversleep
Show her what she means to me
Catch up on all the things I've always missed
Just start livin', that's the next thing on my list

Under an old brass paperweight
Is my list of things to do today

# My Son

*Story by Jan Howard*
*Song written by Jan Howard*
*Recorded by Jan Howard*

"My Son" was written as a letter to my son Jimmy, who was in Vietnam. My middle son Carter, who I've always called Corky, was home on leave from Vietnam and he was going back. I had two sons in Vietnam at the same time. This was in 1968. I didn't have a melody or anything. Corky said, "You need to put that to music. Jimmy would be proud."

So I just put a little melody to it and recited the rest. I sang it to Bill Anderson, who said, "You need to record that." There was just one problem. I couldn't sing it without crying. When I got in the studio, I told Owen Bradley I couldn't get through it. He said, "If you can get one take, we'll do it. Just one good take." So I sang it one time and I couldn't do it anymore.

Then Owen said, "Now Jan, it's just another song." And I said, "No, it isn't. That's Jimmy's life." So that was it. That was the way it was done.

I immediately sent Jimmy a little seven-and-a-half-inch reel-to-reel tape with the song on it. He wrote back and said that he had gotten the tape, but he hadn't had a chance to listen to it yet. I didn't tell him what it was. I just said, "I have a surprise for you." He said in his letter that he was looking for someone who had a reel-to-reel recorder so he could play it. And that was the last I heard from him.

A few weeks later, two people came to my house. They knocked on the door and I opened it. There were two officers standing there. It's still hard for me to talk about. They said, "Ms. Howard, we regret to inform you..." and I just knew what had happened. But I had two sons there. So I said, "For God's sake, tell me which one it was?" They said it was Jimmy.

A few months later, I got a letter from someone in Jimmy's troop who said that Jimmy had borrowed his tape recorder to play the song, and Jimmy was so moved that he cried. I understand that they played it every day in Vietnam, like the national anthem, for quite some time after that. That brought me some comfort, knowing that he had heard the song before he died. He was a wonderful, wonderful boy.

I didn't sing that song for a long, long time after that. The only time I did was when I had a special request from a parent who had lost someone.

My youngest son, David, had a nervous breakdown after Jimmy was killed. He could never deal with it and he took his own life. My middle son brought Jimmy home and served out the rest of his military term in the States.

It's a wound that never heals. It doesn't matter how long it's been. I never watched anything about Vietnam. I never watched any of the movies. I don't read the books. I don't need to. I know all I need to know about Vietnam.

# My Son

(Singing) My son, my son. I pray that you'll come home to me
My son, my son

(recitation) It seems only yesterday
the most important thing on your mind
was whether you'd make the baseball team

or get the new school jacket like all the other kids had
And I remember how your eyes lighted up when you got your
    first
rod and reel for that big fishing trip
Just you and your dad

And I remember wiping the tears away
when you hurt yourself on your sled
In those days it seems the house was always filled
with laughter and joy, filled with your friends
They were all such good boys
And then came the day that you
walked down the aisle, to receive that all-important diploma.
I was so proud but I couldn't
believe that tall young man was my son
My wonderful son.
And then I remember the little girl
that was always around kind of tagging after you
She's not so little anymore but she's still around
Who knows, maybe someday?
Then you received the call
that I guess we knew would come someday
But it came so quick and now you're so very far away
In a land that, until a short time ago, I didn't even
know was there.
I know the time will pass
You'll be home again. But until that time, my darling, take
care. Take special care

(singing) My son my son I pray that
you'll come home to me. My son, my son.

# Not That Different

Story by Karen Taylor-Good and Joie Scott
Song written by Karen Taylor-Good and Joie
    Scott
Recorded by Collin Raye

JS: I was born and raised in Chicago and I was working in advertising with Leo Burnett. I was a city girl but I fell in love with country music. I had known Karen for a while. She used to sing a lot of jingles for our advertising agency. So we struck up a long-distance relationship writing songs together. I was writing for Paul Craft's music publishing company then. There's this school right outside Chicago called Keshet, and it's for kids with special needs. Every year, they would do a fundraising event and I would be asked to write a piece of music for the event. I was sitting at my desk and I was thinking, "If I were a child with special needs, what would I want to say to the world? What would I want to convey?" The thought came to my mind, "I'm really not that different than you. I still have the same emotions. I laugh the same. I cry the same. I feel the same." I thought that's what an individual like that might want to say. So I started writing the chorus to the song. And it all came out in one piece. But then I got stuck on some of the verses, so I called Karen.

KTG: I had met this wonderful woman up in Chicago and she

was writing these tender, incredibly moving lyrics, and I was singing them, things like "Taco Salad, oooh what a treat. Made just for you and a boy can eat: Taco Bell." Then we went on to a little bit more meaningful writing. One day, Joie called me and said, "Karen I have this idea for a song. I thought it was just going to be for this school project, but I think it might be something bigger."She sang me the chorus that she had written. And I couldn't believe it. I got goose bumps.

JS: We had that long-distance writing relationship for a while. We wrote some of this song in Chicago and we wrote some of it over the phone. I actually ended up writing a different song for the Keshet school fundraiser. We both knew that we had something pretty special with "Not That Different." It had a pretty universal theme. When we took it in the direction of a love song, it reminded me a little of my husband, Avi, and myself. He was a school principal in Chicago, and I was a big-city girl. And when it was suggested that we go out, I knew who he was, and I thought, "Oh, my gosh, we're really way too different. This is never going to work." But of course, it worked beautifully. So there are some elements that I drew from my personal life. There's a line in the song that says, "She had always dreamed of loving someone more exotic, and he just didn't seem to fit the part." When he first heard that line, he said, "You're not really going to keep that, are you?"

KTG: We finished it and I took the song to Cliff Audretch over at Sony. They liked me at Sony because I had a hit with Patty Loveless. So I was pitching the song for Patty. I played it for Cliff and he said, "No. I don't hear this song for Patty." I was getting ready to be really depressed. Then he said, "But I really hear it for Collin Raye." I said, "You're kidding? Really?" Fortunately, he's a great A&R guy and he was absolutely right. Even though Joie and I took the song in a romantic direction on purpose, the chorus has such a bigger meaning. The whole song has a much bigger meaning. We knew that Collin Raye, because he has such a wonderful heart, would get that. And he showed that with the way they did the video. In the video, there were people in wheelchairs and a Holocaust survivor with a number branded on his arm, and it was very moving.

JS: So Collin cut the song and it went to #1 in 1996. He included it on his greatest hits album and it's been recorded by a number of other artists since then. A little while after that, I began toying with the idea of moving to Nashville, which I eventually did. But I came here the first time on a dare. Someone actually dared me to go to Nashville because they said it was so "not me." But it ended up being an incredible, overwhelming experience, for a lot of reasons. One of the things that really struck me was there was this huge rainbow across the sky. It was a sign to me that said: "I'm doing the right thing. I am in the right place." And, the name of the school in Chicago — Keshet — it's the Hebrew word for "rainbow."

# Not That Different

She said we're much too different; we're from two separate
    worlds
And he admitted she was partly right
But in his heart's defense he told her what they had in common
Was strong enough to bond them for life
He said "Look behind your own soul and the person that you'll
    see
Just might remind you of me"

CHORUS:
I laugh, I love, I hope, I try
I hurt, I need, I fear, I cry
and I know you do the same things too
So we're really not that different, me and you

She could hardly argue with his pure and simple logic

But logic never could convince a heart
She had always dreamed of loving someone more exotic
and he just didn't seem to fit the part
So she searched for greener pastures but never could forget
What he whispered when she left

CHORUS

BRIDGE:
Was it time or was it truth
Maybe both led her back to his door
As her tears fell at his feet
She didn't say "I love you" what she said meant even more

CHORUS

61

# Old Dogs, Children and Watermelon Wine

*Story by Tom T. Hall*
*Song written by Tom T. Hall*
*Recorded by Tom T. Hall*

I wrote this song in 1972, during the Democratic National Convention in Miami Beach, Florida. There was a park across the street from the convention center called Flamingo Park. They hired me, and George Jones and Tammy Wynette—this was when they were still together—and Ray Price to entertain. It was a daytime show that started late in the afternoon.

One of the interesting things that happened that day was, when the show was over, I gave away my P.A. system. We were having a lot of trouble with it that day, so I told the audience, which was composed of hippies and yippies and other partying types of that era, that they could have the P.A. system, and they took us up on it. We picked up our instruments and got on the bus and the crowd came on stage and carried away the P.A. system. I could see people walking off with mikes and stands and speakers and monitors. It just all disappeared into the night in Miami.

I went back to the hotel where we were staying. The convention was going on, so there were hardly any people in the hotel that night. This must have been about 9:00 or 10:00 at night and I decided to have a nightcap, so I walked into the little bar there in the lobby. There were only two people in there. The bartender was watching *Ironsides* on television, and he was standing there in a very theatrical pose, watching the show and cleaning one glass over and over, which is what bartenders do when they want to look busy.

I went over and ordered a drink. I remember it was Seagram's 7, Canadian blended whiskey, just like in the song, I went back and sat down and there was this old, African-American gentleman who was there cleaning up. There was very little to do there that evening, so he came over to my table and wiped off my table and said, 'Do you mind if I sit down?" I said, "No, go right ahead."

He said, "How old do you think I am?" That's where the song begins.

We talked until my drink was finished. I said goodnight and went back to my room. But before I left, I wrote the words "watermelon wine" on my bar napkin and stuck it in my jacket pocket.

The next morning, I got on a plane for Atlanta on my way back to Nashville. On my way up to Atlanta, I was looking for something in my pocket, and I found that napkin. I had nothing to do on the plane and I started looking for something to write on. The band was on the bus and they were driving back to Nashville, but I had a recording session in Nashville that next day so I had to fly back. I didn't have much with me. I got a sick bag out of the seat pocket in front of me and started writing.

I wrote down exactly what happened, which is the way I write most story songs. I let whoever is listening figure out what it was all about. I knew he said that he had turned sixty-five eleven months ago. I didn't know what that line meant; I just knew he said that. I put it in the song, and later I realized that he was probably telling me that he was retired and maybe on retirement or social security and didn't need the job, that he was just killing time or picking up some extra change.

I went into the recording session the next day and told Jerry

Kennedy, "Here's a song I wrote on the plane," and he liked it, so we cut it. I think the song was less than 24 hours old when I recorded it, but it turned out to be a pretty good song for me.

## Old Dogs, Children and Watermelon Wine

"How old do you think I am?" he asked. I said, well, I didn't
    know.
He said "I turned sixty-five about eleven months ago."
I was sittin' in Miami pourin' blended whiskey down
When this old grey black gentleman was cleanin' up the lounge
There wasn't anyone around 'cept this old man and me
The guy who ran the bar was watching *Ironsides* on TV
Uninvited he sat down and opened up his mind
On old dogs and children and watermelon wine

"Ever had a drink of watermelon wine?" he asked.
He told me all about it though I didn't answer back
"Ain't but three things in this world that's worth a solitary dime
That's old dogs and children and watermelon wine."

He said, "Women think about theyselves when menfolk ain't
    around
And friends are hard to find when they discover that you're
    down."
He said, "I tried it all when I was young and in my natural
    prime
Now it's old dogs and children and watermelon wine.
Old dogs care about you even when you make mistakes
God bless little children while they're still too young to hate"
When he moved away, I found my pen and copied down that
    line
'Bout old dogs and children and watermelon wine.

I had to catch a plane up to Atlanta that next day
As I left for my room I saw him pickin' up my change
That night I dreamed in peaceful sleep of shady summertime
Of old dogs and children and watermelon wine

# Old Hippie

*Story by David Bellamy*
*Song written by David Bellamy*
*Recorded by the Bellamy Brothers*

At the time we wrote the first version of this song, we were probably too young to be called "Old Hippies," but now we definitely aren't. The song came from our backgrounds, mine and my brother Howard's, and a lot of what our friends went through, too. It was more of a composite character, really. We had one friend who had come home from Vietnam a few years before, and another one who was out doing some illegal things, and then there was the adjustment to the changing music that came from our perspective, so we drew from several different people.

I didn't think this song would be a hit. The only person I showed it to was Howard, and I remember saying, "I don't know if this will work for a single or even an album cut, but I wanted to show it to you because it means a lot to me personally." And he said, "Oh, man, this is a great song." Then we showed it to our producer, Jimmy Bowen, and he said, "That's pretty cool. It's different."

When we put it out, it became a hit pretty fast. When we play a show, these guys who were probably 70 or 75 years old would come up to us and say, "Man, you wrote that song about me." I always thought that was funny, because this was in 1985. I thought it was weird that so many people would relate to it from different age groups. Even now, people come up and say the same thing.

Thirty or forty years ago, it seemed that most people were into the same kinds of things, but now everything is so fragmented. Howard and I still live in our own era. I am pretty open-minded about new music, but I don't hear much that is on a par with what I consider the really great music that came out of the 1960s and 1970s. That's why it says, "disco leaves him cold" and "he's got friends into new wave," and so on. So the song is a composite of a whole generation that was getting older.

I thought it was strange that it did so well in the country market, because it had references to John Lennon and so many things outside the country market, but the radio stations started playing it and it never stopped. It still gets a lot of airplay today.

In 1995, we did "The Sequel," and had references to Bill Clinton and his presidency, and Woodstock II, Billy Ray and Garth, and things like that. It did pretty well, also. One of the reasons I decided to do the sequel was because people kept writing newer versions of the song and sending them to me. I wish I had saved them because there were literally hundreds of them. This was before e-mail, and people would just type up new lyrics and send them to me, so I thought maybe we should do an updated version. I still get people re-writing it to this day.

We did a gospel album in 2007 and did the third version: "Old Hippie: Saved." Together, we call them "The Trilogy." The last one is not as well known as the first two, but it really reflects where we are now.

# Old Hippie

He turned thirty-five last Sunday and in his hair he found
    some gray
But he still ain't changed his lifestyle. He likes it better the old way
So he grows a little garden in the back yard by the fence
He's consuming what he's growing nowadays in self defense

He gets out there in the twilight zone
Sometimes when it just don't make no sense

He gets off on country music 'cause disco left him cold
He's got young friends into new wave, but he's just too friggin'
    old
And he dreams at night of Woodstock and the day John
    Lennon died
How the music made him happy and the silence made him cry
Yeah he thinks of John sometimes
And he has to wonder why

CHORUS:
He's an old hippie
and he don't know what to do
Should he hang on to the old?
Should he grab on to the new?
He's an old hippie.
This new life is just a bust
He ain't trying to change nobody
He's just trying real hard to adjust

He was sure back in the sixties that everyone was hip
Then they sent him off to Vietnam on his senior trip
And they forced him to become a man while he was still a boy
And behind each wave of tragedy he waited for the joy
Now this world may change around him
But he just can't change no more

CHORUS

Well, he stays away a lot now from the parties and the clubs
And he's thinking while he's joggin' 'round
He sure is glad he quit the hard drugs
Cause him and his kind get more endangered everyday

And pretty soon the species will just up and fade away
Like the smoke from that torpedo, just up and fade away

CHORUS

•••

# Old Hippie II: The Sequel

He'll be forty-five come Wednesday and his gray hair is getting
    thin
But he's still hanging in there, don't feel too bad for the shape
    he's in
He's seen yuppies in the White House, but he thinks they're
    gonna fail
He just don't trust a President that never has inhaled
And he prays to God to stop his crime
but it seems to no avail

Well, he still loves country music, but he's been left out in the
    dark
'Cause they don't play Merle and George no more. He don't
    know Billy Ray from Garth
And he's heard of Woodstock II, but it never could compete
'Cause he was there the day that Hendrix played the anthem
    with his teeth
Back when all those grunge bands
couldn't even keep a beat

CHORUS:
He's an old hippie
Even older than before
Wondering what to pay attention to
And what should be ignored

He's an old hippie
Still adjusting to the change
He's just trying to find some balance
In a world gone totally insane

He still thinks back on the sixties, but not in the same way
'Cause they built a wall to his war, then forgot the MIA's
And he's trying to be a nice man but it's too much of a bore
Cause fax machine and cell phones ain't what he was put here
for
And in a world selling sex and youth, he's the last old dinosaur

CHORUS

Well, he comes on home from work now, takes some time up
with the kids
Try to teach them right from wrong, hope they don't learn it
the way that he did
And his eyes are on the future but it's looking pretty sad
And with every day that passes he becomes more like his dad
Hopes that when this century turns around, things won't be so
bad

CHORUS

• • •

# Old Hippie III: Saved

He'll be fifty-five this weekend, can't believe he's lived this long
Now he hangs out with the grandkids, instead of tokin' on his bong
He still thinks about his crazy days, but thanks his God above
That he's traded in his loving for a greater kind of love
He still shoots them that old peace sign, still gentle as a dove

He loves all kinds of music, country rock with a little roll
Nowadays he's partial to the melodies that saved his soul
Life has put him through the ringer; friends have fallen
    through the cracks
And with all the trips he's taken, he's been to hell and back
He don't feel that cool no more; he don't care and that's a fact

CHORUS:
He's an old hippie, getting older every day
But his eyes are on the prize and his faith ain't gonna stray
He's an old hippie, he knows what his life is for
Trying' to get right with The Man
before he goes knockin' on heaven's door

He's confused by the issues from Vietnam to Desert Storm
But he prays every night for the guys and gals in uniform
He ain't trying to convert you, just glad for your new start
And he won't be preaching to you like some born-again old fart
He'll just tell you about the love he's found deep within his
    heart

CHORUS

Well, he skips the crowds and the gatherings, spends some
    quiet time alone
His family is his universe, and heaven is his home
He's seen and done it all, been in the belly of the whale
He's looked the devil in the eye and sent him back to hell
He thanks dear Jesus every day, that he's lived to tell the tale

CHORUS

# On Angel's Wings

Story by Karen Taylor-Good
Song written by Karen Taylor-Good
and Jason Blume
Recorded by Collin Raye, Karen Taylor-Good

The song was written about my mama, Molly Berke, who passed away in January of 2010. She had been suffering from dementia for the previous ten years. Earlier in her life, she belonged to Mensa, the society for people with high IQs. She was very proud of her smarts, and was just very, very sharp in a lot of ways. She ended up legally blind from macular degeneration and then we eventually had to move her to a dementia care unit.

That whole journey just crushed me and made me very angry. I was railing at God half the time, crying a lot, and not understanding at all… until I went into a writer's room at SESAC in Nashville with my co-writer Jason Blume, back in the early 2000s. He is also one of my dear friends, so just talking about it with him—and going through half a box of Kleenex—helped. I said, "I still believe that God is not mean and vindictive, but I just can't see the purpose behind this." I asked Jason, "Do you think we could write a song that would help me look at this differently?" This song was the gift we were given that day.

I know the song was heaven-sent. It was an answer to my prayer, like it says in the lyrics: "the answer came down from above." I knew that the chorus was true: "people and places / memories and faces

/ are just way too heavy it seems / to carry on angel's wings." The bridge just slayed me: "Oh, the wonders she'll see / and I know she'll remember to watch over me."

Back then, I was writing for Warner/Chappell Music and I always sent everything through Collin Raye to see what he thought of the songs. He is one of my favorite male artists and a dear friend. He has recorded six or seven of my songs. So I pitched it to Collin and he wanted to do it. At the same time, one of my song pluggers pitched it to a really big female artist and she wanted to do it, too, but I fought for Collin, and won. Later, I ended up putting it out myself as well. I wrote a book about my life as a grown-up, dealing with teenage children, aging parents, etc., and included a 14-song CD. It's titled *On Angel's Wings*. Each of the book's fourteen chapters is about one of the songs, how it came to be written and what it meant to me. The lyrics are included, too, and then there is a little love note for anyone who is going through something similar.

I make a point of singing "On Angel's Wings" everywhere I go and sharing it with everyone I can, because it really helps people going through Alzheimer's or dementia with their loved ones. I have just signed a record deal with a company in Germany and I know what the hook will be to get me on NPR, even though I hate having to reveal my age to do so. The hook is "Woman gets first major record deal at age 60!" When I can get on NPR and have them review the CD, and share this song, my life will be complete!

# On Angel's Wings

This is the woman
Who had all the answers
The one I would lean on
For comfort, for strength
She's never forgotten
One grandchild's birthday
Now she can't remember my name

And it makes me so angry
I shake my fist
And cry out to the heavenly one
Why would you play
Such a cold hearted trick
I thought your job was to love
And the answer came down from above

CHORUS:
She's gonna fly
When her time here is through
First she'll have to let go
Of some things she can't use
'Cause people and places
Memories and faces
Are just way too heavy it seems
To carry on angel's wings

This is the woman
Who saw things so clearly
The one who could pick out
One crumb on the floor
She saw through a white lie
Saw me through love's eyes
She hardly can see anymore
And it makes me so sad
And it just isn't fair
Why should so much be taken away?
But when I cry out
For all that she's lost
I silently hear someone say

CHORUS

And oh, the wonders she'll see

And I know she'll remember
To watch over me

CHORUS

# Online

Story by Chris DuBois
Song written by Brad Paisley, Kelley Lovelace,
and Chris DuBois
Recorded by Brad Paisley

Brad had the idea for "Online," so he and Kelley Lovelace and I started working on it together. It's funny because I'd be surprised if any of the three of us have ever been in a chat room or anything like that, but you hear about people who are trying to be something they're not online. The blessing and the curse of the Internet is that you can hide behind your computer screen and be whoever you want to be. It's hard to do background checks on Facebook and Myspace and places like that.

So Brad came to us with the idea and we thought it would be really interesting to write something about somebody who was your basic computer guru, with limited social skills, who portrayed himself to be the complete opposite of that.

That song took a long, long time to write. It probably took about 12 to 15 writing sessions to finish—most of them at Kelley's house.

When we write with Brad, it's usually because he's getting ready to cut a new album and he's going to cut it if it's good. That's the beauty of having Brad in the room when you are writing, because he knows what he will and won't say, so you don't have to guess. When you are writing with another songwriter, you are constantly guessing about what an artist may be willing to say, so it's always nice to have the artist in the room with you.

Brad had gotten to know Jason Alexander when Jason was in his video for the song "Celebrity," so while we were writing the song, we were already talking about the video and all the cool things we could do. We thought Jason would be the perfect guy to cast as the pizza guy in the video. Jason also was able to get Estelle Harris, who played his mother, Mrs. Costanza, on *Seinfeld*, to be in the video, along with William Shatner. That was a hoot. Seeing the video getting made was almost as much fun as writing the song!

# Online

I work down at the Pizza Pit
And I drive an old Hyundai
I still live with my mom and dad
I'm 5 foot 3 and overweight
I'm a sci-fi fanatic
A mild asthmatic
And I've never been to second base
But there's whole 'nother me
That you need to see
Go checkout MySpace

'Cause online I'm out in Hollywood
I'm 6 foot 5 and I look damn good
I drive a Maserati
I'm a black-belt in karate
And I love a good glass of wine
It turns girls on that I'm mysterious
I tell them I don't want nothing serious
'Cause even on a slow day
I could have a three-way
Chat with two women at one time

I'm so much cooler online
So much cooler online

When I get home, I kiss my mom
And she fixes me a snack
And I head down to my basement bedroom
And fire up my Mac
In real life the only time I've ever even been to L.A.
Is when I got the chance with the marching band
To play tuba in the Rose Parade

But online, I live in Malibu
I pose for Calvin Klein, I've been in GQ
I'm single and I'm rich
And I've got a set of six pack abs that would blow your mind
It turns girls on that I'm mysterious
I tell them I don't want nothing serious
'Cause even on a slow day
I could have a three-way
Chat with two women at one time
I'm so much cooler online
Yeah, I'm cooler online

When you got my kind of stats
It's hard to get a date
Let alone a real girlfriend
But I grow another foot and I lose a bunch of weight
Every time I login

Online
I'm out in Hollywood
I'm 6 foot 5 and I look damn good
Even on a slow day
I could have a three-way
Chat with two women at one time

I'm so much cooler online
Yeah, I'm cooler online
I'm so much cooler online
Yeah, I'm cooler online

Yeah, I'm cooler online

# Reuben James

*Story by Alex Harvey*
*Song written by Alex Harvey and Barry Etris*
*Recorded by Kenny Rogers and others*


When I first started writing for United Artists, Billy Edd Wheeler was there and he was the man who really taught me how to write songs. He went to Berea College and later studied drama at Yale. When it comes to writing songs, there's a real art to simplicity. When I think back to Tchaikovsky or Beethoven or Rachmaninoff, or any of the romantic composers that I was moved by, I hear very simple melodies. As far as lyrics, I read a lot of Sandburg and Frost, who wrote simple but profound poems. So did Rimbaud. He was the French street poet that Dylan studied. Dylan also studied Bertolt Brecht. Rimbaud translates just as gutsy as he wrote it in French, which is hard to do.

When Billy Edd was at UA, a fellow named Barry Etris came in with a song called "Reuben James." It was a song about a white man, and for whatever reason, the song didn't quite work. Billy told me about the song and said, "Can you do something with this? It needs a little help." I said, "I don't really like co-writing songs." But I said, "Maybe I could find something from my own heart and experiences that could add to it." So I went back to a memory from my childhood to help me write some of the extra verses.

Across the road from my dad's little country store in West

Tennessee was a little sharecropper's shack and next to that was a blacksmith shop that was run by a couple of black men named Wesley Watkins and Walter DeBerry. My dad had tuberculosis and when he had to go to the hospital, those men really became my fathers. They got me through some pretty rough times, so I was really close to them. I would go and sit in the door of the blacksmith shop, because my dad was gone and my mom was working, and they really became my family.

My dad never really traded with white people much at his store. When he was born, his mother didn't have any milk. A black woman named Majulia, who lived not far from them, had just had a baby named Jimmy Lee. So when he was a baby, my dad suckled on one breast and Jimmy Lee suckled on the other. That's where I got the lines, "And although your skin was black / You were the one that didn't turn your back / On the hungry white child with no name, Reuben James."

As a result, my dad really grew up thinking he had a black twin. He preferred dealing with black people and he built his store, I think, so they could have a place to trade. He built it in the middle of this section of land that was owned by the DeBerry family. They had been given some land after the war and they had split it up. They each had about twelve acres and lived all around that store. They farmed the land and made a good living, but what impressed was how they always carried themselves with such grace and dignity. They were deeply religious people and were always very proud of the fact that they were landowners at a time when not many black people owned land.

One of them, Mose DeBerry moved into that sharecropper shack across from my dad's store when he got older. I went to see him right before he died and the only thing in that shack was a bunk and a chair and a couple of books, and on either side of the bunk were two pictures: one of Martin Luther King, Jr. and one of John F. Kennedy. I'll always remember that because here was this simple country fellow with no real formal education, out in the middle of nowhere, with pictures of those two men right beside his bed.

I found out that Kenny Rogers was coming to Nashville; I think it was to do *The Johnny Cash Show*. I went down and sat at his dressing room door for almost three days. He would come in and see me sitting there and he would go into his dressing room. Finally, he looked at me and said, "Who are you?" I said, "Oh, I'm just somebody who wants to play you a song." And he said, "Well come on in and play it."

I played it for him and he cut it. It wasn't long after that, he said, "I really like the way you sing, and I'd like to do an album with you." So I got on a plane and went out to L.A. for a year or two and did my first album on Capitol, which he helped produce.

That song's been covered about 27 times at last count. Although it did pretty well for us, it's probably not one of my favorites, just because of all the doggone work it took to whittle that thing down. I've never worked that hard on a song before.

# Reuben James

Reuben James
In my song you'll live again
And the phrases that I rhyme
Are just the footsteps out of time
From the time when I knew you, Reuben James

Reuben James
All the folks around Madison County cussed your name
You're just a no-account, sharecropping colored man
That would steal anything he can
And everybody laid the blame on Reuben James

CHORUS:
Reuben James
You still walk the fertile fields of my mind
The faded shirt, the weathered brow

The calloused hands upon the plow
I loved you then, and I loved you now
Reuben James

Flora Grey
The gossiper of Madison County died with child
And although your skin was black
You were the one that didn't turn your back
On the hungry white child with no name,
Reuben James

Reuben James
With your mind on my soul
And a Bible in your right hand
You said "Turn the other cheek
For there's a better world awaitin' for the meek."
In my mind these words remain from Reuben James

CHORUS

Reuben James
One dark cloudy day they brought you from the field
And to your lonely pinebox came
Just a preacher and me in the rain
Just to sing one last refrain for Reuben James

# She Thinks I Still Care

*Story by Dickey Lee*
*Song written by Dickey Lee*
*Recorded by George Jones, Elvis Presley,*
*Anne Murray and others*

I used to tell a story to the audience when I played this song live. I would say, "This song is about the first girl I really fell in love with, and she really messed me up. But things worked out okay because George Jones had a #1 record with it. Then Anne Murray had a big hit with it, and then Elvis had a big hit with it. So I finally made enough money from the song to take out a contract on her and I had her killed." That usually gets a big laugh.

I had an apartment in Memphis in 1962 and I was going to Memphis State. I met a girl there who I really liked, but it wasn't reciprocated. Her name was Beverly Meyer. We're actually still friends today. I don't see her regularly, but we keep in contact. The funny thing about that song was that I wasn't thinking about writing a hit at all. I was just writing a song about her.

The first guy I pitched it to was Elvis. I gave it someone who knew Elvis and he said he would make sure he heard it. I didn't hear anything else about it, so I just forgot about it. Years later, I was talking to Elvis and he was saying how much he liked it and that he wanted to record it one day. I said, "Well, you're the first guy I sent it to."

He said, "What are you talking about?"

I said, "Well, I gave it to so-and-so to play for you," and Elvis said, "Well, that S.O.B. He never let me hear it." Elvis eventually did cut it, but it was on his last album. He put it out on the *Moody Blue* album.

George Jones got a copy of it, though, and cut it in 1963. Anne Murray cut it in the 1970s as "He Thinks I Still Care," and it works just as well.

Years ago, I was told that this had been covered over 500 times and it's hard to say how many more since then. James Taylor covered it on a live album he did back in the 1990s. When he introduces this song, he says, "When George Jones sings this song, even my dog cries." James nearly always does his own material so I think I was the only songwriter listed on the album besides him.

I think all songwriters have had their hearts broken at least once. But it sure helps when a broken heart can make you that much money.

## She Thinks I Still Care

Just because I asked a friend about her
Just because I spoke her name somewhere
Just because I rang her number by mistake today
She thinks I still care

Just because I haunt the same old places
Where the memory of her lingers everywhere
Just because I'm not the happy guy I used to be
She thinks I still care

But if she's happy thinkin' I still need her
Then let that silly notion bring her cheer

But how could she ever be so foolish
Oh where would she get such an idea?

Just because I asked a friend about her
And just because I spoke her name somewhere
Just because I saw her then went all to pieces
She thinks I still care
She thinks I still care

# Simple Man

Story by Charlie Daniels
Song written by Charlie Daniels,
John L. Gavin, Taz DiGregorio,
and Charles Hayward
Recorded by Charlie Daniels

This song was born out of a lot of anger and frustration. I had just gotten disgusted with the level of violent crime in this country and our inaction to do anything serious about it. We just keep turning the same people loose in the streets until they finally go and murder somebody. We don't need more laws. We just need to enforce the ones we have. But it's like there's a plea bargain for this, and a technicality for that and we just keep turning people loose to go out and keep committing crimes. Some drug dealer who smuggles a ton of cocaine into the country gets a million-dollar lawyer or a team of lawyers and comes up against some public prosecutor whose caseload looks like the Sears Roebuck catalog, and he wins.

We also need to clean up our prisons. People shouldn't go into prison and be able to join gangs and things like that. That's not what it's for. It's punishment. It just goes on and on and on. We seem to literally manufacture a criminal class. They learn how to be good criminals in our prisons and that shouldn't be happening.

A big part of it is political will. Everybody is afraid now that somebody is going to point a finger at them and call them names. It takes guts and conviction to stand up and say, "This is wrong, and deep down in your heart, you know this is wrong." You can hide behind political correctness.

I wrote a column about this a while back. I said you can call a rattlesnake a green snake if you want to. But it's not going to change the fact that he is a rattlesnake and he will still bite you. Some problems in this country need more attention and more clarification than others do. They are not all the same. Can you imagine if 80% of the electorate would actually turn out for an election? It would scare Capitol Hill to death. All they do is aim their advertising at whatever group they know is going to the polls. But if everybody went, if people said, "We've got a law and order candidate here, and we're going to vote for him. We don't like you and we don't like what's happened under your tenure. So we're going to kick you out of office," then things might change.

Our political system was never designed for career politicians. It was designed for somebody to go and serve a term or maybe two terms and then go back home and go to work and let the druggist or the farmer or the plumber go up. Then we can get somebody fresh off the street who knows what's going on now, not what was going on thirty years ago when they were elected. Then they wouldn't get into these power groups and do all these back-door deals and sell out the people. That's not what it was about. The system is inherently corrupt. They are power hungry; they've power drunk. So we need term limits. The President only serves four or eight years and it's the most important office in the world. Why isn't that good enough for everybody else? Serve eight years and then get the heck out of there and let someone go back there who knows what is going on in the streets of Nashville, Tennessee or Miami. The people up there literally do not know what's going on. They are insulated. Let somebody who's been dealing with these problems go up there and deal with it.

It's not the FBI, and it's not the police that are the problem; it's the will of the politicians. They don't have the will. All they want is power and whatever group they have to appeal to in order to get the power, they'll appeal to them.

So that's what I was thinking about when I wrote that song. People just need to go out and vote to change things. If people don't vote, then they can't complain about what's happening.

# Simple Man

I ain't nothing but a simple man
Call me a redneck, I reckon that I am
But there's things goin' on that make me mad down to the core
I have to work like a dog to make ends meet
There's crooked politicians and crime in the street
And I'm madder than hell and I ain't gonna take it no more
We tell our kids to just say no
And then some panty waist judge lets a drug dealer go
And he slaps him on the wrist and he turns him back out on
    the town
Well, if I had my way with people sellin' dope
I'd take a big tall tree and a short piece of rope
And hang 'em up high and let 'em swing till the sun goes down

CHORUS:
Well you know what's wrong with the world today
People done gone and put their Bibles away
They're livin' by law of the jungle not the law of the land
Well the good book says it, so I know it's the truth
An eye for an eye and a tooth for a tooth
You'd better watch where you go
And remember where you've been
That's the way I see it I'm a simple man

Now, I'm the kind of man that wouldn't harm a mouse
But if I catch somebody breakin' in my house
I've got a twelve gauge shotgun waitin' on the other side
So don't go pushin' me against my will

I don't want to have to fight you but I dang sure will
So if you don't want trouble then you'd better just pass me on
    by
As far as I'm concerned there ain't no excuse
For the raping and the killing and the child abuse
And I've got a way to put an end to all that mess
You just take those rascals out in the swamp
Put them on their knees and tie 'em to a stump
And let the rattlers and the bugs and the alligators do the rest

CHORUS

# Smoky Mountain Rain

*Story by Dennis Morgan*
*Song written by Dennis Morgan and Kye Fleming*
*Recorded by Ronnie Milsap*

I've written a lot of songs with Kye Fleming, and I remember we were working on two different songs at the same time. One was called "Appalachian Rain," and it just wasn't happening; it wasn't gelling. The other song was called "I Wonder What She's Doing Now." We were working on both of those on and off.

We heard that Ronnie Milsap was looking for material. He's from East Tennessee. And Tom Collins was involved with this, too. He was producing Ronnie at the time, and he is also from East Tennessee, so the Smoky Mountains came into the conversation, and "Appalachian Rain" turned into "Smoky Mountain Rain."

I've done some hitchhiking in my life, all over the country, but I don't think I've ever actually hitchhiked from L.A. back to Knoxville. I just remember having a lot of trouble blending the two song ideas, but once the title of "Smoky Mountain Rain" came, the rest of it came fairly quickly.

Kye and I would sit and write every day for hours and hours, just bouncing around ideas. We had three different offices on Music Row where we used to write, and we wrote this in the Pi-Gem Publishing music office. We were both very serious about writing, and our combined imaginations played a big part in this song. I've never dated anyone from Knoxville, but I think you're always subconsciously thinking about lost love from your past when you are writing songs.

I recently went back and listened to "I Wonder What She's Doing Now" and I realized there was a reason that song wasn't coming together. It was just a bad song.

Tom Collins eventually took "Smoky Mountain Rain" to Ronnie and he loved it. It ended up being a #1 for him. We recently found out that it has been named one of the official state songs of Tennessee. We were very honored when we heard that. That puts it right up there with "Tennessee Waltz" and "Rocky Top," which have also been Tennessee state songs. To be in that kind of company is quite humbling.

When you write every day, you don't ever really throw anything away. You just put it in the back burner of your mind. When you've written enough and learned enough, it's just like combustion. Then when it comes time for the idea, you're ready for it and you pull it out, and that's what happened with this song.

# Smoky Mountain Rain

I thumbed my way from LA back to Knoxville
I found out those bright lights ain't where I belong
From a phone booth in the rain I called to tell her
I've had a change of dreams I'm comin' home
But tears filled my eyes when I found out she was gone

CHORUS:
Smoky Mountain rain keeps on fallin'
I keep on callin' her name
Smoky Mountain rain I'll keep on searchin'
I can't go on hurtin' this way
She's somewhere in the Smoky Mountain rain

I waved a diesel down outside a café
He said that he was goin' as far as Gatlinburg
I climbed up in the cab all wet and cold and lonely
I wiped my eyes and told him about her
I've got to find her
Can you make these big wheels burn?

CHORUS

BRIDGE:
I can't blame her for lettin' go
A woman needs someone warm to hold
I feel the rain runnin' down my face
I'll find her no matter what it takes!

CHORUS

# Somebody's Prayin'

*Story by Ricky Skaggs*
*Song written by John G. Elliott*
*Recorded by Ricky Skaggs*

This was written by a dear friend of mine, John Elliott. He used to lead worship at Belmont Church in Nashville, right about the time that Michael W. Smith and Amy Grant were also going there and active in that church. John left Nashville in the early 1990s to move to Decatur, Texas near Fort Worth. He's raising his family there now. They are a wonderful family, and he writes a great devotional on his website.

John recorded "Somebody's Prayin'" on one of his albums. I either heard it on his record or I heard John sing it somewhere and was really moved by it. It felt like something I'd like to record. So when I produced my album *My Father's Son* with Mac McAnally, which was my last album for Sony, I knew that would be a really strong song for that album.

We've heard of incredible stories from people about how the song gave them hope when they thought they didn't have much hope left. I was playing at Dollywood theme park in Pigeon Forge, Tennessee about ten years ago. There was a lady in the audience who had sent a letter to us. It said, "I've got an amazing story to tell you. You might not believe this, but it's all true and I have documented evidence to prove it." I started reading the rest of the letter and I found out that this lady was basically sent home to die. She had cancer and the doctors told her there wasn't much hope. She heard the song and wanted to get the music and listen to it over and over again. She listened to the song day and night with headphones on, over and over and over.

After a period of time, she felt she had to go back to the doctors and be checked again. When she did that, she had no trace of cancer whatsoever. She was from East Tennessee and was there at Dollywood with her grandchildren and said she wanted to meet me. When she came backstage, she brought a copy of the doctor's report. It said she had absolutely no cancer, and she showed it to me. She said, "This song has healing in it." She said, "The words in the song gave me hope. I just prayed and asked God to heal me through this and He did." That just shows how powerful a song can be.

## Somebody's Prayin'

Somebody's prayin', I can feel it
Somebody's prayin' for me
Mighty hands are guiding me
To protect me from what I can't see
Lord I believe, Lord I believe
That somebody's prayin', for me.

Angels are watchin', I can feel them
Angels are watchin' over me
There's many miles ahead 'til I get home
Still I'm safely kept before your throne
'Cause Lord I believe, Lord I believe
Your angels are watchin' over me.

Well, I've walked through barren wilderness
When my pillow was a stone
And I've been through the darkest caverns

Where no light has ever shown.
Still I went on 'cause there was someone
Who was down on their knees
And Lord. I thank you for those people
Prayin' all this time for me.

Somebody's prayin', I can feel it
Somebody's prayin' for me
Mighty hands are guiding me
To protect me from what I can't see
Lord I believe, Lord I believe
Somebody's prayin' for me...

# Something in Red

*Story by Angela Kaset*
*Song written by Angela Kaset*
*Recorded by Lorrie Morgan*

I'd been writing in town professionally as a staff writer for one company or another for about fifteen years. I had gotten a few album cuts but had not had a hit. I was signed with a publishing company and when my contract came up for renewal, they chose not to renew it. I guess it was the first time that I really got canned from a writing gig.

That hit me pretty hard. It happened in the fall, so I went through a pretty tough winter both emotionally and financially. In the spring, I went looking for a new publishing deal. Of course, as luck would have it, one of our cars died, too. One day I was driving my husband to work. He was working out of town, so I was driving him to a half-way point where he was going to get a ride with someone who was going to take him the rest of the way. It was just another one of those gray Nashville days and if I had had any money, I probably would have gone and done a little shopping—a little retail therapy—but I was broke so I couldn't even do that!

And I was driving down I-40 in Nashville and I remember looking up and seeing some of the first hints of green. It was just some ivy or weeds or something. It fed my soul. I thought, "Wow, there really is going to be a spring. There is going to be a break to all this darkness and gloom."And then I remember thinking, "It's so good to see something in green."

And right away, my brain went, "Incoming! Song idea!" So I thought I might write a song called "Something in Green" that would be about jealousy, where a woman is out shopping and the clerk asks if she can help her and she says, "I'm looking for something in green." I really liked that idea but then I realized that I couldn't write a whole song just about jealousy. I needed another place to start. So I took the story back a few notches in my mind. I thought, "If this woman were in the store looking for something else, what other colors might she choose?" I thought colors would be a fun thing to work with. There are so many colors that have emotional significance, and they were also good rhyming words, too. I didn't have to deal with orange or chartreuse or burgundy!

Red seemed to be the color of attraction and the color that calls attention to itself. So when I said the words, "I'm looking for something in red," I knew that would be the starting point. So instead of going shopping, I spent the rest of the day writing that song and I finished it by the time my kids got home from school. It was one of those rare occasions when you get an idea when you're by yourself, and you don't have a co-writer to help you along with it, but you're still able to finish it in one day. It was a good day.

The song was really quite transformative. To quote another famous song, "You can't always get what you want, but sometimes you get what you need." That time, I got what I needed to help me get through the day. And I also was able to get a new publishing deal. When my new publisher heard this song, they were ready to ink a deal.

I pitched it to Lorrie Morgan and she actually passed on it three times. Her producer at the time, Richard Landis, told her to listen to it again. She said, "I did and I already passed on it." Then he told her to go back and listen to it all the way through very carefully again, and she did. When she did, she called him up right away and said, "I'm so glad nobody else decided to cut this," and she took it into the studio and cut it. It went to #7, but stayed there a really long time. That can be just as good as a #1 hit.

The most interesting thing about this song is that I have had a number of men come up to me and say that it really moved them. I was surprised at that because I thought it was just going to appeal to women.

When I play it live, it really seems to bring out a lot of tears. After it had been a hit, the label forwarded a letter to me from a woman. She said, "I'm surprised the writer of this song didn't know the best way to end it. I'm sending her another way to end it, and if the song ever gets recorded again, I'd be happy to come in as a co-writer on it." She had written the song with the woman looking for something in black and the guy dying! I had actually considered that at one point but it just seemed so dark that it would take away from the rest of the verses. And it also seemed to me that to kill the guy off right after they had a baby together would be pretty mean, too.

# Something in Red

I'm looking for something in red
Something that's shocking to turn someone's head
Strapless and sequined and cut down to there
Stockings and garters and lace underwear
The guaranteed number to knock the man dead
I'm looking for something in red

I'm looking for something in green
Something to out-do an ex-high school queen
Jealousy comes in the color of jade
Do you have some pumps and a purse in this shade?
And a perfume that whispers "Please come back to me"
I'm looking for something in green

I'm looking for something in white

Something that shimmers in soft candlelight
Everyone calls us the most perfect pair
Should I wear a veil or a rose in my hair?
Well, the train must be long and the waist must be tight
I'm looking for something in white

I'm looking for something in blue
Something real tiny, the baby's brand new
He has his father's nose and his chin
We once were hot lovers now we're more like friends
Don't tell me that's just what old married folk do
I'm looking for something in blue

I'm looking for something in red
Like the one that I wore when I first turned his head
Strapless and sequined and cut down to there
Just a size larger that I wore last year
The guaranteed number to knock a man dead

I'm looking for something
I've gotta have something
I'm looking for something in red

# Southern Voice

Story by Bob DiPiero
Song written by Bob DiPiero
and Tom Douglas
Recorded by Tim McGraw

**"S**outhern Voice" was actually a concept that my co-writer, Tom Douglas, had. We had a writing session at his house out by the Harpeth River, and he said, "I got this idea and it's called 'Southern Voice.'" I don't know where exactly it caught fire. We were doing the verses and we wrote, "Hank Williams sang it, Number 3 drove it," and all of a sudden we just started doing these shout-outs like "Chuck Berry twanged it, Will Faulkner wrote it."

When that started rolling, I remember just writing the lyrics and not having any melodic thing going on at all. I remember thinking, "This is interesting. Let's just follow this down the rabbit hole for a while."

For Tom to come up with anything with any up-tempo groove is not normal for him. He'll tell you that. He's very much a slow, ballad kind of guy, but he really wanted to write something that rocked. And I wanted to write something that had more meat on the bones lyrically, so it was a great combination of what we wanted to do.

At first, I had no idea what the song would sound like, but phonetically how the words were falling created a natural groove in my head. Then we got to the chorus and, personally, I always wanted to use the word "Apalachicola" in a song. I'm such a word hound; I love words and their power and their shape and their sound. To me, Apalachicola just sounds good and it's so rhythmic.

I don't want to get too songwriter-y, and get a focus group in here to decide what people we should really target in the song, but we wanted a really good cross-section, at least in terms of our own understanding, of great people from the South, and from different walks of life: stock car drivers, guitar players, novelists, social heroes like Rosa Parks, and spiritual figures like Billy Graham. I was envisioning the *Sgt. Pepper's Lonely Hearts Club Band* album cover, and seeing all these faces, and trying to decide which of these faces we wanted to use, and which ones hadn't been used.

Probably the first listen-through of the song, casual listeners are just hearing the groove, and like the way it sounds or, if they're a big Tim McGraw fan, they might not hear those references. But by the second or third listen, they are delving into the lyrics a little more. That's what makes a song a hit. The more you listen to it, the more you get out of it.

For me, coming from Ohio, but living more of my life in the South than I did in the North, I took in everything that was Southern over the past thirty years. All these things just came out in the song. Finally, what we decided on musically was pretty much straightforward—three-chord rock and roll and the melody was pretty simple and easy to remember.

When we took it to Tim, he immediately put it on hold, so it had a very arduous trek to the radio from that point. Tom saw Tim and Faith at a restaurant right after that and Tim said, "I loved your song and it's going to be the name of the album and the name of the tour," and we were just blown away.

He did actually cut it right after that, but then somebody at his label decided they were going to put out a *Tim McGraw Greatest Hits* album first, so that delayed *Southern Voice* by at least a year and a half. And during that time, he continued to find new songs and record them, so we were concerned that he would become too familiar with it or burn out on it, or maybe he would decide to take the album in a different direction, but he didn't. He put out the *Southern Voice* album about a year and a half later, but he put out another song as a single first. So it was a little over two years from the time the song was recorded until the time it actually was heard on the radio, but by February of 2010, it had hit #1.

The song is a nod to Lynyrd Skynyrd and the Allman Brothers. One of the high points of my career was seeing Tim perform that song on *The Jay Leno Show* with Greg Allman. Greg, to me, is one of the greatest guitar players that ever drew a breath, and that's why I mentioned the Allman Brothers in that song. To hear him sing that song on the show was pretty mind-blowing.

# Southern Voice

Hank Williams sang it, Number 3 drove it
Chuck Berry twanged it, Will Faulkner wrote it
Aretha Franklin sold it, Dolly Parton graced it
Rosa Parks rode it, Scarlett O chased it

CHORUS:
Smooth as the hickory wind
That blows from Memphis
Down to Apalachicola
It's "Hi y'all. Did ya eat well?
Come on in. I'm sure glad to know ya"

Don't let this old gold cross
And this Allman Brothers t-shirt throw ya
It's cicadas making noise
With a southern voice

Hank Aaron smacked it, Michael Jordan dunked it
Pocahontas tracked it, Jack Daniels drunk it
Tom Petty rocked it, Dr. King paved it

Bear Bryant won it, Billy Graham saved it

CHORUS

Don't let this old gold cross
And this Crimson Tide t-shirt throw ya
It's cicadas making noise
With a southern voice

Jesus is my friend. America is my home
Sweet iced tea and Jerry Lee
Daytona Beach, that's what gets to me
I can feel it in my bones.

Smooth as the hickory wind
That blows from Memphis
Down to Apalachicola
It's "Hi y'all. Did ya eat well?
Come on in child. I'm sure glad to know ya."

Don't let this old gold cross
And this Charlie Daniels t-shirt throw ya
We're just boys making noise
With a southern voice

Yeah, yeah, yeah, yeah
Southern voice
I got a southern voice
A southern voice

# Strawberry Wine

Story by Matraca Berg
Song written by Matraca Berg
and Gary Harrison
Recorded by Deana Carter

This song came from spending summers at my grandpa's farm in Wisconsin. I have an aunt that is close to my age in Wisconsin and we used to hang out together. That's where I met this fellow. I didn't actually meet him on my grandma's farm, but it sounded good in the song.

This is a song about first love. There is something about the summertime and being away from home in a completely foreign environment, which it was. It was very rural there. There is something so innocent about the way people pass their time there. There was a place called the Gravel Pit where all the kids used to hang out because there were no movie theaters. There was nothing to do. We used to sneak out through the cornfields to get to his car if we wanted to go out, and then we would go to the Gravel Pit.

Everything else in the song was completely true. We actually drank Boone's Farm Strawberry Hill wine. It was awful. The farm was sold as my grandparents got older. Their kids didn't really want to farm. It's just too hard to make a living farming these days.

It was really sad because I felt like I couldn't go back there and revisit any of those memories. That was what the song was about.

There is an innocence lost when you are a young girl and fall in love for the first time, but there is also an innocence lost about a way of life that will never be again, at least in our family. Everybody went off to college and that was that. I think I was longing for that farm and those times as much as I was lost love.

When the song became a hit, it was a pretty big deal in Luck, Wisconsin, to have a hit song about the area. My aunt still lives there, but she is a nurse, not a farmer. She actually built a house on some of my grandfather's hunting property. The boy moved away, but I think his parents still live there.

My publishing company had a little guitar pull and invited record labels and producers and artists to come and listen to our new songs. There were Kim Carnes, Jim Photoglo, Tim Mensy, and me and some other writers. We set up a tent and Deana Carter was the only artist who showed up, so she heard the song first. She had already made her first record and kept this song in the back of her mind. It made the rounds to several other female artists and they all passed, including Trisha Yearwood and Pam Tillis. It just wasn't right for them, so it was still waiting for her when it came time to do her second album. It was CMA Song of the Year in 1997 and nominated for a Grammy.

# Strawberry Wine

He was working through college on my grandpa's farm.
I was thirsting for knowledge and he had a car.
I was caught somewhere between a woman and a child.
One restless summer we found love growin' wild.
On the banks of the river on a well-beaten path.
It's funny how those memories they last.

Like strawberry wine, seventeen.
The hot July moon saw everything.
My first taste of love, oh bittersweet.

Green on the vine.
Like strawberry wine.

I still remember when thirty was old.
And my biggest fear was September when he had to go.
A few cards and letters and one long distance call.
We drifted away like the leaves in the fall.
But year after year I come back to this place.
Just to remember the taste.

Of strawberry wine, seventeen.
The hot July moon saw everything.
My first taste of love oh bittersweet.
Green on the vine.
Like strawberry wine.

The fields have grown over now.
Years since they've seen the plow.
There's nothing time hasn't touched.
Is it really him or the loss of my innocence
I've been missing so much?
Yeah…
Like strawberry wine and seventeen.
The hot July moon saw everything.
My first taste of love oh bittersweet.
Green on the vine.
Like strawberry wine.

# That's Just About Right

*Story by Jeff Black*
*Song written by Jeff Black*
*Recorded by Blackhawk*

I had a lot of wonderful musicians who took me under their wing when I first came to town, people like bassist Dave Pomeroy and bluegrass legend Sam Bush. After I had been here a while, I made some demo recordings for my publisher in town. I was really proud of the session. They were acoustic-based and I felt like they were a great collection of songs. In my mind, they were a true expression of the art I was trying to create.

I sat down and started playing these for the publisher and he listened to the first song for about a minute, then hit the stop button, and shook his head. Then he played the second song for about a minute or minute and a half, and he did the same thing. He listened to the third song and did the same thing, hitting the stop play button. After that, he sat back and lit a cigarette and he said, "Black, you know what your trouble is? You're thinking too much."

That's when I knew I was on the right track. At the same time, I didn't know whether I should trash the office or just lie down on the floor. I had just picked up everything and left everything I loved, my home and my family, and all that I knew was true. I couldn't help but wonder, "What have I done?"

I was beside myself. I didn't own a piano at the time and really couldn't play one very well, but I went upstairs to this little writing room there at the publisher where they had this tiny piano, and I started playing some chords. I liked the way it sounded and "That's Just About Right" fell out of the sky. I wrote that song down as fast as I could, as fast as it would come out of my pen. I really never changed much about the draft. I wrote that song in about fifteen or twenty minutes.

I've always been very Zen about my songwriting and almost always write by myself. I've always looked at my songwriting as a journal of sorts. I was wondering what I was doing and what to make of this whole meeting of art and commerce, and all of the sudden, I couldn't write it down fast enough.

The song is a composite of several different influences. I have a friend who had gone to the art institute in Kansas City and he had moved to Chicago and was working on being an illustrator. He and I have had several long conversations about art and commerce and how you find yourself in the midst of it. You may feel as though you're on your path and then all of a sudden you're blindsided by the real world and responsibility. As a creative person, it's never really good to get your head out of the clouds, but sometimes it's good to get yourself a little closer to the ground every once in a while to check your balance in an attempt to center yourself on a planet that's flying around the sun at 65,000 miles an hour. I believe all the questions start sounding like answers more and more as the days go by and, hopefully, we gain some perspective. It's simply how we look at things and trying to remember that is the hardest part.

Part of the struggle is that all of us in our day-to-day are pushed to stare at a white empty canvas, no matter what you do for a living, and it can be terrifying. It's such a short time that we spend on this planet, and happiness is what we're all after. When it gets down to it, there's nothing completely original. Everything's been done, so the only thing that really matters, the only original thing left, is our individual point of view. That is what the song is about: being comfortable with your point of view. Feeling comfortable in your own skin. I tell this story a lot when I play the song live. Whether your creative medium of choice is pastel, or watercolor, or songs or stories or whether you draw funny little pictures while you're talking on the telephone, it's finding a comfort in that. A comfort in knowing that you belong.

We live in a society that tries to put the "thumbs-down" on people and that process is designed to make people doubt themselves and think "I could never sing," or "I could never write a poem or write a story" or "I could never paint a picture." That's ridiculous. Of course you can. We all have something to say. We all have an original point of view. It's natural for us to be creative. And we can't be attached to the outcome and constantly comparing ourselves with other people. It's not about perfection. It's just about expressing yourself.

# That's Just About Right

My old friend lives up in the mountains
He flew up there to paint the world
He says, "Even though interpretation's what I count on
This little picture to me seems blurred
Hard lines and the shadows come easy
I see it all just as clear as a bell
I just can't seem to set my easel to please me
I paint my Heaven but it looks like hell"

CHORUS:
Your blue might be gray, your less might be more
Your window to the world might be your own front door
Your shiniest day might come in the middle of the night
That's just about right

He says, "Man I ain't comin' down until my picture is perfect

And all the wonder is gone from my eyes
Down through my hands and on to the canvas
Still like my vision, but still a surprise"
"Real life," he says, "is the hardest impression
It's always movin' so I let it come through
And that, my friend, I say, is the glory of true independence
Just to do what you do what you do what you do"

CHORUS

My old friend came down from the mountain
Without even lookin' he found a little truth
You can go through life with the greatest intentions
But you do what you do what you just gotta do

CHORUS

# That's My Job

*Story by Gary Burr*
*Song written by Gary Burr*
*Recorded by Conway Twitty*

Every word in this song was based on my life, except the title. That came from the Muse, but everything else in there was based on my life and my relationship with my father.

My dad passed away in 1986 and a few days after that I went down to my basement, where I used to go and write songs. I was living in Connecticut at the time, and I picked up my guitar and started singing the song and writing it as I went, and I pretty much sang it out just the way it was recorded. I've never had that happen before.

The description of the house in the song, with the mirror at the end of the hall, is the house I grew up in. As a little boy, I would have these bad dreams that my parents had died, and I would go in their room and they would calm me down and let me get into their bed and sleep with them.

When I was in college, I had a chance to move to California to be in a band, so I decided to drop out of school to move to California. My parents obviously didn't want me to go. They thought I was making a huge mistake. My mom and dad sat me down and told me all the reasons why I shouldn't go, and tried to talk me out of it. They were just fit to be tied. I listened to them, and then I told them that this is what I was going to do. I had made up my mind. I was going out west. Then they looked at me and said, "How can we help?" They bought me two amplifiers, so when we got to California we could have something to play into. All the guys in the band had sold our equipment to get the money to go to California.

As for the song, there are some serious grammatical errors in it, but I never went back to rewrite it. The reason I never rewrote it is because I never thought anyone would record it. I thought it was too personal. And it was too long. It had a very non-country structure. But I turned it in because that's what I was supposed to do—to play it for the people who were publishing me. I had no expectations, though. A couple of guys and I had formed a publishing company and they were in New York at the time, but they had some outlets in Nashville, so they sent it down there.

I always heard that Conway Twitty was the guy to pitch to. Everyone I knew always said that Conway would really listen to a song that had a strong lyric and that he would cut it regardless of whether it was commercial or not. If he liked it, he would do it. So they pitched it to him on a whim. I think he was the first person we pitched it to. And boom, it was on the radio and my boyhood home was being described in a song on country radio stations all around the country.

I got married pretty young. When my dad passed away, I was already a dad myself. But when your father goes, then you're the "man." It really puts things into perspective. It certainly made me think of a time in the future when my kids would be going through this. And I want them to be able to say the same things and to have the same feelings about me that I had about my dad.

## That's My Job

I woke up cryin' late at night, when I was very young
I had dreamed my father had passed away and gone.
My world revolved around him. I couldn't lie there anymore

So I made my way down the mirrored hall and tapped upon
     his door.

And I said, "Daddy, I'm so afraid.
How would I go on, with you gone that way?
Don't wanna cry anymore
So may I stay with you?"

CHORUS:
And he said, "That's my job. That's what I do.
Everything I do is because of you
To keep you safe with me.
That's my job, you see."

Later we barely got along, this teenage boy and he
Most of the fights, it seems, were over different dreams
We each held for me.
He wanted knowledge and learning. I wanted to fly out west
Said "I could make it out there, if I just had the fare
I got half, will you loan me the rest?"

And I said, "Daddy, I'm so afraid
There's no guarantee in the plans I've made
And if I should fail, who will pay my way back home?"

CHORUS

Every person carves his spot, and fills the hole with life
And I pray someday I might light as bright as he.

I woke up early one bright fall day and spread the tragic news
After all my travels, I settled down within a mile or two.
I make my livin' with words and rhymes, and all this tragedy
Should go into my head and out instead, as bits of poetry.

But I say, "Daddy I'm so afraid.
How will I go on, with you gone this way?
How can I come up with a song to say, 'I love you'?"

That's my job, that's what I do
Everything I do is because of you
To keep you safe with me. That's my job, you see.
Everything I do is because of you
To keep you safe with me.

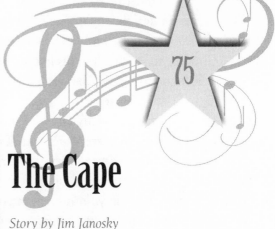

# The Cape

*Story by Jim Janosky*
*Song written by Guy Clark, Jim Janosky, and*
*Susanna Clark*
*Recorded by Guy Clark, Kathy Mattea*

Susanna Clark and I were just visiting one day and we got to talking about our childhoods and the pranks we used to play. Then we started talking about how, when we were kids, we used to really think we could fly. That led to a conversation about the amazing faith that little kids have, and how they really believe those kinds of things could happen. We had several more conversations about this and started writing down random notes and phrases and lines on the idea of childhood faith.

I told her the story of a guy I used to work with up in Pennsylvania. We worked at a butcher shop together. Once, when he was a kid, he tried to be a tightrope walker. He put a rope between two beams in his barn and took the tires off his bicycle and tried to go across that tightrope on the rims of his bicycle. He got about a foot and ended up unconscious on the floor of his barn. His mother woke him up just so she could beat him! She said, "What made you think you could do this?" He said, "I just believed I could!"

So we kept talking about the idea of childhood faith and it stewed for a while. Over the course of several meetings, we got four or five verses down on this theme of thinking you could fly. Later,

Susanna showed it to Guy, and he got pretty interested in that idea. He took all of our notes and then we met once or twice after that. Guy basically congealed it all into "The Cape."

Guy started singing it in his live shows and got some really good feedback from it. One day, he was rehearsing it at a gig in New York and Kathy Mattea heard it. She later put it on her *Walking Away A Winner* album, and then Guy later put it on his *Dublin Blues*. Her version was a lot more up-tempo version of it. I've always liked Guy's a little better, because it's more earthy and natural.

What we were trying to get at with the song was to maintain that faith in yourself, in your dream, in your idea, even in God—no matter what happens. In this song, the guy is older and still has that childlike faith. He still thinks he can fly, metaphorically, and believes that life is just a leap of faith, and he'll probably still believe it until he's dead. That's certainly been a theme of my life. "The Cape" is really a symbol of that ability to maintain your belief, no matter how tough things get, and it gets harder as you get older. And if you really keep that faith, you'll be able to fly; you won't crash and burn.

I found a letter I got a few years ago from a cancer survivor. It reads, "Jim, I am the patient featured in a film about lung cancer that Dr. Alan Kramer is making in the *Living with Cancer* series. Let me add my thanks to you and Guy and Susanna for allowing us to use that wonderful song, 'The Cape' in the film. I was turned on to the song this spring by a friend who knows me very well and thought that it sounded made-to-order for me; in particular, about the leap of faith. Later, I was lucky enough to attend (the bluegrass festival) MerleFest in North Carolina and heard Guy singing it. I was blown away by him. I was diagnosed at age 65 with Stage 4 lung cancer and given only 8-10 months to live. I never quite accepted that, though, and worked hard with my doctors. I am trying to do something to change my chances. I have been very lucky and am now a five-year survivor. That is what our film is all about: the conjunction of my hard work and luck, along with the medical world's advances in treatment and drugs. In a month, I will be celebrating my 70th birthday, my five-year survival, and life in general here in Sonoma Valley with a few hundred of my closest friends and family. My friend is going to sing his version of 'The Cape' and we are going to show rough cuts of the film. Thanks again for everything. Wells Whitney."

I just found out that recently that Mr. Whitney is actually now a *twelve*-year survivor and at 77 is still doing great. It's good to hear something like that. It gives you a really nice, warm feeling. There's so much rejection in the songwriting world. Getting a letter like that makes up for about 400,000 rejections!

# The Cape

Eight years old with flour sack cape
Tied all around his neck
He climbed up on the garage
Figurin' what the heck
He screwed his courage up so tight
The whole thing come unwound
He got a runnin' start and bless his heart
He headed for the ground

CHORUS:
He's one of those who knows that life
Is just a leap of faith
Spread your arms and hold your breath
And always trust your cape

All grown up with a flour sack cape
Tied all around his dream
He's full of piss and vinegar
He's bustin' at the seams
He licked his finger and checked the wind
It's gonna be do or die
He wasn't scared of nothin', boys
He was pretty sure he could fly

CHORUS

Old and grey with a flour sack cape
Tied all around his head
He's still jumpin' off the garage
And will be till he's dead
All these years the people said
He's actin' like a kid
He did not know he could not fly
So he did

# The Dance

*Story by Tony Arata*
*Song written by Tony Arata*
*Recorded by Garth Brooks*

The way "The Dance" got written and recorded was almost like a movie script, which was kind of ironic, since I got the idea for the song after watching a movie.

I had gone to college in Statesboro, Georgia and played in a band in college. When I graduated, I continued to play in the clubs. One night, I heard that Jim Glaser was looking for material for his next album. His record company was in Atlanta and I got a little cassette tape to him and he decided to record "The Man in the Mirror." That was the reason I first came to Nashville: to meet Jim Glaser. We decided to go ahead and move here for good in 1986.

One night my wife and I went to hear a bunch of songwriters at The Bluebird Café in Green Hills. I was blown away, and I decided I wanted to move back to Georgia because there was no way I could write songs like those guys. But my wife talked me into staying.

A little while later, my wife was out of town, I think, and I decided to go out and see a movie. The movie was *Peggy Sue Got Married* with Nicholas Cage and Kathleen Turner. In the movie, Peggy Sue gets divorced when she's in her forties, and then has a chance to go back to high school and change her decisions. When Nicholas Cage asks her to dance, she starts to say no, and then she looks down at the locket with the pictures of her kids in it. She realizes if she says no and doesn't marry him, the kids' pictures will fade.

I went away from the theater thinking about that scene for a long time. There are so many times in life when we want to avoid the pain, but if we do, a lot of times we will have to miss a lot of the joy in life, too.

A little while after I wrote that, I was singing at an open mike night at a little club called Douglas Corner over on Eighth Avenue in Nashville. And there sitting at the bar was this stocky guy wearing a cowboy hat. A lot of guys look like fake cowboys with hats on, but Garth didn't. He looked like the real deal. We talked for a while, and later we were playing at The Bluebird Café together. It was on a Sunday night. We were doing the early show, when nobody was in the room. I played "The Dance" and he came up to me later and said, "Man, if I ever get a record deal, I want to record that song." And I thought, "Okay, sure." He was selling boots and I was lifting 50-pound boxes for a living. We had the music industry right where we wanted them, right?

Anyway, a year or so after that, I was working at a company called Tom Jackson and Associates, writing articles about busses, and I got a call one day from Garth and he said, "I just signed with Capitol and I want to record 'The Dance.'"

I said, "You're kidding me!" But he wasn't. So he took it into the studio. A couple of months after that, he called me again and said he had just finished the album and wanted me to come to his manager's office and listen to it. I remember I didn't even recognize it at first because of the piano intro. But it was beautiful.

The great thing about "The Dance" is that it was recorded by a songwriter and produced by a songwriter, Allen Reynolds, so they really nailed it. When the album was finished, they released several singles that did really well. They were actually starting to work on his second album and didn't have plans to release "The Dance" as a single. But Allen Reynolds wanted to put out one more single. Jimmy Bowen was head of Capitol by then and he said no. But Allen talked to Bowen and said, "Would you just do me a favor and go see Garth sing it live before you make your final decision?" Bowen went to see Garth sing it and the crowd went wild, so he said he would go ahead and release one more song. I'm sure glad he did.

When they finished the video for "The Dance," Garth called me again and said he wanted me to see it. I loved what they did with it, using clips of John F. Kennedy and Martin Luther King, Jr. in the video. At the end, Garth's voice comes on and says something about how his life is like "The Dance"—that he could have missed some of the heartaches if he hadn't chased his dreams, but that he wouldn't have missed it for the world. I just bawled when I saw the video.

"The Dance" won Song of the Year from the Academy of Country Music and the Country Music Association and it was the most played song on country radio that year. It was also nominated for a Grammy. My wife and I went that year. I remember walking along the Avenue of the Americas in New York City and seeing all the stars lining up on the red carpet outside. Everything seemed so surreal.

We get letters all the time where people tell us they played the song at their father or mother's funeral. I really believe in fate. It's kind of interesting because *Peggy Sue Got Married* is a lot about fate, and the song is about fate, and the way it got written and recorded seemed to be guided by fate, like it was meant to happen. It didn't seem like it really had that much to do with me. All the stars were lined up just right, and all I really had to do was show up.

# The Dance

Looking back on the memory of
The dance we shared 'neath the stars above
For a moment all the world was right
How could I have known that you'd ever say goodbye?

And now I'm glad I didn't know
The way it all would end, the way it all would go
Our lives are better left to chance. I could have missed the pain

But I'd have had to miss the dance

Holding you I held everything
For a moment wasn't I a king?
But if I'd only known how the king would fall
Hey, who's to say, you know I might have changed it all

And now I'm glad I didn't know
The way it all would end, the way it all would go
Our lives are better left to chance. I could have missed the pain
But I'd have had to miss the dance

Yes my life is better left to chance
I could have missed the pain but I'd have had to miss the
    dance

# The Devil Went Down to Georgia

*Story by Charlie Daniels*
*Song written by Charlie Daniels, Tom Crain,*
*Taz DiGregorio, Fred Laroy Edwards,*
*Charles Hayward, and James Marshall*
*Recorded by The Charlie Daniels Band*

We were in the recording studio doing an album. We had written and rehearsed and arranged all the songs. Then we came to the glaring realization that we did not have a good fiddle tune, and we needed one. So the band and I took a couple of days off and went into a rehearsal studio and wrote this song. My style of writing at the time was, if I had an idea, I wanted to hear the music for it right now. It helped motivate me.

The idea of "The Devil Went Down to Georgia" came into my head and I just kind of started it and we added a beat and Taz DiGregorio came up with that riff at the beginning of the devil's part and that's how it went, everybody adding their ideas.

I had read a poem by Stephen Vincent Benét called "The Mountain Whippoorwill" when I was a kid. I think I read it in literature class when I was in the ninth grade or somewhere along there. It's a poem about a fiddle contest. Being a young fiddle player, it kind of stuck with me. That possibly could have had something to do with me developing the lyric to the song. It's hard to say, really, what motivates the idea for a song. You just kind of pull it out of the air.

The music really plays off the lyrics in this song; it's not just repeating the melody. It's a stylized thing. We were recording at Woodland Studios in Nashville. I started writing the lyrics and we put the music together. I'm sure we tightened up a little and tweaked the lyrics, but we had a pretty good idea where we were going from the beginning as far as the story. Everybody contributed musical ideas to it.

As for some of the refrains, like "Chicken in the bread pan, pickin' out dough. Granny does your dog bite? No child, no"—that's just an old square dance refrain. "Fire on the mountain, run boys run"—that's just a timing thing the callers used to say at square dances when they didn't really have anything else to say.

Mark O'Connor ended up recording "The Devil Comes Back to Georgia" as a sequel. I played on that, and Johnny Cash and Marty Stuart and Travis Tritt did some of the singing, but that was really Mark's song. "Big Bad John" and a few other songs like that had sequels to them. Those are the kind of ballads that you could just change the story a little bit and do a new version.

I used seven fiddles on the devil's part on the original recording. Nowadays, you could probably do it electronically, but then we used seven different fiddles to play the devil's part. He wasn't actually playing anything. He was just making a lot of noise. The line says, 'Then a band of demons joined in and sounded something like this," so we just thought what would a band of demons sound like? Probably just a lot of noise.

## The Devil Went Down to Georgia

The devil went down to Georgia, he was looking for a soul to
steal.
He was in a bind 'cause he was way behind, he was willing to
make a deal.
When he came across this young man sawin' on a fiddle and
playin' it hot.

And the devil jumped up on a hickory stump and said, "Boy let
    me tell you what.
I bet you didn't know it, but I'm a fiddle player too.
And if you'd care to take a dare, I'll make a bet with you.
Now you play a pretty good fiddle, boy, but give the devil his
    due.
I'll bet a fiddle of gold against your soul, 'cause I think I'm
    better than you."
The boy said "My name's Johnny and it might be a sin,
But I'll take your bet, you're gonna regret, 'cause I'm the best
    that's ever been."

Johnny, rosin up your bow and play your fiddle hard.
'Cause hell's broke loose in Georgia and the devil deals the
    cards.
And if you win you get this shiny fiddle made of gold.
But if you lose, the devil gets your soul.

The devil opened up his case and he said "I'll start this show."
And fire flew from his fingertips as he rosined up his bow.
And he pulled the bow across his strings and it made an evil
    hiss.
Then a band of demons joined in and it sounded something
    like this.
When the devil finished, Johnny said, "Well you're pretty good
    ol' son.
But sit down in that chair, right there, and let me show you
    how it's done."

Fire on the mountain, run boys, run.
The devil's in the house of the risin' sun.
Chicken in the bread pan, pickin' out dough.
"Granny, does your dog bite?"
"No, child, no."

The devil bowed his head because he knew that he'd been beat.
He laid that golden fiddle on the ground at Johnny's feet.
Johnny said, "Devil just come on back if you ever want to try
    again.
"I told you once, you son of a gun, I'm the best that's ever been."

And he played fire on the mountain, run boys, run.
The devil's in the house of the risin' sun.
Chicken in the bread pan, pickin' out dough.
"Granny, will your dog bite?"
"No, child, no."

# The Famous Lefty Flynn's

*Story by Jamie Johnson*
*Song written by Jamie Johnson and Morry Trent*
*Recorded by The Grascals*

One day back around 1994 or 1995, I was at this little tavern back home, The Railroad Inn in Milan, Indiana. There was this guy sitting at the bar, and he came up to me and said, "You're Lee Johnson's little brother, the singer, right?" And I said, "Sure am." And he introduced himself. When he did, I just looked at him in amazement. I used to hear my brothers telling stories about this guy all the time and how tough he was. It seemed like he beat up pretty much everybody in town, including all the big, mean guys I knew growing up. In my imagination, I thought he must be huge, but he was about my size. I said, "You're the guy that's beating all these people up?" He said, "That's me."

At the time, I thought his name was Flynn, but I found out recently that his name was actually Flint. That event stuck in my mind for several years. Then six or seven years ago, I got the idea to write a song about a bank robber who was little and didn't look like a bank robber. I'm left-handed, so I called him Lefty Flynn. The rest of the song—the singer going to prison and sharing a cell with this guy and breaking out and going to Mexico—pretty much came from the imagination of me and my co-writer, Morry Trent, who is also left-handed. We were just trying to be Tom T. Hall and make it interesting to the listener.

I actually had both of the characters in the song living at one point. They were sitting in the bar in Mexico together and enjoying life. I played it for Larry Shell, who co-wrote "Murder on Music Row" and all sort of hits. He is quite a character. He said, "That's a good song, son, but somebody's gotta die. You're gonna have to kill one of them off." So we did. I played with it for another year or so and we cut it and it eventually ended up being the title cut of the album we released in the spring of 2010.

I was really looking forward to taking this song back home and playing it for this guy who inspired it, but I heard that he passed away a couple of years ago, so he never got to hear the song. And The Railroad Inn just closed down recently, too. It was a bar and restaurant and hotel, and it took a lot of jobs. It's kind of sad, really, because there's not much else there. Maybe I can make enough money from the song to buy the place. If I do, maybe I could even name it "The Famous Lefty Flynn's." Talk about life imitating art.

# The Famous Lefty Flynn's

The walls are mighty high in Fort Worth Prison
And the cells are awful small for two grown men
The Warden slammed that heavy door behind me
And said "allow me to introduce to you the famous Lefty Flynn"

Well I'd read about ole Lefty in the papers
How he'd robbed all the banks out in the West
I figured he'd be bigger than a mountain
With chiseled arms and battle scars tattooed upon his chest

But he was small and looked just like a movie star
His teeth were pearly white and his hair was black as coal

And I'll never forget the day that I shook his hand
And began my education from the Famous Lefty Flynn

I guess I must've asked a million questions
And he took to me — I was his only friend
He told me all about his hiding places
And all the money that he stole and never got to spend

He said there was an old abandoned farm house
And in the backyard was a dried up well
A million dollars lay there at the bottom
And we made a pact to not look back and break out of that cell

We barely made it out with lawmen on our tails
Well, the bullets were a flyin' and they shot ole Lefty down
With a heavy heart, I headed for that pot of gold
And on across the border to the Gulf of Mexico

Now I'm living like a king in old Tampico
I'll never have to steal or run again
And just like we planned, I built that little tavern
Where the neon light says, "Welcome to the Famous Lefty
    Flynn's"

# The Good Stuff

*Story by Craig Wiseman*
*Song written by Craig Wiseman and Jim Collins*
*Recorded by Kenny Chesney*

I was writing with Jim Collins, a buddy of mine — a great song-writer. I was writing for Sony at the time. I was running late and Jim was out in front smoking a cigar with the security guard, Rusty Martin, who I had just gotten to know. I knew Rusty was a retired Mississippi highway patrolman. He found out I was a Mississippi boy, too, and he was always a really nice guy. I also knew he wasn't old enough to retire; he was maybe in his late forties.

I started asking around and found out that he had come up here because his wife had been battling cancer for a long time and was being treated at Vanderbilt in Nashville. They were coming up here so much, they were thinking of moving here, but his wife passed away before that happened.

I didn't know all those details then, but Jim knew some things and I knew some things and we just started putting Rusty's story together. At that point, I'd been married probably 10 or 12 years and Jim had been married about 15 or 16. We talked about what it would be like to have to sit and watch your wife pass away in front of you. We sat in silence for a few moments and then we said, "Well, let's get back to writing."

Jim said, "I got this idea for a song. It's called 'The Good Stuff.'"

We both thought it was going to be a different song, but ended up going in another direction.

I picked up the guitar and wrote the first line, "Me and my lady had our first big fight. So I drove around until I saw the neon light." I said, "Well, we can't just have them have a fight and he goes to a bar. How clichéd is that?"

The other part of that story comes from an experience I had at a blackjack table. I was at a casino and was playing at a table with one of my songwriter friends. We were talking to the dealer and we said, "How would you play that hand?"

He said, "I wouldn't play it. I don't gamble."

I said, "You're a dealer and you don't play cards?"

He said, "I'm in recovery. I was a gambling addict." Then he said, "I can do one better than that. My other job is at a liquor store and I'm a recovering alcoholic."

I said, "Are you kidding me? What's up with that? That would be a little challenging."

He said, "I figure I'm faced with the results of that temptation enough that it actually gives me some peace." That stuck in my mind. So when we started writing the song again, I thought about that dealer and put him in the place of the bartender in the song. We decided that they weren't going to drink in the song. Jim told me the idea he had about the customer asking for the good stuff and the bartender says, "That's not the good stuff. This is," and he explains what that means. Then we got the idea of them sharing a glass of milk because it seemed so different that it just might work. That was me pushing the envelope a little.

We always knew it would end with the bartender telling the young guy, "When you get home, she'll start to cry / When she says 'I'm sorry,' say 'So am I.' / And look into those eyes so deep in love... and drink it up, 'cause that's the good stuff."

We knew Kenny Chesney was cutting and thought it might be right for him, so we put it down and sent it over to him.

The story took on a different angle altogether, but it was emotionally inspired by Rusty's story of losing somebody so close to him.

I told Jim, "Before we do anything, I want to play this for Rusty. I know it's not exactly his story, but I still want to clear it with him." Ironically, we were thinking of names for the bartender's wife, and we actually wrote down "Bonnie" because I thought of somebody I knew from church. We found out later that Rusty's wife's name was Connie. So that was kind of strange.

I brought Rusty in to hear the demo and he just sat there silently and then he took a CD and left. I didn't know if I had offended him or what. He took the song home and played it for his daughter and she liked it. So he brought it back to us on Monday and said, "Okay. That's fine."

I called the funeral home that did Connie's burial and found out what kind of stone they used and we had a footstone made for her that read, "The Good Stuff."

When we had a #1 party for the song, we invited Rusty and gave it to him there. I worried that it might be too much, but I really wanted to do that for him. It was at the ASCAP building. Sometimes those parties can get to be a little boring, you know, but this time it was different. When we gave it to him, I remember looking up and seeing people coming out of their offices and they were all crying. It was a pretty memorable party.

We always say that this song came from three happy marriages, and two of them are still going.

# The Good Stuff

Well, me and my lady had our first big fight
So I drove around 'til I saw the neon light.
A corner bar, and it just seemed right.
So I pulled up.

Not a soul around but the old bar keep
Down at the end an' looking half asleep
And he walked up, and said, "What'll it be?"

I said, "The good stuff."

He didn't reach around for the whiskey;
He didn't pour me a beer.
His blue eyes kinda went misty,
He said "You can't find that here.

'Cause it's the first long kiss on a second date.
Momma's all worried when you get home late.
And droppin' the ring in the spaghetti plate
'Cause your hands are shaking so much.
And it's the way that she looks with the rice in her hair.
And eatin' burned suppers, the whole first year
And askin' for seconds to keep her from tearin' up
Yeah, man, that's the good stuff."

He grabbed a carton of milk and he poured a glass.
An' I smiled an' said, "I'll have some of that."
We sat there an' talked as an hour passed
Like old friends.

I saw a black an' white picture and it caught my stare,
It was a pretty girl with bouffant hair.
He said "That's my Bonnie,
Taken 'bout a year after we were wed."

He said, "Spent five years in the bottle,
When the cancer took her from me.
But I've been sober three years now,
'Cause the one thing stronger than the whiskey

Was the sight of her holding my baby girl.
The way she adored that string of pearls,
I gave her the day that our youngest boy, Earl,
Married his high school love.

And it's a new tee-shirt saying 'I'm a Grandpa.'
Being right there as our time got small,
And holding her hand, when the Good Lord called her up,
Yeah, man, that's the good stuff."

He said, "When you get home, she'll start to cry.
When she says 'I'm sorry,' say 'So am I'
And look into those eyes, so deep in love,
And drink it up.
'Cause that's the good stuff.
That's the good stuff."

# The Grand Tour

*Story by Norro Wilson*
*Song written by Norro Wilson, George Richey,*
*and Carmol Taylor*
*Recorded by George Jones, Aaron Neville*

**G**eorge Richey came up with the title. He said, "We need to write a song called 'The Grand Tour.'" And we immediately got it as soon as he said it. I've always thought that if you come up with a unique concept for a song, it will write itself. We did it in two days. We would just go from one thought to the next, like "see the picture on the table, don't it look like she'd be able / to touch me and say 'good morning dear.'" It's like "Paint Me A Birmingham," which I think is a fabulous song. The writer of that was saying, "paint me a picture of that. I want to live in that little community and have a white fence and a swing." What the singer was saying was, "This was what it was like when life was good," "Over there sits the chair, when she'd bring the morning paper to me," and things like that.

We wrote it exclusively for George. That song had George Jones all over it. I can sound like George. I can't sing like him, but I've always been able to do his inflections and he's always gotten a kick out of that.

Right after that song was cut, I went to the Opry with Freddy Weller, It was the first time that he had ever sung there, so I went with him to support him. And everybody at the Opry knew about the song that night and they were all saying, "Well, I guess you'll be able to buy another Cadillac soon," because they all knew it was going to be a big song.

When I found out Aaron Neville was going to record it a few years ago, I thought that was fabulous. I really like him and I like his style of singing. The producer who did Aaron's record apparently knew Billy Sherrill and remembered that song, so he played it for Aaron and he loved it.

Since that song did pretty well for Aaron, we later pitched him, "A Picture of Me Without You," which had the same three writers as "The Grand Tour." He had just lost his wife to cancer, though. He said, "I love the song but I can't cut it, because I don't think I would ever get through it." I'd love to hear what he could have done with it, but of course, we can't fault him for feeling that way.

# The Grand Tour

Step right up, come on in
If you'd like to take the grand tour
Of the lonely house that once was home sweet home
I have nothing here to sell you
Just some things that I will tell you
Some things I know will chill you to the bone

Over there sits the chair
Where she'd bring the paper to me
And sit down on my knee and whisper, "Oh, I love you."
But now she's gone forever
And this old house will never
be the same without the love that we once knew

Straight ahead, that's the bed
Where we'd lie and love together
And lord knows we had a good thing going here

See her picture on the table
Don't it look like she'd be able
Just to touch me and say, "Good morning dear."

There's her rings, all her things
And her clothes are in the closet
Where she left them when she tore my world apart
As you leave, you'll see the nursery
Oh, she left me without mercy
Taking nothing but our baby and my heart
Step right up, come on in.

# The Highwayman

*Story by Jimmy Webb*
*Song written by Jimmy Webb*
*Recorded by The Highwaymen (Waylon
      Jennings, Willie Nelson, Johnny Cash,
      and Kris Kristofferson)*

"The Highwayman" was written after a vivid dream experience that I had. It was very unusual. I don't go around writing songs about my dreams very often. I woke up, and there happened to be a piano in the room with me, and I just went over and wrote the first verse about The Highwayman. Then the idea came to me that this guy, for whatever reason, would live more than one lifetime, and I would weave his soul through these different lives.

I loved it, and it charged me immediately with a lot of energy. It creates a lot of space and time to work in, which is what you are looking for whenever you've only got three minutes to tell a story.

Willie and Waylon and Kris went to help out on a Johnny Cash record that he recorded when he was ill. Glen Campbell was in Nashville helping out with that project and he was in the studio, and it was my understanding that he played the song for them first. This was really where the Highwaymen were born.

I'm not sure how they decided to later name their album and the foursome "The Highwaymen." I can only say it was a big deal for me. It was a big injection into my career.

It is another strophic song, like "By the Time I Get to Phoenix."
It's a true ballad with the three verses and the story contained with no
traditional chorus, and it later won a Grammy for 1985. I remember
Waylon, when he heard it was being nominated for Country Song of
the Year, being surprised and saying, "Which country is that?"

## The Highwayman

I was a highwayman. Along the coach roads I did ride
With sword and pistol by my side
Many a young maid lost her baubles to my trade
Many a soldier shed his lifeblood on my blade
The bastards hung me in the spring of twenty-five
But I am still alive.

I was a sailor. I was born upon the tide
And with the sea I did abide.
I sailed a schooner round the Horn to Mexico
I went aloft and furled the mainsail in a blow
And when the yards broke off they said that I got killed
But I am living still.

I was a dam builder across the river deep and wide
Where steel and water did collide
A place called Boulder on the wild Colorado
I slipped and fell into the wet concrete below
They buried me in that great tomb that knows no sound
But I am still around...I'll always be around...and around and
        around and around and around

I fly a starship across the universe divide
And when I reach the other side
I'll find a place to rest my spirit if I can
Perhaps I may become a highwayman again

Or I may simply be a single drop of rain
But I will remain
And I'll be back again, and again and again and again and
again.

# The House That Built Me

*Story by Allen Shamblin*
*Song written by Allen Shamblin and Tom*
*Douglas*
*Recorded by Miranda Lambert*

Since I graduated from high school in 1977, I have had a ritual where I go back every year to my hometown of Huffman, Texas. I'll go through the Dairy Queen drive-through and then drive by the house my dad built on Sunny Glen Drive. It's just a way I recalibrate myself, and it seems like over the past few years, since 9/11, with the world going the way it has, it's more and more important for me to go back there. It's a touchstone for me.

"The House That Built Me" was actually written about seven or eight years ago. I brought in the title, but it was truly a co-written song. Tom Douglas and I both drew on our experiences from our childhood homes while we were in the writing process. The upstairs bedroom where I learned to play guitar, the dog buried in the back-yard, the fingerprints—all of that is drawn straight from our lives. We actually buried a couple of dogs in my backyard. I was crazy about dogs growing up, and still am.

In the song, the singer says he (or she) is broken, and that came from our lives, too. When you've lived as long as Tom and I have, there are certain things that just break your heart, and home seems to be the place to go to feel better. I have a home in Tennessee now and a family here, but when I go back to those earliest memories of my childhood home, it just seems very healing to me. It brings me great comfort the older I get.

Maybe part of that brokenness or grieving is the breakdown of community. I miss the days when we could get on our bikes and stay gone all day and nobody thought a thing about it. Everybody knew everybody in our neighborhood. The world's not like that anymore. We have to keep a much closer eye on our children than my parents had to keep on me.

The song has an unusual format. That just came out in the writing. The lines that repeat, "I thought if I could touch this place"—work like a chorus, but it's hard to define. That's just the way it came out. We weren't really analyzing it in the process. We were just following one line to the next, following the heart of the song wherever it led us. We went where the emotion took us lyrically and melodically. It's usually better to do it that way. Most of the time, when you are writing a song, the head will steer you wrong, but the heart will always steer you right.

So it was pitched for a while and it just wasn't connecting with people the way we thought it would. Then two years ago, Tom called me up and said, "Let's take another look at 'The House That Built Me.'" We could see the holes and the weak spots so clearly after letting it sit for a few years. Within an hour and a half we had rewritten it.

Tom went in and demoed it with just a piano and a light drum groove and sent it to Scott Hendricks, who is a great producer. Scott put it on hold for Blake Shelton. Blake was picking Miranda up at an airport one day and Miranda got in Blake's truck and he started playing the compilation CD of the songs he had on hold. I think it was the third or fourth song on the CD. When Miranda heard it, she said, "Blake, I want this song," so they called Scott Hendricks from the truck and Blake said, "Scott, I need to talk to you about something. Miranda just heard 'House that Built Me.' She was pretty moved by it

and says she'd like to have it." So Blake and Scott graciously released
the song to Miranda.

Miranda really made it hers. Frank Liddell and Mike Wrucke
ended up producing it for her and they did a simple acoustic version
of it and it worked great. The fact that it was a woman singing, I
think, really helped the song connect with the public better anyway.
It worked better for the video, too. It's a pretty bold request for a man
to come up to someone's house and ask to walk through it, so that
might not have worked as well with a male.

# The House That Built Me

I know they say you can't go home again
But I just had to come back one last time
Ma'am I know you don't know me from Adam
But these handprints on the front steps are mine

Up those stairs in that little back bedroom
Is where I did my homework and I learned to play guitar
I bet you didn't know, that under that live oak
My favorite dog is buried in the yard

I thought if I could touch this place or feel it
This brokenness inside me might start healing
Out here it's like I'm someone else
I thought that maybe I could find myself
If I could just come in I swear I'll leave
Won't take nothing but a memory
From the house that built me

Mama cut out pictures of houses for years
From *Better Homes and Gardens* magazine
Plans were drawn and concrete poured
Nail by nail and board by board

Daddy gave life to mama's dream

I thought if I could touch this place or feel it
This brokenness inside me might start healing
Out here it's like I'm someone else
I thought that maybe I could find myself
If I could just come in I swear I'll leave
Won't take nothing but a memory
From the house that built me

BRIDGE:
You leave home and you move on and you do the best you can
I got lost in this old world and forgot who I am

I thought if I could touch this place or feel it
This brokenness inside me might start healing
Out here it's like I'm someone else
I thought that maybe I could find myself
If I walk around I swear I'll leave
Won't take nothing but a memory
From the house that built me

# The Most Beautiful Girl

*Story by Norro Wilson*
*Written by Norro Wilson, Rory Bourke,*
*and Billy Sherrill*
*Recorded by Charlie Rich*

The world doesn't know it now, but I was a recording artist for every label except CBS. What it taught me is that, although I thought I could sing, I wasn't a stylist like a George Jones or a Willie Nelson. When you hear Willie Nelson, you never forget his voice. And you have to have a hit song, too.

I had recorded this song that Rory Bourke had written called "Sunset and Vine." I always was a pretty good mimic. When I did nightclubs, I would do impressions and things like that all the time, and this song was my impression of The Beach Boys. I went up to Chicago to meet Rory, who was the national sales and promotions director of Smash Records, a subsidiary of Mercury. I went there to do a promotional tour and see the DJs, and so on.

After we did the radio tour, I was staying with Rory and his wife in their guest bedroom. In those years, I would take a drink now and then and, one morning, there was a knock at my door. I opened the door, and there was Rory and his wife. She was holding a cup of coffee and he was holding a little glass of orange juice. Rory had his guitar in his hand and he said, "Let's write a song." Now, I couldn't think of anything else in the world that I wanted to do less than write a song at that moment. But I was on his turf, so I said, "Okay."

He told me had an idea and he strummed, "I woke up this morning, realized what I had done / I stood alone in the cold grey dawn and knew I'd lost my morning sun. / I lost my head and I said some things, now comes the heartache that the morning brings." That's as far as he had gotten. And, I didn't really even consider myself a writer at the time, but maybe I got lucky. I sat right up and said, "What if that guy wakes up in an apartment building and then walks outside and goes up to the first guy he sees and says, 'Hey, Mister, did you happen to see the most beautiful girl in the world? And if you did, was she crying?'" And we went on to finish it. It's a very short song if you look at the lyrics. It's not too wordy or involved, but it had magic to it.

The song lay around for six or seven years. I tried to get Joe Stampley to cut it, but it was too pop for him. We had no problem with that. He wanted to be a country singer and it was a pop song, which has really been my background. I was always more pop than country.

Then Billy Sherrill heard it. He heard the intro, "Hey Mister, did you happen to see the most beautiful girl in the world?" and he said, "What kind of crap is that — 'Hey Mister'? Why don't you just say, 'Hey, did you happen to see....' It don't matter who he's talking to. People will get it." Well, that was the answer! That was just what the song needed. That really kicked it in the butt.

Billy was producing Charlie Rich then, so he took it to him and they began working on it in the studio. They took a lot of the flavor of the piano work from Charlie's first hit, "Behind Closed Doors" and they worked some of it into "Most Beautiful Girl," which kind of became Charlie's signature sound. When they went in to cut "Most Beautiful Girl," they took several hours trying to get the piano intro just how Billy wanted it. But man, did it work.

# The Most Beautiful Girl

Hey, did you happen to see the most beautiful girl in the
    world?
And if you did was she crying, cryin'?
Hey, if you happen to see the most beautiful girl, that walked
    out on me
Tell her I'm sorry, tell her I need my baby
Oh, won't you tell her, that I love her.

I woke up this morning, and realized what I had done
I stood alone in the cold gray dawn
And I knew I'd lost my morning sun
I lost my head and I said some things
Now come the heartaches that the morning brings
I know I'm wrong and I couldn't see
I let my world slip away from me.

Hey, did you happen to see the most beautiful girl in the
    world?
And if you did was she crying, cryin'?
Hey, if you happen to see the most beautiful girl, that walked
    out on me
Tell her I'm sorry, tell her I need my baby
Oh, won't you tell her, that I love her.

Did you happen to see the most beautiful girl in the world?
And if you did was she crying, cryin'?
Hey, if you happen to see the most beautiful girl, that walked
    out on me
Tell her I'm sorry, tell her I need my baby

Oh, won't you tell her, that I love her

Did you happen to see the most beautiful girl in the world?
And if you did was she crying, cryin'?

# The River

*Story by Victoria Shaw*
*Song written by Victoria Shaw*
*and Garth Brooks*
*Recorded by Garth Brooks*

I wrote "The River" with Garth Brooks at my little house in East Nashville. We were sitting around trying to come up with any kind of song idea but we were blank. After about an hour he said, "Put some music on," so I put on this new James Taylor album I had just gotten. If you listen, you can hear we had James as our muse.

As soon as we locked in, the song wrote itself. We were done in two hours. Garth's first record hadn't even come out yet. He told me he would put it on his second album, but it never made it, so I was thrilled when it showed up on *Ropin' the Wind*. This song was, and is, one of Garth's signature songs.

I still get people telling me all the time how "The River" was used at their graduation or at a funeral or it inspired them to leave a job or a town they were unhappy in and start a new life.

Garth and I were two wide-eyed dreamers when we wrote this. The song was, and still is, our philosophy of life.

# The River

You know a dream is like a river
Ever changin' as it flows
And a dreamer's just a vessel
That must follow where it goes
Trying to learn from what's behind you
And never knowing what's in store
Makes each day a constant battle
Just to stay between the shores

CHORUS:
I will sail my vessel
'Til the river runs dry
Like a bird upon the wind
These waters are my sky
I'll never reach my destination
If I never try
So I will sail my vessel
'Til the river runs dry

Too many times we stand aside
And let the waters slip away
'Til what we put off 'til tomorrow
Has now become today
So don't you sit upon the shoreline
And say you're satisfied
Choose to chance the rapids
And dare to dance the tide

CHORUS

There's bound to be rough waters
And I know I'll take some falls

But with the good Lord as my captain
I can make it through them all

CHORUS

# The Song Remembers When

*Story by Hugh Prestwood*
*Song written by Hugh Prestwood*
*Recorded by Trisha Yearwood*

I was an English major in college and a lot of poets influenced my lyric writing. I've loved poets like Frost, and Edwin A. Robinson, and Emily Dickinson. I got the idea for "The Song Remembers When" from a poem by Anne Sexton called "Music Swims Back to Me." There's a line in the poem where the narrator says, "The song remembers more than I."

I had a couple of major heartbreaks in my life. I think everyone has had those relationships where you hear a song that triggers emotions and memories. The lines that read, "we were rolling through the Rockies, we were up above the clouds"—that came from a real moment in time. My wife and I were driving through Rocky Mountain National Park. We drove from Estes Park, Colorado, and as we got higher, we were literally driving through the clouds and eventually we were above the clouds.

We were listening to the radio and I actually heard one of my songs, "Hard Rock Bottom of Your Heart," performed by Randy Travis. So this was just an incredible moment, looking out over the mountains and then hearing one of my songs on the radio. The station was actually out of Denver, and I started to use Denver in the song, but we had also been to Jackson Hole, Wyoming on that trip and I decided Jackson sounded better.

The first verse, "I was standing at the counter, I was waiting for the change," was also based on an experience I had when I heard one of my songs for the first time. I was at a Shoney's restaurant and something that I had written came over the speakers. So I remembered that scene and thought, "I'll use that as the first verse." All of those scenes got jumbled around and ended up in this song, which was about a painful break-up.

We had a lot of trouble getting that song recorded. I was writing for BMG then and I went through a little bit of a depression because I thought that was as good a song as I would ever write and we could not get it cut. I actually had a couple of big producers who called me and asked me if I would consider re-writing it to make it more radio-friendly and more chorus-y. It doesn't really even have a chorus. But I just loved it the way it was and I didn't want to change it.

Then Kathy Mattea recorded it and I really very happy about it, until I found out it didn't make it on her record. That really sent me into a nosedive, with a lot of self-doubt. She told me later the label actually liked the song, but it didn't really match the flavor of the album.

We had pitched it to Trisha Yearwood for a previous album and that didn't happen either, but the second time around, she cut it. It later won the Nashville Songwriters Association Song of the Year, and even won an Emmy because Trisha did it in a TV special. Since then, it's almost become her signature song. When an artist gets identified with a song that closely, a lot of other artists don't want to touch it. If I were an artist and I heard Trisha sing it, I wouldn't want to try to cover it either. She really nailed it.

# The Song Remembers When

I was standing at the counter

I was waiting for the change
When I heard that old familiar music start
It was like a lighted match
Had been tossed into my soul
It was like a dam had broken in my heart

After taking every detour
Getting lost and losing track
So that even if I wanted
I could not find my way back
After driving out the memory
Of the way things might have been
After I'd forgotten all about us
The song remembers when

We were rolling through the Rockies
We were up above the clouds
When a station out of Jackson played that song
And it seemed to fit the moment
And the moment seemed to freeze
When we turned the music up and sang along

And there was a God in Heaven
And the world made perfect sense
We were young and were in love
And we were easy to convince
We were headed straight for Eden
It was just around the bend
And though I have forgotten all about it
The song remembers when

I guess something must have happened
And we must have said goodbye
And my heart must have been broken
Though I can't recall just why

The song remembers when

Well, for all the miles between us
And for all the time that's passed
You would think I haven't gotten very far
And I hope my hasty heart
Will forgive me just this once
If I stop to wonder how on earth you are

But that's just a lot of water
Underneath a bridge I burned
And there's no use in backtracking
Around corners I have turned
Still I guess some things we bury
Are just bound to rise again
For even if the whole world has forgotten

The song remembers when
Yeah, and even if the whole world has forgotten
The song remembers when

# The Streak

*Story by Ray Stevens*
*Song written by Ray Stevens*
*Recorded by Ray Stevens*

I was on a plane flying from L.A. to Nashville. Back in those days, they used to carry several of the weekly magazines on board, like *Time* or *Newsweek*. Now they have their own magazines. And in the back, they always had these little news blurbs about events across the country. One of the blurbs was about a college student in California who took off his clothes and ran through a crowd and they called it "streaking." I thought, "Now there's an idea," so I started making some notes.

When I got home, all of the news broadcasts were talking about streaking, so I thought I'd better finish the song, so we could get in the studio and cut it. I write a lot of comedy songs. When I sit down to write, I usually get the title or concept in mind first and then, of course, that dictates whether the song is going to be funny or serious. I try to have the tempo and the melodic structure reflect the silliness or the seriousness of the song. You can't put a slow, dragging, love-song melody to a comedy song like this. And of course this had to be a funny song.

By the time I got my record released, there were already fifteen other streaking records out. I think mine was one of the ones that made it, though, because I had a little more time to think about it and polish the song. Most of the others were just hastily thrown together, and didn't really have any other meaning to them other than just trying to cash in on a fad.

Later, when videos became more popular, we did a video for the song and put it in a package called *Comedy Video Classics* and it sold something like four million copies.

# The Streak

(Reporter):

Hello, everybody, this is your action news reporter with all the news that is news across the nation, on the scene at the supermarket. There seems to have been some disturbance here. Pardon me, sir, did you see what happened?

(Witness):

Yeah, I did. I's standin' over there by the tomaters, and here he come, running through the pole beans, through the fruits and vegetables, nekkid as a jay bird. And I hollered over t' Ethel, I said, "Don't look, Ethel!" But it's too late, she'd already been incensed.

(Chorus)

Here he comes, look at that, look at that
There he goes, look at that, look at that
And he ain't wearin' no clothes

Oh, yes, they call him the Streak
Look at that, look at that
Fastest thing on two feet
Look at that, look at that

He's just as proud as he can be
Of his anatomy
He goin' give us a peek

Oh, yes, they call him the Streak
Look at that, look at that
He likes to show off his physique
Look at that, look at that
If there's an audience to be found
He'll be streakin' around
Invitin' public critique

(Reporter):

This is your action news reporter once again, and we're here at
the gas station. Pardon me, sir, did you see what happened?

(Witness):

Yeah, I did. I's just in here gettin my car checked, he just
appeared out of the traffic. Come streakin' around the grease
rack there, didn't have nothin' on but a smile. I looked in there,
and Ethel was getting her a cold drink. I hollered, "Don't look,
Ethel!" But it was too late. She'd already been mooned. Flashed
her right there in front of the shock absorbers.

(Chorus)

He ain't crude, look at that, look at that
He ain't lewd, look at that, look at that
He's just in the mood to run in the nude

Oh, yes, they call him the Streak
Look at that, look at that
He likes to turn the other cheek

Look at that, look at that
He's always makin' the news
Wearin' just his tennis shoes
Guess you could call him unique

(Reporter):

Once again, your action news reporter in the booth at the gym,
covering the disturbance at the basketball playoff. Pardon me,
sir, did you see what happened?

(Witness):

Yeah, I did. Half time, I's just goin' down there to get Ethel a
snow cone. And here he come, right out of the cheap seats,
dribbling, right down the middle of the court. Didn't have on
nothing but his PF's. Made a hook shot and got out through
the concessions stand. I hollered up at Ethel, I said, "Don't
look, Ethel!" But it was too late. She'd already got a free shot.
Grandstandin', right there in front of the home team.

(Chorus) (Witness):

Oh, yes, they call him the Streak Here he comes again.
Look at that, look at that Who's that with him?
The fastest thing on two feet (voice: "Ethel? Is that you, Ethel?")
Look at that, look at that (voice: "What do you think you're
    doin'?")
He's just as proud as he can be (voice: "You git your clothes on")
Of his anatomy
He's gonna give us a peek

Oh, yes, they call him the Streak (voice: "Ethel! Where you
    goin'?")
Look at that, look at that (voice: "Ethel, you shameless hussy")

He likes to show off his physique (voice: "Say it isn't so")
Look at that, look at that (voice: "Ethel! Ethelllllll!!!")
If there's an audience to be found
He'll be streakin' around
Invitin' public critique

# The Thunder Rolls

*Story by Pat Alger*
*Song written by Pat Alger and Garth Brooks*
*Recorded by Garth Brooks*

**G**arth and I made up this story. It's just an old fashioned country cheating song where he gets his comeuppance. The title actually comes from a line I wrote in another song for Kathy Mattea, "Like a Hurricane." Garth said, "We should write a song about a guy who is cheating on his wife and every time he does it, the thunder rolls." And we sat down and wrote it in about an hour and a half. We wrote it at Allen Reynolds' office. There was a lot of room to pace there, and Garth likes to pace a lot when he writes. I think we even demoed it the same day.

We initially pitched this song to Tanya Tucker and we heard she was going to do it on her *Greatest Hits* album. So we thought, "This is great. This will sell at least a million copies." Tanya's producer, Jerry Crutchfield, thought it should be a little more dramatic, so he asked us to write another verse at the end. We actually wrote three or four different versions and turned one in. She has a gun at the end and the lyric reads, "Tonight will be the last time / she'll wonder where he's been," but we don't really say what happens. We imply that she shoots him, but I always like to leave a little to the imagination.

Garth didn't have a record deal at the time, so we were really excited about Tanya doing it. After the fact, Allen felt the original version of the song was fine, but Tanya wanted the extra verse, so we wrote it for her. For whatever reason, though, she ended up shelving it for a future album. By the time she got around to putting that next album out, Garth had been signed by the same label, Capitol, and he asked for the song back. Tanya did eventually put her version out. It's on her boxed set, but I don't think it was ever pushed as a single.

The way we wrote it originally is the way it appears on Garth's record. After Garth cut it, they put an incredible amount of time and money into the video. It was one of the most expensive videos done at the time. There was a big controversy over what happens at the end, with the domestic violence. So they cut the last verse, but Garth always sang it in all of his live shows and still does.

It went on to be a much more popular video than it would have been if they had just left it alone. It became a big news item and actually raised quite a bit of awareness about domestic violence.

It's a pretty dramatic song. Now, when I play it live, I sing that extra verse, too. I don't even go back to the final chorus; I just end it there, and it usually gets pretty quiet in the room.

# The Thunder Rolls

Three thirty in the morning
Not a soul in sight
The city's lookin' like a ghost town
On a moonless summer night
Raindrops on the windshield
There's a storm moving in
He's headin' back from somewhere
That he never should have been
And the thunder rolls
And the thunder rolls

Every light is burnin'
In a house across town

She's pacin' by the telephone
In her faded flannel gown
Askin' for miracle
Hopin' she's not right
Prayin' it's the weather
That's kept him out all night
And the thunder rolls
And the thunder rolls

CHORUS:
The thunder rolls
And the lightnin' strikes
Another love grows cold
On a sleepless night
As the storm blows on
Out of control
Deep in her heart
The thunder rolls

She's waitin' by the window
When he pulls into the drive
She rushes out to hold him
Thankful he's alive
But on the wind and rain
A strange new perfume blows
And the lightnin' flashes in her eyes
And he knows that she knows
And the thunder rolls
And the thunder rolls

CHORUS

She runs back down the hallway
To the bedroom door
She reaches for the pistol

Kept in the dresser drawer
She tells the lady in the mirror
"He won't do this again."
Cause tonight will be the last time
She'll wonder where he's been

# This One's for the Girls

*Story by Hillary Lindsey*
*Song written by Hillary Lindsey, Aimee*
*Mayo, and Chris Lindsey*
*Recorded by Martina McBride*

When Aimee Mayo and Chris and I first sat down to write, "This One's for the Girls," we were thinking of writing something that would be an inspiration only for younger girls. Then, the more we started talking about it, the more we decided to touch on every generation. The line that talks about "living on dreams and Spaghettios / wonderin' where your life is gonna go"—that was me, at that same age, living in an apartment, and living on SpaghettiOs. I still occasionally eat them, because I love them. I was living in a really creepy apartment near Music Row. It was very convenient but was roach-infested and everything. So that part was pretty autobiographical.

I think when we wrote the line about "every laugh line on your face," we were probably thinking of our moms, but also being at the age when we were starting to develop our own little laugh lines or crow's feet.

When we wrote the lines about high school being so rough and mean and holding onto your innocence as long as you can, both

Aimee and I felt this way when we were teenagers—maybe not feeling like you were part of the "in-crowd." I don't know how Chris felt, being a man and all. He probably felt the same way. There's just so much facing young women today, from peer pressure to bullying to negative feedback from the media, so we were just trying to write a positive song that they can listen to and feel encouraged by.

We want girls to feel comfortable being who they are, being comfortable in their own skin, and not trying to be someone they're not. It's kind of addressing us girls, too, because heaven knows, we're usually our worst critics. We can be pretty hard on ourselves and sometimes hard on each other, too. So this song was meant to be an encouragement to girls of all ages to just be themselves.

# This One's for the Girls

This is for all you girls, about thirteen.
High school can be so rough, can be so mean.
Hold onto, onto your innocence.
Stand your ground, when everybody's givin' in.
This one's for the girls.

This is for all you girls, about twenty-five.
In little apartments just tryin' to get by.
Livin' on, on dreams and Spaghettios.
Wonderin' where your life is gonna go.

CHORUS:
This one's for the girls,
Who've ever had a broken heart;
Who've wished upon a shootin' star:
You're beautiful the way you are.
This one's for the girls,
Who love without holdin' back
Who dream with everything they have.

All around the world,
This one's for the girls.

This is for all you girls, about forty-two.
Tossin' pennies into the fountain of youth.
Every laugh, laugh line on your face,
Made you who you are today.

CHORUS

Yeah, we're all the same inside
From one to ninety-nine:

CHORUS

# Time Marches On

*Story by Bobby Braddock*
*Song written by Bobby Braddock*
*Recorded by Tracy Lawrence*

**"T**ime Marches On" was a huge record for me. It's probably already a little dated. It was timely when I wrote it because it was about the people who were going through those transformations around 1996. The people that started out as hippie kids were starting to get old then and they're a whole lot older now!

When I was a kid in a small town in Florida, a lot of the country people moved up north looking for work. And by the time I wrote that song, there were people from the North moving down into the area to retire. So that's where the line "the South moves north, the North moves south" came from.

We were at a family reunion once and my ex-wife's sister had a bumper sticker on the back of her car that said, "Sexy Grandma." I thought that was pretty funny, so I put that in the song, too.

I thought the songs that were mentioned in each verse reflected the time periods: Hank Williams for the 1950s and Dylan for the 1960s, and then back to Hank again. I decided to add the B-3 organ lick right after the line "Dylan sings 'like a rolling stone'" on the demo because it sounds like what he did on that song. They decided to keep it on Tracy's record. Of course, on Dylan's, it wasn't in a minor key, but it falls in a minor on "Time Marches On," so it sounds a little different, but it's still the same lick. I also used a Don Helms-style pedal-less steel guitar lick on the Hank Williams line, but they didn't use that on the record.

On my demo, Brent Rowan played that little acoustic thing that sounds like a clock ticking at the beginning of the song. Then Brent Mason played on the record. They are two of the best session players in town, but it's kind of ironic that Brent Mason got credit for playing a Brent Rowan lick.

Tracy just had a hit with my "Texas Tornado," and I played the song for Don Cook, his producer, and he liked it. I think Tracy had already heard it somewhere and liked it anyway, so that's how he decided to cut it. Tracy did a great job on it. He sang it with a lot of conviction, even though he was too young to really have gone through much of that.

There was a major artist that is really hot today—I won't say who—who heard it and he passed on it. When he heard Tracy's song, he asked his producer, "Why didn't I get to listen to that?" His producer said, "Well, you did. You passed." So that goes to show that sometimes an artist will hear a song differently in different situations.

# Time Marches On

Sister cries out, from her baby bed.
Brother runs in with feathers on his head.
Mama's in her room learning how to sew.
Daddy's drinking beer, listenin' to the radio.
Hank Williams sings "Kaw-Liga" and "Dear John"
Time marches on, time marches on.

Sister's using rouge and clear complexion soap.
Brother's wearing beads and he smokes alot of dope.
Mama is depressed, barely makes a sound.
Daddy's got a girlfriend in another town.

Bob Dylan sings "like a rolling stone."
Time marches on, time marches on.

BRIDGE:
South moves north, North moves south
A star is born, a star burns out.
The only thing that stays the same is everything
changes, everything changes.

Sister calls herself a sexy grandma.
Brother's on a diet for high cholesterol.
Mama's out of touch with reality.
Daddy's in the ground beneath the maple tree.
As the angels sing an old Hank Williams song.
Time marches on, time marches on.
Time marches on, time marches on.

# Unanswered Prayers

*Story by Pat Alger*
*Song written by Garth Brooks, Pat Alger,*
*and Larry Bastian*
*Recorded by Garth Brooks*

I had an experience where I ran into my high school girlfriend. I had grown up in Georgia. This girl and I dated all through high school, and we both assumed we would get married. But after high school, I went off to Georgia Tech and she went to Emory. Once we were both in the big city, we lost contact and moved on. When we saw each other again, I think we both realized it probably wouldn't have worked. She's a wonderful person and I actually introduced her to the guy who ended up being her husband, who was a friend of mine.

If she and I had stayed together, my life probably wouldn't have taken the path that it took. I probably would have gotten a job as an architect in a suburb of Georgia and just stayed there. I don't think I would have ended up in the music business, writing songs for Garth Brooks, that's for sure. And if someone had told me I would end up in the Nashville Songwriters Hall of Fame 30 years later, I couldn't have even conjured up an image of what that would look like. But I think I discovered that I loved music a lot more than architecture by about my sophomore year. For the next 10 years, I was a troubadour, singing my songs all over the country and even in Europe, and then I finally ended up here in Nashville.

Around 1988, Garth and his manager, Bob Doyle, had been talking to producers and Allen Reynolds was one of them. I was coming out of an office on Music Row and they were coming out of another. Allen said, "This is Garth Brooks. He's a pretty good songwriter. You two should try to get together and write sometime."

Garth was playing at a small club in the basement of a building on Church Street that night. There were about 30 or 40 people in the club and Garth just knocked their socks off. Afterwards I said to him, "Hey, let's get together as soon as possible."

Allen had a comfortable little office on Music Row with a studio above it called Jack's Tracks. That's where he did a lot of his recording. Allen said, "Why don't you guys go upstairs where they have some windows and try writing." First we wrote a couple of songs for other people. Then Garth told me about a conversation he had earlier with another writer, Larry Bastian, about those fortuitous circumstances where things don't work out like you hoped they would, but you're glad later. So I shared with him my experience with my high school girlfriend, and I think he had had a similar experience with an old flame, too, so we started working on "Unanswered Prayers."

Garth didn't even have a record deal at the time we wrote it. Then he was signed by Capitol Records and they said they were going to put the song on his first album, but didn't. So I just assumed he wasn't interested any longer. But Garth always had a plan. Things just don't happen by chance for him. He and Allen had saved up a lot of really strong songs for Garth's second album. A lot of artists have a really big first album, but then the second one is usually about half as good. *No Fences*, his second album, ended up selling a lot more than the first. It had "Friends in Low Places," and "The Thunder Rolls," and a bunch of others. And they included "Unanswered Prayers," too.

Garth is a great collaborator and really put his stamp on the song. Over the years, "Unanswered Prayers" has been one of his signature songs and very closely identified with him, so it hasn't been covered by many other artists. I did it myself, but I don't know of many others.

I've had a lot of people share stories with me over the years who have had similar circumstances where they were hoping for their life to go in one direction and then it goes in another, but it turns out to be a blessing in disguise. And now the song has even inspired a made-for-TV movie. When you play it live and everybody in the room is singing along with the lyric, you realize what an impact it's had on so many lives.

## Unanswered Prayers

Just the other night at a hometown football game
My wife and I ran into my old high school flame
And as I introduced them the past came back to me
And I couldn't help but think of the way things used to be

She was the one that I'd wanted for all time
And each night I'd spend prayin' that God would make her
    mine
And if he'd only grant me this wish I wished back then
I'd never ask for anything again

CHORUS:
Sometimes I thank God for unanswered prayers
Remember when you're talkin' to the man upstairs
That just because he doesn't answer doesn't mean he don't care
Some of God's greatest gifts are unanswered prayers

She wasn't quite the angel that I remembered in my dreams
And I could tell that time had changed me
In her eyes, too, it seemed
We tried to talk about the old days
There wasn't much we could recall

I guess the Lord knows what he's doin' after all

BRIDGE:
And as she walked away, I looked at my wife
And then and there I thanked the good Lord
For the gifts in my life

CHORUS

Some of God's greatest gifts are all too often unanswered...
Some of God's greatest gifts are unanswered prayers

# Uncle Pen

*Story by James Monroe*
*Song written by Bill Monroe*
*Recorded by Bill Monroe, Porter Wagoner,*
*Ricky Skaggs and others*

U ncle Pen — Pendleton Vandiver was his name — lived in a little cabin not far from where my dad grew up, in Rosine, Kentucky. He had three or four acres of land. The cabin sat high on a hill above the town, just like the song says. Pen was my dad's mother's brother. My father said he had brown eyes like I have. All of the Monroes have blue eyes.

My dad lost his parents pretty young. His mother died when he was nine, and his daddy died when he was just 16. That's when he moved in with Uncle Pen. That was the last place my father stayed before he left Kentucky around the age of 18. Pen used to take my dad with him on horseback or muleback and they would play shows in that area. They would play parties and square dances together. Whatever Uncle Pen got paid, he would give my father half.

My father was known for his mandolin, but he played fiddle, too, and guitar sometimes, and he would play fiddle and guitar with Pen. The music always came from the Vandiver side; it wasn't on the Monroe side. It was on the Dutch side. Uncle Pen was a self-taught musician. Back in those days, not many people took formal music lessons. My grandfather could dance, too, and my grandmother played a little accordion and fiddle, and could sing, too.

My father told me Pen was a wonderful man, and a good uncle to my dad. Pen would cook breakfast for my dad in the morning and then cook him dinner, too. Pen was divorced at the time. Uncle Pen had some health problems, so later in life he would get paid to play music and he would also go from town to town trading things. He would trade knives or guns or whatever. He would buy them and then sell them at a profit.

My dad wrote the song to pay tribute to his uncle. It was really a memorial in the form of a song. It was a big hit for my dad, but a lot of other people recorded it, too. Porter Waggoner had a pretty big hit on it, and Ricky Skaggs had a good hit out of it. It's had over a million airplays. BMI gave us the million-air award for "Uncle Pen," and that's pretty unusual for a bluegrass song.

I think it's been so popular because it's a real story. You can just feel it when you play it. It all fits together perfectly, the story and the music. The song is made for a fiddle. It's got that shuffle timing and you can't really even play the song without a fiddle. I've tried it, and you can't do it.

# Uncle Pen

Oh, the people would come from far away,
To dance all night 'til the break of day.
When the caller would holler, "Do-Si-Do"
They knew Uncle Pen was ready to go.

CHORUS:
Late in the evening, about sundown,
High on the hill, an' above the town,
Uncle Pen played the fiddle, Lord, how it'd ring,
You could hear it talk, you could hear it sing!

INSTRUMENTAL BREAK

Well, he played an old tune they called the "Soldier's Joy"
And he played the one they called the "Boston Boy."
Greatest of all was the "Jennie Lynn"
To me, that's where the fiddlin' begins.

CHORUS

I'll never forget that mournful day
When old Uncle Pen was called away,
He hung up his fiddle and he hung up his bow,
And he knew it was time for him to go.

CHORUS

# Walk on Faith

*Story by Mike Reid*
*Song written by Mike Reid and Allen*
*Shamblin*
*Recorded by Mike Reid*

I never made a decision to pursue a career in music. After I decided to quit playing football when I left the Cincinnati Bengals, I didn't know what I was going to do for a living. I started playing and singing at clubs in the Cincinnati area and eventually moved to Nashville. The first real hit I wrote was a song called "Inside" for Ronnie Milsap and later I won a Grammy for Ronnie's recording of "Stranger in My House" in 1983.

In 1990, I wrote "Walk on Faith" with Allen Shamblin. He brought the idea in one day and we wrote it together. It's the kind of song that encourages people to hang in there through tough times, whether it's in a marriage or from a spiritual perspective. There's no really great story to tell about it, as far as a story behind the song, but this one has a very touching story *after* the song.

I ended up recording that song on an album of mine called *Turning for Home* in 1991. The label put it out as a single and it hit #1 and was there for a couple of weeks. So I went out on the road opening up for K.T. Oslin and Kathy Mattea at the time. We were up in the Northeast somewhere. After the shows, we would line up and sign autographs for people or sign their CDs. And there was a girl—she couldn't have been more than 20 or 21 — who came through the line that night. When she came through, she was carrying a baby. I asked her name before I signed the CD. I wrote her name and then wrote, "Walk on Faith."

After I signed her CD, she thanked me and then she looked at me and said, "I just want you to know that song is the reason I decided to keep this baby." It was a startling moment for me. There wasn't much I could say, so I just stood up and gave her a hug.

I've thought about that night a lot since then, because that baby today would be close to 20 years old. I don't know if songs really make people do things one way or another, but I believe the power of a song lies in its ability to help people identify important things inside them that they have lost touch with.

I just did a show with Billy Dean and Gary Nicholson out in Napa Valley and there was fellow there who was a hugely successful winemaker. He came up to us afterward and he said, "What you songwriters do is remind us what we feel. For us, our lives are usually about marketing and strategies and that kind of thing," he said, "and when we sit down on a night like this and listen to songs like these, you help remind us of things we feel, and have felt, but have forgotten." That's about the most wonderful thing for someone to say to a songwriter.

# Walk on Faith

We have come to this place in our love
Where faith must be stronger than fear
For if true love is our destination
Through every storm it must always be clear
The surest way to get there from here (is to)

CHORUS:
Walk on faith
And trust in love

Just keep on putting one foot down
In front of the other
When the valley's so wide
We stumble in stride
And everything inside
wants to give up
Walk on faith and trust in love

Farther on beyond the shadows of our doubt
We will live where true love never dies
Though the road we must travel is uncertain
There is a truth in our hearts that never lies
It is by such grace we are bound to arrive

CHORUS

# Walking Away a Winner

*Story by Bob DiPiero*
*Song written by Bob DiPiero and Tom*
*    Shapiro*
*Recorded by Kathy Mattea*

When I wrote "Walking Away a Winner" I was either in the middle of, or quickly careening toward, a messy break-up. I was hoping that I was going to take the high road, like the singer in "Walking Away a Winner" did. The line "with my pride intact and my vision back"—who could say that in real life? But I could say it in a song. So I was whistling past the graveyard, so to speak.

We wrote it in 1992 or 1993, and Kathy Mattea cut it in 1994. It was written quickly because the idea was pretty well fleshed out from the start. I was writing with Tom Shapiro, who is one of the best songwriters of our generation. When you're writing with someone of his caliber, once you latch onto a really strong idea, the song kind of creates its own kind of internal energy. So then it's just a matter of riding it and then going back and tweaking the weak parts later.

"Walking away from a losing game"—some people just can't do that. To me, it's a song of empowerment. Even though Kathy sang it, it could be from a guy's point of view, too. That's the powerful part of the song—the singer is saying, "I might be losing here, but I didn't get all my teeth kicked out. I've learned from it. I don't think I'll go there again."

"When love is on the table, the stakes are high," because you are just laying yourself out there for someone and, of course, this includes the possibility of getting hurt, too. That's what this person in the song is going through, but they're taking something positive out of it. That's where I think the power of that song lies.

I've talked with a lot of people who have said, "That really helped me during a difficult part of my life. I was feeling defeated and broken and that song really helped me get through it." That's all you can hope for when you write a song: that it will affect someone's life personally like that.

## Walking Away a Winner

Any time love is on the table the stakes are high
And I thought this was love so I laid it all on the line
You nearly took everything I had. Never knew I could hurt so
    bad
But at least I left with every piece of this heart of mine

CHORUS:
I'm walking away a winner
Walking away from a losing game.
With my pride intact and my vision back, I can say
I know where I'm going and I know I'll be all right.
I'm walking away a winner, walking back into my life.

It was a hard way to go when I didn't know when to leave
And if you knew all along baby, you weren't telling me
Now I know what I can live without.

I'm heading down the right road now
Still believing in the way that a real love is meant to be

CHORUS

# What A Difference You've Made In My Life

*Story by Archie Jordan*
*Song written by Archie Jordan*
*Recorded by Ronnie Milsap*

When I was living in Nashville, I went to a Bible study every week at the home of my friend Alan Moore. We met in his basement, and one week there were about 25 of us, and someone stood up and told this story. He was from a well-to-do family in Nashville. He was doing very well, making lots of money and living the American dream. He had a beautiful wife and daughter and a beautiful home, but he had gotten to drinking and doing drugs. One thing led to another and he lost his job. He went through his savings and then lost his home. Everything went downhill. His wife got disgusted with him and divorced him and left the state with their daughter.

He was telling us this story and he looked at us and said, "One day, I woke up and realized that I had nothing—no money, no home, and I had nobody. I finally came to the end of my rope, and I turned my life over to God and oh, what a difference He made in my life."

Right at that moment, I started writing this song. I started getting music and lyrics in my head while he was still talking. If I ever wrote an inspired song, this was it. I continued writing it on the way home, and played it for my publisher the next morning. He loved it. He said, "Not only is this a great gospel song, but it can be about your wife or your mom or dad, or one of your children."

I started to think maybe I should start with a verse like "You do this and you do that for me, and what a difference you've made in my life," building a laundry list. But when I thought about it, I knew the song should start with the title. And when I got through singing the chorus, I thought, "I think it wants to do the same thing again in the next verse when it says, 'What a change you have made in my heart,' and then repeat that at the end for the phrase again."

Then I knew I would do a bridge and then go back to that first verse again. It was like an old AABA form, like "Raindrops Keep Fallin' On My Head," and it seemed a little redundant, but nothing else really fit.

I got a chance to write several songs with Hal David, who used to write the lyrics to all those great songs by Burt Bacharach, and he told me one time, "Always go where the song wants to go. Don't have any preconceived notions about it." And he was right. He wrote the lyrics to "It Was Almost Like A Song," which was another big hit for Ronnie Milsap. Hal came to Nashville several times a year and my publisher got me an audition with him, and I put down three of my best melodies on a tape and he liked what he heard, so we ended up collaborating on a few songs.

I did a simple piano and vocal melody and gave it to Ronnie Milsap. When we cut the demo, we went over to the old RCA Studio B, where Elvis and Roy Orbison and those guys used to record. But when we recorded the master, we did it at Woodland Studios in Nashville. They rented another grand piano and Ronnie played one piano and I played the other. We are both playing on the record.

B.J. Thomas later recorded "What A Difference You've Made In My Life," and it was a big gospel hit for him. A number of other people recorded it after that. It was nominated for a CMA Award, but didn't win. That's okay. I was just glad to get that story out.

I went to a church in Statesboro, Georgia, one time and there was a pastor who stood up and started telling a story about a mission trip he took to Russia. Several members of his church went to a remote part of Russia. While they were there, these Russians at this little tiny church said, "We heard this American song and we learned it and want to sing it to you." So, they started singing, in broken English, "What A Difference You've Made In My Life." Small world.

# What A Difference You've Made In My Life

What a difference you've made in my life
What a difference you've made in my life
You're my sunshine day and night
Oh what a difference you've made in my life

What a change you have made in my heart
What a change you have made in my heart
You replaced all the broken parts
Oh what a change you have made in my heart

Love to me was just a word in a song
That had been way over-used
But now I've joined in the singin'
'Cause you've shown me love's true meanin'
That's why I want to spread the news

What a difference you've made in my life
What a difference you've made in my life
You're my sunshine day and night
Oh what a difference you've made in my life

# Where've You Been?

*Story by Jon Vezner*
*Song written by Jon Vezner and Don Henry*
*Recorded by Kathy Mattea*

**M**y grandparents moved from Minneapolis to Tucson when they were in their mid-seventies. They lived there until their early nineties. Then my grandmother fell and broke her hip. She also had what I think was dementia instead of Alzheimer's, even though the symptoms are similar. My aunt went down and brought her back to Minneapolis and put her in the hospital there because she refused to eat. She was this short, strong-willed German woman and I think she just didn't want to live like that. My grandfather stayed with my aunt up in Minneapolis. When that happened, I think this was the first time — except for maybe one trip earlier in his life — that they had ever spent a night apart.

I had been thinking about moving to Nashville. So, I made a trip here, and I was here for about a week when, during that time, my grandfather had a seizure and they realized he had a massive brain tumor. It was benign, but it was too big to operate on. They put him in the hospital and he was in the same hospital as my grandmother, but on a different floor. When we'd go in to see my grandmother, she acted like she knew my dad but nobody else. And she hadn't seen my grandfather since he had been put in the hospital. That went on for a week or two and one night, I said to the nurse, "Can I bring him up to see her?"

"I don't see why not," she said.

I wheeled him up to the elevator and there were these big glass windows. This was in the Metropolitan Medical Center in Minneapolis. My grandfather always had this boyish sense of wonder, as my dad did, and I think I do, too. He looked out over the city at night through those windows and he kept saying, "Look at that. Isn't that something?" His eyesight wasn't that great, but he could see the lights and the glare on the glass.

I took him to my grandmother's room and, as I wheeled him in, their eyes just locked. I could see that. She didn't even look at me. She just looked right at him and he looked at her. She had kind of a scowl on her face. He picked up her hand and he started stroking her hair and he said "Look at them hair," not "her hair," but "them hair."And he kept saying, "Nobody has hair like grandma."

She kept looking at him and finally she said, "Where've you been?" Almost like she was ticked off at him. That was about the only thing she said to him and, to our knowledge, it might have been one of the last things she said.

I went back to Nashville and I told Kathy about it. We were just dating then. And I thought about putting it into a song, but it seemed almost too personal. I hadn't been in Nashville that long, maybe two years. One day, Don Henry and I were writing and I told him about it and he said, "We've gotta write that."

I had some fears about it. I didn't want to take advantage of it and I was a little afraid about what the family might say, but we went ahead and wrote it. We made up the part about being a salesman, and we changed their names. Their names were Bill and Bertha, so that probably wouldn't work. Edwin was a cousin of my grandmother's, and I've always loved that name. And Claire was just a name we loved.

We put our songwriter hats on and tried to figure out a couple of other ways to work in the "where've you been" lines earlier in the song and we finished it. We wrote it really fast.

I was writing for Wrensong at the time, and I played it for my publisher, Ree Guyer, and she basically just leaned against the door and slid down to the floor and sobbed when she heard it. I was a music major and I loved cello, so we decided to put a cello and a nylon string guitar on it when we did the demo.

Kathy hadn't heard the song, and there was a party for Kathy and Allen Reynolds' first #1 single, which was "Going, Gone." Afterward, I said, "Hey, can I play you guys something?" Kathy leaned over and mouthed the words "you did it" to me while Allen was listening. Interestingly, Allen didn't want to record it. He thought it was too sad. And I heard stories about other people who heard it. I think Willie Nelson heard it and he cried, but he passed on it because it was too sad. People were afraid of it.

Then I got invited to do an NEA (Nashville Entertainment Association) showcase at The Bluebird. Kathy came down, and it stopped the house. That same night, someone else cancelled and a new guy named Garth Brooks filled in for him and that's the night he got his record deal. If you look at *The Bluebird Café Scrapbook*, that night is listed.

In 1988, Kathy won Single of The Year for "Eighteen Wheels and a Dozen Roses," and in 1989 she won Female Vocalist and her new record had just come out. We heard "Where've You Been?" on the radio coming back from the CMA Awards in 1989 and, exactly one year later it won Song of the Year at the CMA.

Kathy played it at *Austin City Limits* and they had to stop taping because they couldn't get the people to sit down. The show producer, Terry Locona, came up and he said, "I've *never* seen that happen."

It actually only got up to #13 on the country charts, but it crossed over. It was the first country song in a long time to cross over and it hit #15 on the Adult Contemporary charts. Later, it won an ACM award and a Grammy. It then won the Nashville Songwriters Association International Song of the Year and then I won NSAI Songwriter of the Year that year.

Kathy gets a lot of "Claires" and "Edwins" who come up to her and tell her how much that song meant to them. I get a lot of people who come up to me and say, "I remember exactly where I was when I first heard that and I had to pull over," and things like that. It's kind of strange. It's almost like 9/11 or the Kennedy thing. I'm not putting it up at that level of course, but we hear a lot about that song.

## Where've You Been?

Claire had all but given up
when she and Edwin fell in love
She touched his face and shook her head
in disbelief she sighed and said
"In many dreams I've held you near, but now at last you're
     really here

CHORUS:
Where've you been?
I've looked for you forever and a day
Where've you been?
I'm just not myself when you're away"

He asked her for her hand for life
and she became a salesman's wife
He was home each night by eight
but one stormy evening he was late
Her frightened tears fell to the floor
until his key turned in the door

CHORUS

They'd never spent a night apart
For sixty years she heard him snore
Now they're in a hospital

in separate beds on different floors

Claire soon lost her memory
Forgot the names of family
She never spoke a word again
Then one day they wheeled him in
He held her hand and stroked her head
In a fragile voice she said…

CHORUS

# Wichita Lineman

*Story by Jimmy Webb*
*Song written by Jimmy Webb*
*Recorded by Glen Campbell, Dwight Yoakam,*
*James Taylor, and others*

One night I was getting a special award at the Songwriters Hall of Fame in New York. They told me Billy Joel was going to sing "Wichita Lineman." I thought, "Wow, this will be great. I'm going to get to sit back and hear Billy Joel's version of this." He came out on stage and started playing it, then he deconstructed the song line by line. He said, "When the guy says, 'I need you more than want you,' that's kind of a dis toward the girl, isn't it?" Then he sang the next line, "and I want you for all time," and he said, "Well, I guess he *really is* crazy about her," or something to that effect. He was just kind of probing the song to try to understand it better, as many of us songwriters do. I don't know if I really understand the song's appeal.

I grew up in Oklahoma, and I was around that whole world of humming wires and the trucks and trains on their endless journeys across the Plains states. I remember the sound of the wires and looking up and seeing these men working on them. I also remember seeing them from the perspective of the front seat of an automobile, cruising along in the Panhandle at 60 miles per hour and seeing a little dot on a pole and seeing him come closer and closer until you are on him and then he's gone in an instant. Sometimes he would be talking on a little telephone. It's a lonely, romantic, prairie gothic image. I definitely tapped into it and used it with "Wichita Lineman," which is also a love story about a guy who can't get over a woman.

I was living in a house on Camino Palmero in Hollywood. Glen Campbell and Al DeLory had asked me to come up with another song after "By the Time I Get to Phoenix," which was a hit for them. They were in the studio, and they needed a song. I was living in a kind of communal environment with 25 or 30 of my best friends, and there were a couple of clowns who came into my music room and spray-painted my piano green, I think, because of "MacArthur Park"—"all the sweet, green icing flowing down." They thought it was pretty funny. So I spent the afternoon trying not to brush up against the piano and writing a song at the same time. That whole afternoon was a comedy, with a sticky green piano and several desperate calls from the recording studio.

I remember getting the first verse and a part of the second verse and then thinking, "I don't know if this needs a bridge or a chorus or another verse or what." But I decided to just put it down and send it over to the studio to see if they liked it so far. If they didn't like it, there was no use spending any more time on it.

When they called from the studio, they said they wanted another "town song" like "By the Time I Get to Phoenix." I told them I didn't know if I could really do that. I thought maybe I could connect it a little more subtly. I knew I could do a cheap imitation of "Phoenix," but that's not really what I wanted. Or I could do a "By the Time I Get to Phoenix II" which is more of what I tried to do, just swinging the camera in a different direction to see what it would see.

I didn't hear anything from them for a while, so I assumed they didn't want it. I ran into Glen some time later and said, "So whatever happened with that 'Wichita Lineman' thing? I guess you didn't like it, huh?"

He said, "Didn't like it? We recorded it."

I said, "What do you mean you recorded it? That wasn't finished."

Glen just looked at me and said, "Well, it is now." Glen just put this big, fat guitar solo in the middle of it that repeated the last line, and came out sounding pretty minimalist and slightly unfinished. But something about it obviously worked.

## Wichita Lineman

I am a lineman for the county.
And I drive the main road.
Searchin' in the sun for another overload.

I hear you singing in the wire.
I can hear you echo through the whine.
And the Wichita lineman,
is still on the line.

I know I need a small vacation.
But it don't look like rain.
And if it snows, that stretch down south,
won't ever stand the strain.

And I need you more than want you.
And I want you for all time.
And the Wichita lineman,
is still on the line.

# Wind Beneath My Wings

Story by Larry Henley
Song written by Larry Henley and Jeff Silbar
Recorded by Bette Midler, Gary Morris, Lou
Rawls, Gladys Knight and others

I was at the writers' office on Music Row one day and I walked past Jeff Silbar's office. He was strumming his guitar, and after a particular chord, I said, "Play that again."

He said, "Play what again?"

And I said, "That chord you just played. I just want to hear it one more time." And when he struck that chord, my mind went, "It must have been cold there in my shadow." I wasn't even sure what it meant really.

This was around 1982. I had been working on "Wind Beneath My Wings" for a couple of years and I couldn't figure out how to get it started. We wrote a little bit on it that night. We wrote the first couple of lines and the first line in the chorus, I think. Then Jeff's mother came in and he had to go with her somewhere. I was leaving for Texas the next day to go fishing. And I couldn't get the song off my mind. It was driving me crazy. I kept trying to write it in my head. I stayed up all night trying to write that.

The next morning, my friend and I went fishing. We were about

50 miles out in the Gulf of Mexico. We'd been fishing for an hour without a bite and I told him, "I don't think we're going to catch any fish." Then I said, "Do you have a piece of paper and a pencil?" He brought me a paper sack and a pencil. And I finished "Wind Beneath My Wings" on that paper sack. Then I signed it and gave it to his wife and said, "Keep this because it might be worth something someday, because I think it's the best thing I ever wrote."

When we demoed the song, Roger Whittaker happened to be cutting and Chet Atkins was producing him, so our publisher took the song right over to him. He was the first one to cut it. I don't think he released it as a single, unless it was released in Europe. Then we did a mass mailing to everybody who we knew was recording, and they *all* cut it!

We thought Lee Greenwood was going to have the biggest single on it, but then Gary Morris heard about the song and he sent somebody from Warner Bros. over to get a copy of the tape. The next thing we knew, Gary Morris was going to put it out as a single. I didn't even know who Gary Morris was at the time, but he did a great job on it. I won Song of the Year for it, and Gary won Single of the Year, too.

Then, in 1989, they were looking for songs for the movie *Beaches*, and Bette Midler was going to star in it. I think her hairdresser told her about the song. The next thing I knew, they called me and told me Bette had cut our song. By that time, it had been cut so many times I didn't get that excited about it anymore. I knew they were going to use it in a movie, but I didn't even know if the song fit with the movie. I had a few songs that were in movies before and nothing really ever came of them.

When I heard Bette's version, I didn't really like the way she had changed the lyric. She changed a couple of the lines and she made it fit the movie. And after it came out in the movie, it charted on the pop charts. It came out at like #50 and then it moved up very quickly. By the time it got to about #20, I thought, "Well, maybe it's not so bad that she changed the lyric after all." By the time it hit #1, I had completely forgotten what I was even mad about. And it did fit the movie perfectly. The next year, the song won a Grammy.

A few years after that, a friend and I were taking a pot-bellied stove to a church in the jungle in Hawaii. We went into the church and put the stove down and I looked up on the mantle of this church and someone had written down the lyrics to my song on the mantle of this church. I said, "Where did you get that?" He told me somebody had mailed it to him from Brazil. He didn't even know it was a song; he just thought it was a poem. And I said, "Let me sign that for you. I wrote that song."

He didn't want me to have it. He thought I was lying, I guess. But I finally did take it apart and signed it for him. But just to think that I found the lyrics to my song out in the middle of the jungle like that was incredible to me.

# Wind Beneath My Wings

It must have been cold there in my shadow,
to never have sunlight on your face.
You were content to let me shine;
you always walked a step behind.

So I was the one with all the glory,
while you were the one with all the strength.
A beautiful face without a name
A beautiful smile to hide the pain.

CHORUS:
Did you ever know that you're my hero,
and everything I would like to be?
I can fly higher than an eagle,
'cause you are the wind beneath my wings.

It might have appeared to go unnoticed,
but I've got it all here in my heart.
I want you to know I know the truth

I would be nothing without you.

CHORUS

# You Had Me From Hello

*Story by Skip Ewing*
*Song written by Kenny Chesney and Skip Ewing*
*Recorded by Kenny Chesney*

Kenny Chesney and I were at the same publishing company, and I knew him before he got his record deal. We had written a song together called "Me and You" that had been a hit for him. I liked what he did and he liked what I did, so we decided to start writing together again.

One day he called me and said, "Have you seen that movie *Jerry McGuire*?" I said I had, and then asked him why, and he said, "You know that one line in there—'you had me at hello'—that is an amazing song idea."

That movie was pretty popular by then, so I said, "Well, everybody's seen that movie, everybody knows that line right now, so everybody's going to want to write that." And, in his inimitable way, he said, "Well, then, let's be the first ones."

As soon as he said that, I felt something. I usually go with my gut, and if I feel something like that, I'll go with it. Before we even got together, I already had some ideas working in my head, but I wanted to change it to "You Had Me *From* Hello," because there was something about going from "me" to "at" that I didn't like. It seemed it would be better to go from a vowel to a consonant rather than from a vowel to another vowel. Vocally, I thought it would work better for the singer, and also poetically it sounded better.

When we wrote it, we really weren't thinking about the movie that much. We were just thinking about how someone can take your breath away and steal your heart at the same time. And the singer in this song says, "The moment you looked into my eyes, you owned me." I love those kinds of lines, expressing those kinds of feelings.

The challenge is to say something that will make the listener think the person singing the song understands *them*. If you are close enough to someone and you end up falling for them—boy, that's universal. Everyone has done that. We've all been hurt by it, but what a wonderful element of our lives that is. And it's such a powerful feeling to hear "You had me from hello."

Unlike many artists, when Kenny has an idea like that, he is already imagining what he can do with that song, so he is really writing for himself. We knew that he was going to cut it. It's not that he can't write for someone else, but he's a very soulful person. He has a lot of depth to him and he's a pretty cool guy. We finished the song, he cut it and it was a big hit for him.

At the time we wrote it, we both knew who Renée Zellweger was and who Tom Cruise was, but we didn't know that much about either of them. At least Kenny didn't. I was a pretty big fan of Renée Zellweger, but had never met her. So one thing led to another and Kenny and Renee were in a relationship with each other, and I sat there thinking, "I was a big fan of hers. Don't I at least get to *meet* her?"

When I play this live, sometimes I make a joke about this and say, "Here we write this song and Kenny Chesney ends up having a love affair with Renée Zellweger and all I get is my name in super small print somewhere in the middle of *People* magazine. What's up with that?"

# You Had Me From Hello

One word, that's all you said,
Something in your voice caused me to turn my head.
Your smile just captured me, and you were in my future, far as
    I could see.
And I don't know how it happened, but it happens still.
You asked me if I love you, if I always will.

CHORUS:
Well, you had me from "Hello"
I felt love start to grow
The moment that I looked into your eyes.
You owned me.
It was over from the start.
You completely stole my heart,
and now you won't let go.
I never even had a chance, you know
You had me from "Hello"

Inside I built a wall so high around my heart, I thought I'd
    never fall.
One touch and you brought it down.
The bricks of my defenses scattered on the ground
And I swore to me I wasn't going to love again
The last time was the last time I'd let someone in.

But you…

CHORUS

You had me from "Hello."
That's all you said
Something in your voice caused me to turn my head

You had me from "Hello"
You had me from "Hello"
Girl, I've loved you from "Hello"

# You Won't Ever Be Lonely

*Story by Andy Griggs*
*Song written by Andy Griggs and Brett Jones*
*Recorded by Andy Griggs*

I was doing a lot of playing on the road when I first came to Nashville and when I was home for a little break around 1998 I met a guy named Brett Jones. We got together one day over on Music Row to write and he pulled out his guitar. I kept admiring it and I just couldn't stop talking about it. He said, "Yeah, it's a J-200 Gibson 1963 model and I've had it forever," and he talked about what a great sound it had and gave me a big story about it. Then he let me play it, and he started playing my Martin. Then he said, "If you record this song that we write today, it's gonna be a hit."

And I told him, "Look, you've gotta dream bigger than that. It's not just gonna be a hit; it's gonna be a #1.

Then Brett laughed and said, "I tell you what, Griggs. If this song goes to #1, I will give you this guitar." So I said, "Yeah, okay," and we started to write and I didn't think anymore about it.

He asked me, "What do you do about a woman who is home when you're out on the road? How do you keep her happy?" Then we started talking about his wife and how hard it is being away from loved ones. I said, "Well, you can't really tell a woman that you'll *always* be there—physically there. That's just a lie. A woman can't offer a guy that, and a guy can't offer a woman that either."

We kept talking and writing and I said, "You know, sometimes things happen at home when you're away and you can always call her and say, "Honey, I wish I was there, but I'm not. But I won't ever leave you lonely. Even if I am away, if you're down, I'll be there in spirit or emotionally. I'll be in touch one way or another, whether through a cell phone call or a prayer, or an e-mail or whatever. If you need me, we can take pictures of each other being silly or brushing our teeth or whatever." So that was the idea we started with.

We finished the song and it was chosen to be a single release. The first time I heard the song on the radio, I was going hunting. It was about 4:30 in the morning. I was driving by myself, eating a honey bun for breakfast. The DJ said, "Here's a new guy named Andy Griggs and his new single." I just pulled over and started crying. Every week, I watched it go further and further up the charts. But I had forgotten all about the guitar. I was just excited that the song was doing so well. Eventually, it got all the way up to #1 on the *Cashbox* charts and #2 on *Billboard*.

Brent showed up at a #1 party we had on Music Row and he was carrying that guitar. I just looked at him and said, "Listen. Thanks for the song. Thanks for the offer, but the answer is no. I just can't take that guitar from you."

But he said, "No, this guitar belongs to you. I made a deal. Please don't hurt my feelings. You have to take this guitar."

So I said, "Well, since you put it that way, maybe I will." And I took it and gave it a nickname. He had always called me Catfish and I always called him Bullfrog, so I named the guitar Jeremiah in honor of him.

A little while after that song hit, I got a letter from a lady. I think she was from New Mexico. She told me that she had left her husband one day in the early morning. And before she could get out of town, she turned on the radio and heard "You Won't Ever Be Lonely." She started crying and turned back around and went home and her husband was there waiting for her. He had just gotten up and was worried about her. She said in the letter they were still together and doing fine. That was the first time that I heard about one of my songs really changing somebody's life. Her name was Laura. She never gave her last name, but Laura in New Mexico, that was probably the most rewarding letter that I ever got.

Up until then, mostly what that song meant to me was a chance to get a new guitar and some nice royalty checks, but after that it really took on a new meaning for me.

# You Won't Ever Be Lonely

Life may not always go your way
And every once in awhile you might have a bad day
But I promise you now you won't ever be lonely
The sky turns dark and everything goes wrong
Run to me and I'll leave the light on
And I promise you now you won't ever be lonely

For as long as I live
There will always be a place you belong
Here beside me
Heart and soul baby you only
And I promise you now you won't ever be lonely

It's still gonna snow and it's still gonna rain
The wind's gonna blow on a cold winter day
And I promise you now you won't ever be lonely
You're safe from the world wrapped in my arms
And I'll never let go
Baby, here's where it starts
And I promise you now you won't ever be lonely

BRIDGE:
Here's a shoulder you can cry on

And a love you can rely on
For as long as I live
There will always be a place you belong
Here beside me
Heart and soul baby—you only
And I promise you now you won't ever be lonely
No, no, you won't ever be lonely

# You're Gonna Miss This

*Story by Ashley Gorley*
*Song written by Ashley Gorley and Lee Miller*
*Recorded by Trace Adkins*

One afternoon in 2006 my wife and I were living in a house that always needed something fixed. This one afternoon, there was a handyman there—might have been a plumber—and my kids and my dogs were running around him while he was trying to work and getting into his tool box and everything. So I apologized to him several times. Finally, he said, "Oh, that doesn't bother me. I have several grown kids and I miss not having them around the house."

That scene stayed in my head for a while. I had a writing appointment with Lee Miller at his office a couple of days later. Writers will often have the idea fleshed out a little better when they come to a writing session, but I didn't have anything. I didn't even have the title. All I had was this scene in my head of the handyman telling me that he missed his kids.

We started on this song after we had been working on another song most of the day. I started describing the idea I had to him and he just sat there and listened. At one point, he looked at me and said "You're Gonna Miss This." Right there, we knew we had the title. I was playing my guitar, and I started strumming it, and came up with a groove and a melody that we thought would fit. From there we wrote the bridge and then kind of wrote backward from there.

We thought up a few different scenarios to end up with that bridge. We started thinking of the things in life that we think we're going to miss. Our kids were still pretty small, but we both started looking back on that time in life when you get into high school and you start thinking you can't wait until you turn 18 so you can do your own thing and make your own rules. Then you get out on your own and have a job and a lot of pressures and you realize how great it was when all you had to worry about was Mom dropping you off at school and going to practice that night and maybe doing a little bit of homework. And we decided that would be the first verse—the one about the young girl who is in the car with her mother and says, "I can't wait to turn 18." And her mother turns to her and says, "You're gonna wish these days hadn't gone by so fast."

Then we came up with the idea for the next verse where the same young girl is a newlywed and living in a one-bedroom apartment. She says, "I guess this will do." And her father tells her "Baby, slow down, because you're gonna miss this."

The bridge is where the plumber comes in. It's five years later and he is working on her water heater and the kids are screaming and she keeps apologizing. Then he says, "That don't bother me. I've got two babies of my own. One's 36 and one's 23. And you're gonna miss this."

When we finished it and did the full-scale demo, we pitched it to several artists, including Brad Paisley, who had it on hold for a while. But when Trace's manager heard it, he knew that it was a perfect song for Trace's voice. We thought it might just be an album cut but then they put it on his *Greatest Hits* album. One of his singles they had just released wasn't testing well on the radio, so they went ahead and pulled it and put ours out instead. It took off like a rocket. We knew it was a strong single, but we were still really surprised and humbled when the award nominations started coming out. It was nominated for CMA Song of the Year. Although it didn't win there, it did become the ASCAP Song of the Year and the Academy of Country Music chose it as Single of the Year, too.

When Trace was chosen to be on *The Apprentice* with Donald Trump, the song was just peaking toward the end of the taping of the show, so that was great timing for us. Trace was raising money for the Food Allergy and Anaphylaxis Network, which his kid suffers with. Interestingly enough, Lee's kid has a similar serious allergy problem, and for everyone who downloaded a copy of the song that night, the royalties went to that charity. Even though Trace didn't win, he was able to raise a lot of support and awareness for that charity, which was an extra blessing.

So many times in life, it seems like we're so preoccupied about getting to the next stage in our lives that we miss all the precious moments along the way. And that's what Lee and I really wanted to convey with this.

## You're Gonna Miss This

She was staring out that window, of that SUV
Complaining, saying "I can't wait to turn 18"
She said "I'll make my own money, and I'll make my own rules"
Mamma put the car in park out there in front of the school
Then she kissed her head and said "I was just like you, but…"

CHORUS:
You're gonna miss this
You're gonna want this back
You're gonna wish these days hadn't gone by so fast
These are some good times
So take a good look around
You may not know it now
But you're gonna miss this

Before she knows it she's a brand new bride

In a one-bedroom apartment, and her daddy stops by
He tells her "It's a nice place."
She says "It'll do for now"
Starts talking about babies and buying a house
Daddy shakes his head and says "Baby, just slow down"

CHORUS

Five years later there's a plumber workin' on the water heater
Dog's barkin', phone's ringin'
One kid's cryin', one kid's screamin'
She keeps apologizin'
He says, "They don't bother me.
I've got two babies of my own."
One's 36, one's 23.
Huh, it's hard to believe, but ...

CHORUS

101

# You've Got to Stand for Something

*Story by Aaron Tippin*
*Song written by Buddy Brock and Aaron Tippin*
*Recorded by Aaron Tippin*

I have to give my co-writer, Buddy Brock, credit on this one. The initial idea was his. I had just moved to Nashville and was writing for Acuff-Rose Music. I was trying to get Buddy to come up to Nashville from South Carolina, where we were from, and be a part of it, but he wasn't quite ready to make that jump.

I was recently divorced, so I would go back there and have my daughter every other weekend. She was about the same age as Buddy's daughter, so the two of them would play while we wrote songs. One time, Buddy said, "I've got this idea for a song. My dad used to always say, 'You've got to stand for something or you'll fall for anything,' and I think that would be a great title." I told him my dad used to say the same thing and we got to talking about how much they were alike.

We started off going in another direction. It was about a boy who got into trouble and his daddy bailed him out and so on, and I said, "This is not working. It's not real. It needs to be us." So we just took what our dads had taught us and instilled in us as kids and put it down on paper.

I was thinking of my dad when I said, "Daddy didn't like trouble,

You've Got to Stand for Something  **377**

but when it came along / Everyone that knew him, knew which side he'd be on." I remember one time we were at a high school football game. I was about ten years old. The national anthem was playing and there were a couple of old boys standing near us and they were just talking away. The song ended, and everybody sat down except for my dad. He walked right down to him and told them what he thought of their conduct. He said next time they needed to stand up and just shut up, and have some more respect for that flag and this country. That's the type of guy he was. I saw him stand up that way a lot of times.

I had just signed my record deal the week before, and I went in and played the song live for Joe Galante, President of RCA Records. Back then I carried around my lunch pail and a bunch of song lyrics and things like that in a big old beer box. I was known around Music Row for carrying this thing. So I called him and said, "Hey Joe, I need to see you. I want to play this song for you."

He is a busy guy, of course, but he said, "Sure, come on in." So I went into the office and threw this big old beer box on his nice wooden desk, and shoved his stuff out of the way. He just looked at it kind of funny. He listened to the song and then he left the room and he came back with this nice RCA briefcase. He said, "Aaron, I love the song. That's going to be your first single."

I was really excited, of course. Then he handed me that briefcase and he said, "And one more thing. Don't ever bring that damn beer box in my office again." I'll always remember that.

# You've Got to Stand for Something

Now daddy didn't like trouble, but if it came along
Everyone that knew him knew which side that he'd be on
He never was a hero, or this county's shinin' light
But you could always find him standing up
For what he thought was right

CHORUS:
He'd say "You've got to stand for something or you'll fall for
     anything
You've got to be your own man not a puppet on a string
Never compromise what's right and uphold your family name
You've got to stand for something or you'll fall for anything"

Now we might have been better off or owned a bigger house
If daddy had done more givin' in or a little more backing down
But we always had plenty, just living his advice
Whatever you do today you'll have to sleep with tonight

CHORUS

BRIDGE:
Now I know that things are different than they were in daddy's
     day
But I still believe what makes a man really hasn't changed

CHORUS

# Meet Our Authors

**Jack Canfield** is the co-creator of the *Chicken Soup for the Soul* series, which *Time* magazine has called "the publishing phenomenon of the decade." Jack is also the co-author of many other bestselling books.

Jack is the CEO of the Canfield Training Group in Santa Barbara, California, and founder of the Foundation for Self-Esteem in Culver City, California. He has conducted intensive personal and professional development seminars on the principles of success for more than a million people in twenty-three countries, has spoken to hundreds of thousands of people at more than 1,000 corporations, universities, professional conferences and conventions, and has been seen by millions more on national television shows.

Jack has received many awards and honors, including three honorary doctorates and a Guinness World Records Certificate for having seven books from the *Chicken Soup for the Soul* series appearing on the New York Times bestseller list on May 24, 1998.

You can reach Jack at www.jackcanfield.com.

**Mark Victor Hansen** is the co-founder of Chicken Soup for the Soul, along with Jack Canfield. He is a sought-after keynote speaker, bestselling author, and marketing maven. Mark's powerful messages of possibility, opportunity, and action have created powerful change in thousands of organizations and millions of individuals worldwide.

Mark is a prolific writer with many bestselling books in addition to the *Chicken Soup for the Soul* series. Mark has had a profound influence in the field of human potential through his library of audios, videos, and articles in the areas of big thinking, sales achievement, wealth building, publishing success, and personal and professional development. He is also the founder of the MEGA Seminar Series.

Mark has received numerous awards that honor his entrepreneurial spirit, philanthropic heart, and business acumen. He is a lifetime member of the Horatio Alger Association of Distinguished Americans.

You can reach Mark at www.markvictorhansen.com.

**Randy Rudder** has been an arts and entertainment journalist in Nashville for over 20 years. He has an MFA in creative nonfiction writing from the University of Memphis, an MA in literature from Tennessee State University, and a BA in communications from Mount Union College (Ohio). For 18 years, he also taught literature, journalism, and composition at Nashville State Community College, Tennessee State University, and Aquinas College in Nashville.

He has written arts and entertainment features for a variety of academic and popular culture publications, including *Southern Cultures* (University of North Carolina), *Southern Crossroads* (Mercer University Press), *The Pinch* (University of Memphis), *The Washington Post*, *Country Weekly*, *Bluegrass Unlimited*, *American Profile*, *Nashville Lifestyles*, *The Writer*, *Script* magazine, and others.

In 2007, Randy compiled the music anthology, *The Country Music Reader* with Rosanne Cash. That year, he also received the Tennessee Arts Commission Fellowship for Creative Nonfiction. From 2008 to 2010, he worked as a writer/producer for the Christian Broadcasting Network's Nashville office, and is currently co-producing a documentary on the history of The Farm, an intentional community in Summertown, Tennessee founded by San Francisco hippies in 1971.

He lives in Mt. Juliet, Tennessee, near Nashville, with his wife Clare and daughter Abigail. He loves hiking in the Smoky Mountains, listening to country and bluegrass music, and hearing songwriters tell about the stories behind their songs.

**Ken Kragen's** career transcends the music and entertainment industries. A graduate of Harvard Business School, he has successfully managed some of the world's most important entertainers, including Kenny Rogers, Lionel Richie, Trisha Yearwood, Travis Tritt, Olivia Newton-John, The Bee Gees. During the past few years he has devoted an increasing amount of his time to writing, teaching and consulting work for leading corporations and non-profits.

His belief that "it's much easier to do the impossible than the ordinary" has enabled him to organize many historic humanitarian projects including We are the World, Hands Across America, and Netaid. He also played an important role in the original LiveAid and, with his friend Quincy Jones, the 1992 Presidential Inauguration. For this work, Mr. Kragen was honored with the United Nations Peace Medal.

He is the only individual ever elected President of both the Country Music Association and Academy of Country Music. He received the International Citizen's Award from the International Visitors Council of Los Angeles and has also earned two MTV Awards, an American Music Award, several Emmy nominations and Manager of the Year Award from the Conference of Personal Managers.

During his career Mr. Kragen has produced a variety of film and television projects, ranging from the groundbreaking *Smothers Brothers Comedy Hour* on CBS to Kenny Rogers' *Gambler* movies, and numerous series, mini-series and films.

Ken Kragen is the author of the best-selling book *Life is a Contact Sport*.

# Song Lyric Copyrights

Used by permission. All Rights Reserved.

16th Avenue
Lyrics and Music by Thom Schuyler
©1982 Screen Gems-EMI Music Inc.

All-American Boy
Lyrics and Music by Bobby Bare
©1959 Bobby Bare. Dream City Music.

Almost Home
Lyrics and Music by Craig Morgan and Kerry Kurt Phillips
©2003 MAGIC MUSTANG MUSIC INC.; TRIPLE SHOES MUSIC UNIVERSAL
MUSIC-ZTUNES, LLC.

American Honey
Lyrics and Music by Hillary Lindsey, Shane Stevens, Cary Ryan Barlowe
©2009 BUMMERMEN MUSIC; CASTLE BOUND MUSIC; HANNA BEA SONGS.

American Made
Lyrics and Music by Pat McManus and Bob DiPiero
©1983 COMBINE MUSIC CORP./MUSIC CITY MUSIC/EMI MUSIC, INC.

American Saturday Night
Lyrics and Music by Brad Paisley, Ashley Gorley, and Kelley Lovelace
©2009 DIDN'T HAVE TO BE MUSIC (EMI APRIL MUSIC, INC.); TAPEROOM
MUSIC/MUSIC OF WINDSWEPT/ BUG MUSIC INC.; NEW SEAGAYLE MUSIC
(PLAY FAIR CHILD MUSIC); SONGS OF SOUTHSIDE INDEPENDENT MUSIC
(RUMINATING MUSIC, WIXEN MUSIC PUB. INC.)

Back When We Were Beautiful
Lyrics and Music by Matraca Berg
©1997 SONGS OF UNIVERSAL, INC.; EMI LONGITUDE MUSIC (EMI MUSIC, INC.)

Believe
Lyrics and Music by Craig Wiseman and Ronnie Dunn
©2004 BIG LOUD SHIRT/BIG LOUD BUCKS; SHOWBILLY MUSIC (SONY/ATV/TREE MUSIC PUBLISHING).

Bobbie Ann Mason
Lyrics and Music by Mark D. Sanders
©1995 UNIVERSAL MUSIC PUBLISHING GROUP; WARNER CHAPPEL MUSIC, INC.

By the Time I Get to Phoenix
Lyrics and Music by Jimmy Webb
©1967 EMI SOSAHA MUSIC INC.; SONGS OF LASTRADA.

Can't Be Really Gone
Lyrics and Music by Gary Burr
©1995 UNIVERSAL MUSIC PUBLISHING GROUP.

Coward of the County
Lyrics and Music by Billy Edd Wheeler and Roger Bowling
©1979 UNIVERSAL MUSIC PUBLISHING GROUP.

Delta Dawn
Lyrics and Music by Alex Harvey and Larry Collins
©1972 EMI APRIL MUSC, INC. (EMI MUSIC PUBLISHING)

Desperados Waiting for a Train
Lyrics and Music by Guy Clark
©1983 WORLD SONG PUBLISHING INC.; WARNER CHAPPELL MUSIC, INC.

D-I-V-O-R-C-E
Lyrics and Music by Bobby Braddock and Curly Putman
©1969 SONY/ATV/TREE MUSICPUBLISHING

Everlasting Love
Lyrics and Music by Buzz Cason and Mac Gayden
©1967 EMI BLACKWOOD MUSIC GROUP, INC.; RISING SONS MUSIC, INC.

Everything Is Beautiful
  Lyrics and Music by Ray Stevens
  ©1970 AHAB MUSIC, INC.

Gentle on My Mind
  Lyrics and Music by John Hartford
  ©1966 SONY/ATV SONGS LLC; GLASER SP ACCT

Ghost in This House
  Lyrics and Music by Hugh Prestwood
  ©1990 UNIVERSAL MUSIC.

Golden Ring
  Lyrics and Music by Bobby Braddock and Rafe Van Hoy
  ©1979 SONY/ATV/TREE MUSIC PUBLISHING.

Gone Country
  Lyrics and Music by Robert Lee McDill
  ©1994 RANGER BOB MUSIC/UNIVERSAL POLYGRAM INTERNATIONAL
  PUBLISHING INC

Good Ole Boys Like Me
  Lyrics and Music by Robert Lee McDill
  ©1979 RANGER BOB MUSIC/UNIVERSAL POLYGRAM INTERNATIONAL
  PUBLISHING INC.

Green, Green Grass of Home
  Lyrics and Music by Claude (Curly) Putman
  ©1965 SONY/ATV/TREE MUSIC PUBLISHING.

Halfway Home Café
  Lyrics and Music by Johnny Barranco and Paul Overstreet
  ©1998 SCARLET MOON MUSIC; WINGS OF DAWN MUSIC.

Harper Valley PTA
  Lyrics and Music by Tom T. Hall
  ©1967 UNICHAPPELL MUSIC INC. / UNICHAPPELL-NEWKEYS (WARNER/
  CHAPPELL MUSIC INC.)

Have You Forgotten?
  Lyrics and Music by Darryl Worley and Wynn Varble
  ©2003 DARRYL WORLEY AND WARNER-TAMERLANE PUBLISHING CORP.;

PITTSBURG LANDING SONGS (APRIL MUSIC-EMI); EMI APRIL MUSIC INC. (EMI MUSIC PUBLISHING).

He Didn't Have to Be
  Lyrics and Music by Kelley Lovelace and Brad Paisley
  ©1999 LOVE RANCH MUSIC (EMI APRIL MUSIC INC; EMI MUSIC PUBLISHING); SEA GAYLE MUSIC LLC (PLAY FAIRCHILD MUSIC)

He Stopped Loving Her Today
  Lyrics and Music by Curly Putman and Bobby Braddock
  ©1980 SONY/ATV/TREE MUSIC PUBLISHING

Here in the Real World
  Lyrics and Music by Alan Jackson and Mark Irwin (Abramson)
  ©1988 TEN TEN MUSIC GROUP INC. / MARK WEISS; W B MUSIC CORP / WARNER CHAPPELL MUSIC INC.

Hey Cinderella
  Lyrics and Music by Suzy Bogguss, Matraca Berg, and Gary Harrison
  ©1992 WARNER-TAMERLANE PUBLISHING CORPORATION, MARIA BELLE MUSI, PATRICK JOSEPH MUSIC, INC. AUGUST WIND MUSIC, LONGITUDE MUSIC COMPANY, FARMOUS MUSCI COMPANY, LOYAL DUTCHESS MUSIC.

Highway 40 Blues
  Lyrics and Music by Larry Cordle
  ©1979 UNIVERSAL POLYGRAM INTERNATIONAL PUBLISHING INC. (UNIVERSAL MUS. PUB. GROUP)

Holes in the Floor of Heaven
  Lyrics and Music by Steve Wariner and Billy Kirsch
  ©1997 by Red Brazos Music, Inc., Kidjulie Music, Steve Wariner Music Inc; MUSIC OF STAGE THREE; SILVER CHOLLA MUSIC / WAMA INC.; SONGS OF A FAIRCHILD; TENTEX MUSIC LLC (SILVER CHOLLA MUSIC); STEVE WARINER MUSIC

How Do You Get That Lonely?
  Lyrics and Music by Rory Feek and Jamie Teachenor
  ©2003 BLACK IN THE SADDLE SONGS / OLE MEDIA MANAGEMENT L.P.; GIANTSLAYER MUSIC (BLACK IN THE SADDLE SONGS / OLE MEDIA MANAGEMENT L.P.); BUG MUSIC / MURRAH MUSIC CORPORATION

I Believe
  Lyrics and Music by Skip Ewing and Donny Kees

©2002 WRITE ON MUSIC; SONY/ATV ACUFF ROSE MUSIC; SONY/ATV MUSIC PUBLISHING

I Can't Make You Love Me
Lyrics and Music by Mike Reid and Allen Shamblin
©1991 ALMO MUSIC CORPORATION; BRIO BLUES MUSIC (SONGS OF EVERGREEN COPYRIGHTS); HAYES STREET MUSIC, INC.; UNIVERSAL MUSIC-MGB SONGS

I Fall to Pieces
Lyrics and Music by Harlan Howard and Hank Cochran
©1960 SONY/ATV MUSIC PUBLISHING

I Hope You Dance
Lyrics and Music by Tia Sillers and Mark D. Sanders
©2000 SONY/ATV MELODY (CHOICE IS TRAGIC MUSIC); SODA CREEK SONGS (UNIVERSAL MUSIC CORPORATION; UNIVERSAL MUSIC PUBLISHING GROUP)

I Love the Way You Love Me
Lyrics and Music by Victoria Shaw and Chuck Cannon
©1991 TASTE AUCTION MUSIC; UNIVERSAL MUSIC/MGB SONGS

I Run to You
Lyrics and Music by Tom Douglas, Charles Kelley, David Wesley Haywood, Hillary Scott
©2008 DWHAYWOOD MUSIC (WARNER-TAMERLANE); RADIOBULLETS PUBLISHING (WARNER-TAMERLANE PUBLISHING CORP.); SONY/ATV TREE PUBLISHING; TOMDOUGLASMUSIC (SONY/ATV MUSIC PUBLISHING) SHAW ENUFF SONGS (MULTISONGS)

I Was Country When Country Wasn't Cool
Lyrics and Music by Dennis Morgan and Kye Fleming
©1980 UNIVERSAL SONGS OF POLYGRAM INT. INC.

It Matters to Me
Lyrics and Music by Mark D. Sanders and Ed Hill
©1995 UNIVERSAL MUSIC PUBLISHING GROUP; W B MUSIC CORP. / WARNER CHAPPELL MUSIC INC.; MUSIC HILL MUSIC / UNIVERSAL MUSIC MGB NA LLC); UNIVERSAL MUSIC CAREERS / UNIVERSAL MUSIC MGB NA LLC.

Jackson
Lyrics and Music by Billy Edd Wheeler and Jerry Leiber

Jesus Take the Wheel
Lyrics and Music by Hillary Lindsey, Brett James, and Gordie Sampson

Johnny Cash Is Dead and His House Burned Down
Lyrics and Music by Larry Gatlin and John Cash

Letting Go
Lyrics and Music by Doug Crider and Matt Rollings

Little Rock
Lyrics and Music by Tom Douglas

Live Like You Were Dying
Lyrics and Music by Craig Wiseman and Tim Nichols

Long Black Train
Lyrics and Music by Josh Turner

Long Black Veil
Lyrics and Music by Danny Dill and Marijohn Wilkin

Love, Me
Lyrics and Music by Skip Ewing and Max T. Barnes

Mamas Don't Let Your Babies Grow Up to Be Cowboys
    Lyrics and Music by Ed and Patsy Bruce
    ©1975 SONY/ATV TREE PUBLISHING (SONY/ATV MUSIC PUBLISHING)

Man of Constant Sorrow
    Soggy Bottom Boys arrangement by Carter Stanley
    ©1913 APRS (PEERMUSIC)

Marie Laveau
    Lyrics and Music by Shel Silverstein and Baxter Taylor
    ©1954 EVIL EYE MUSIC INC. (THE RICHMOND ORGANIZATION)

Maybe It Was Memphis
    Lyrics and Music by Michael Anderson
    ©1984 CADILLAC PINK MUSIC; ATLANTIC MUSIC CORP.; FIRST RELEASE
    MUSIC PUBLISHING

Mississippi Squirrel Revival
    Lyrics and Music by Buddy and Carlene Kalb
    ©1984 RAY STEVENS MUSIC

Mr. Bojangles
    Lyrics and Music by Jerry Jeff Walker
    ©1968 COTILLION MUSIC INC. (WARNER/CHAPPELL MUSIC INC.)

Murder on Music Row
    Lyrics and Music by Larry Cordle and Larry Shell
    ©1999 WANDACHORD MUSIC; SHELLPOINT MUSIC; PIER FIVE MUSIC INC.;
    SONY/ATV TREE PUBLISHING

My List
    Lyrics and Music by Rand Bishop and Tim James
    ©2001 SOCK AND ROLL SONGS (DONALD SEITZ); SONGWRITERS PADDOCK
    MUSIC (SONG OF WS); WS MUSIC PUBLISHING LLC; WEIGHTLESS CARGO
    MUSIC (DO WRITE MUSIC LLC)

My Son
    Lyrics and Music by Jan Howard
    ©1968 SONY/ATV TREE PUBLISHING (SONY/ATV MUSIC PUBLISHING)

Not That Different
    Lyrics and Music by Karen Taylor-Good and Joie Scott

©1995 BUG MUSIC / SPOOFER MUSIC; MS. KAREN TAYLOR-GOOD (W B M MUSIC CORP.)

Old Dogs, Children and Watermelon Wine
Lyrics and Music by Tom T. Hall
©1972 SONY/ATV ACUFF ROSE MUSIC (SONY/ATV MUSIC PUBLISHING)

Old Hippie
Lyrics and Music by David Bellamy
©1985 BELLAMY BROTHERS MUSIC

On Angel's Wings
Lyrics and Music by Karen Taylor-Good and Jason Blume
©2000 K T GOOD MUSIC; W B M MUSIC CORP. (WARNER/CHAPPELL MUSIC INC.) ZOMBA SONGS, INC.

Online
Lyrics and Music by Brad Paisley, Kelley Lovelace, and Chris DuBois
©2007 DIDN'T HAVE TO BE MUSIC (APRIL MUSIC-EMI / EMI MUSIC PUBLISHING); SEA GAYLE MUSIC LLC (PLAY FAIRCHILD MUSIC)

Reuben James
Lyrics and Music by Alex Harvey and Barry Etris
©1969 United Artists Music Co. Inc., as employer for hire of Alex Harvey & Barry Etris

She Thinks I Still Care
Lyrics and Music by Dickey Lee
©1962 renewed 1990 GLAD MUSIC PUBLISHING & RECORDING LP / PAPPY DAILY MUSIC LP; UNIVERSAL POLYGRAM INTERNATIONAL PUBLISHING INC.

Simple Man
Lyrics and Music by Charlie Daniels, John L. Gavin, Taz (William) DiGregorio, and Charles Hayward
©1989 SONGS OF UNIVERSAL INC.; MISS HAZEL MUSIC

Smoky Mountain Rain
Lyrics and Music by Dennis Morgan and Kye Fleming
©1980 Pi-Gem Music; UNIVERSAL SONGS OF POLYGRAM INT INC.

Somebody's Prayin'
Lyrics and Music by John G. Elliott
©1986 UNIVERSAL MUSIC-MGB SONGS

Something in Red
Lyrics and Music by Angela Kaset
©1990 COBURN MUSIC INC.

Southern Voice
Lyrics and Music by Bob DiPiero and Tom Douglas
©2006 SONY/ATV TREE PUBLISHING; LOVE MONKEY MUSIC;
TOMDOUGLASMUSIC; SONY/ATV MUSIC PUBLISHING

Strawberry Wine
Lyrics and Music by Matraca Berg and Gary Harrison
©1996 GEORGIAN HILLS MUSIC (EMI-LONGITUDE MUSIC); SONGS OF
UNIVERSAL INC.

That's Just About Right
Lyrics and Music by Jeff Black
©1991 WARNER-TAMERLANE PUBLISHING CORP.

That's My Job
Lyrics and Music by Gary Burr
©1980 by Garwin Music, Shenandoah Music; GARWIN MUSIC INC. / IRWIN
BAILEY; SONY/ATV CROSS KEYS PUBLISHING; SONY/ATV TUNES LLC;
UNIVERSAL MUSIC CORPORATION / UNIVERSAL MUSIC PUBLISHING GROUP
Used by Permission

The Cape
Lyrics and Music by Guy Clark, Jim Janosky, and Susanna Clark
©1994 EMI APRIL MUSIC INC. (EMI MUSIC PUBLISHING); SUSANNA CLARK
MUSIC (BUG HOUSE) / BUG MUSIC INC.

The Dance
Lyrics and Music by Tony Arata
©1987 EMI APRIL MUSIC INC.; MORGANACTIVE SONGS INC.

The Devil Went Down to Georgia
Lyrics and Music by Charlie Daniels, John Thomas Crain, Taz (William) DiGregorio,
Fred Laroy Edwards, Charles Hayward, and James Marshall
©1979 SONGS OF UNIVERSAL INC.

The Famous Lefty Flynn's
Lyrics and Music by Jamie Johnson and Morry Trent
©2010 COUNTRY GENTLEMEN MUSIC (ADMINISTERED BY EVERGREEN);
CINDERELLA MAN SONGS

The Good Stuff
Lyrics and Music by Craig Wiseman and Jim Collins
©2002 HOPE N CAL MUSIC / WARNER-TAMERLANE PUBLISHING CORP.;
KELE CURRIER; BIG LOUD BUCKS; UNIVERSAL MUSIC-MGB SONGS

The Grand Tour
Lyrics and Music by Norro Wilson, George Richey, and Carmol Taylor
©1974 EMI AL GALLICO MUSIC CORP; EMI ALGEE MUSIC CORP.

The Highwayman
Lyrics and Music by Jimmy Webb
©1977 UNIVERSAL POLYGRAM INTERNATIONAL PUBLISHING INC.
(UNIVERSAL MUS. PUB. GROUP); SEVENTH SON MUSIC INC. / MUSIC OF
WINDSWEPT (BUG MUSIC INC.)

The House That Built Me
Lyrics and Music by Allen Shamblin and Tom Douglas
©2009 BUILT ON ROCK (ALLEN SHAMBLIN); TOMDOUGLASMUSIC; SONY/
ATV MUSIC PUBLISHING

The Most Beautiful Girl
Lyrics and Music by Norro Wilson, Rory Bourke, and Billy Sherrill
©1973 EMI AL GALLICO MUSIC CORP; EMI ALGEE MUSIC CORP. Used by
Permission

The River
Lyrics and Music by Victoria Shaw and Garth Brooks
©1991 MAJOR BOB MUSIC; MID-SUMMER MUSIC INC.; UNIVERSAL MUSIC-
MGB SONGS

The Song Remembers When
Lyrics and Music by Hugh Prestwood
©1993UNIVERSAL MUSIC CAREERS

The Streak
Lyrics and Music by Ray Stevens
©1974 AHAB MUSIC COMPANY INC.

The Thunder Rolls
Lyrics and Music by Pat Alger and Garth Brooks
©1989 MAJOR BOB MUSIC; UNIVERSAL MUSIC CORPORATION / UNIVERSAL
MUSIC PUBLISHING GROUP; UNIVERSAL POLYGRAM INTERNATIONAL
PUBLISHING INC. (UNIVERSAL MUS. PUB. GROUP)

This One's for the Girls
    Lyrics and Music by Hillary Lindsey, Aimee Mayo, and Chris Lindsey
    ©2003 ANIMAL FAIR (SONY ATV HARMONY); MONKEY FEET MUSIC;
    CHRYSALIS ONE MUSIC; SILVERKISS MUSIC / UNIVERSAL MUSIC CAREERS

Time Marches On
    Lyrics and Music by Bobby Braddock
    ©1995 SONY/ATV SONGS, LLC PUBLISHING

Unanswered Prayers
    Lyrics and Music by Garth Brooks, Pat Alger, and Larry Bastian
    ©1990 MAJOR BOB MUSIC; MID-SUMMER MUSIC INC.; UNIVERSAL MUSIC
    CORPORATION / UNIVERSAL MUSIC PUBLISHING GROUP; UNIVERSAL
    POLYGRAM INTERNATIONAL PUBLISHING INC.)

Uncle Pen
    Lyrics and Music by Bill Monroe
    ©1951 BILL MONROE MUSIC / MUSIC OF EVERGREEN (EVERGREEN GF
    COUNTRY MUSIC LLC); UNICHAPPELL MUSIC INC.; WARNER CHAPPELL
    MUSIC INC.)

Walk on Faith
    Lyrics and Music by Mike Reid and Allen Shamblin
    ©1991 ALMO MUSIC CORPORATION; BRIO BLUES MUSIC (SONGS OF
    EVERGREEN COPYRIGHTS); UNIVERSAL MUSIC-MGB SONGS

Walking Away a Winner
    Lyrics and Music by Bob DiPiero and Tom Shapiro
    ©1992 MIKE CURB MUSIC; SONY/ATV TREE PUBLISHING; MUSIC OF STAGE
    THREE; WARNER-TAMERLANE PUBLISHING CORP.

What A Difference You've Made In My Life
    Lyrics and Music by Archie Jordan
    ©1977 renewed 2005 UNIVERSAL POLYGRAM INTERNATIONAL PUBLISHING
    INC. (UNIVERSAL MUS. PUB. GROUP)

Where've You Been?
    Lyrics and Music by Jon Vezner and Don Henry
    ©1988 SONY/ATV CROSS KEYS PUBLISHING; SONY/ATV TUNES LLC.

Wichita Lineman
    Lyrics and Music by Jimmy Webb

# Photo Credits

Story 4. Hillary Lindsey: photo credit Becky Fluke
Story 6. Ashley Gorley: photo credit Tucker Photography
Story 9. Mark D. Sanders: photo credit Alan Mayor
Story 11. Gary Burr: photo credit Alan Mayor
Story 15. Bobby Braddock: photo credit Alan Mayor
Story 16. Buzz Cason: photo credit Alan Mayor
Story 18. John Hartford and Betty Harford: photo courtesy of Betty Harford
Story 20. Bobby Braddock: photo credit Alan Mayor
Story 21. Bob McDill: photo credit Alan Mayor
Story 22. Bob McDill: photo credit Alan Mayor
Story 24. Ricky Skaggs: photo credit Erick Anderson
Story 25. Tom T. Hall: photo credit Alan Mayor
Story 26. Darryl Worley: photo credit Kristin Barlowe
Story 28. Curly Putman: photo credit Alan Mayor
Story 29. Mark Irwin, right, with Alan Jackson
Story 32. Billy Kirsch, right, with Steve Wariner: photo credit Alan Mayor
Story 34. Skip Ewing: photo credit Anthony Scarlati
Story 35. Mike Reid: photo credit Alan Mayor
Story 36. Harlan Howard: photo credit Alan Mayor
Story 38. Victoria Shaw: photo credit Alan Mayor
Story 39. Tom Douglas: photo credit Alan Mayor
Story 40. Dennis Morgan: photo credit Alan Mayor
Story 41. Mark D. Sanders: photo credit Alan Mayor
Story 43. Hillary Lindsey: photo credit Becky Fluke
Story 44. Larry Gatlin: photo credit Alan Mayor
Story 45. Doug Crider, left, with Suzy Bogguss
Story 46. Tom Douglas: photo credit Alan Mayor
Story 47. Craig Wiseman: photo credit Alan Mayor
Story 48. Josh Turner: photo credit George Holz
Story 50. Skip Ewing: photo credit Anthony Scarlati

Story 55. Buddy Kalb: photo credit Randy Rudder
Story 59. Jan Howard: photo courtesy of The Grand Ole Opry
Story 61. Tom T. Hall: photo credit Alan Mayor
Story 62. David Bellamy: photo credit Alan Mayor
Story 66. Dickey Lee: photo credit Alan Mayor
Story 68. Dennis Morgan: photo credit Alan Mayor
Story 69. Ricky Skaggs: photo credit Erick Anderson
Story 72. Matraca Berg: photo credit Alan Mayor
Story 76. Tony Arata: photo credit Ben Kreinen
Story 78. Jamie Johnson: photo credit Keoni K
Story 79. Craig Wiseman: photo credit Alan Mayor
Story 80. Norro Wilson: photo credit Randy Rudder
Story 81. Jimmy Webb at 1991 NSAI Dinner: photo credit Alan Mayor
Story 83. Norro Wilson: photo credit Randy Rudder
Story 87. Pat Alger: photo credit Randy Rudder
Story 88. Hillary Lindsey: photo credit Becky Fluke
Story 89. Bobby Braddock: photo credit Alan Mayor
Story 90. Pat Alger: photo credit Randy Rudder
Story 91. James Monroe and Bill Monroe: photo credit Alan Mayor
Story 92. Mike Reid: photo credit Alan Mayor
Story 98. Skip Ewing: photo credit Anthony Scarlati
Story 100. Ashley Gorley with Lee Miller: photo credit Stephanie Greene

# Improving Your Life Every Day

eal people sharing real stories—for seventeen years. Now, Chicken Soup for the Soul has gone beyond the bookstore to become a world leader in life improvement. Through books, movies, DVDs, online resources and other partnerships, we bring hope, courage, inspiration and love to hundreds of millions of people around the world. Chicken Soup for the Soul's writers and readers belong to a one-of-a-kind global community, sharing advice, support, guidance, comfort, and knowledge.

Chicken Soup for the Soul stories have been translated into more than forty languages and can be found in more than one hundred countries. Every day, millions of people experience a Chicken Soup for the Soul story in a book, magazine, newspaper or online. As we share our life experiences through these stories, we offer hope, comfort and inspiration to one another. The stories travel from person to person, and from country to country, helping to improve lives everywhere.

# Share with Us

We all have had Chicken Soup for the Soul moments in our lives. If you would like to share your story or poem with millions of people around the world, go to chickensoup.com and click on "Submit Your Story." You may be able to help another reader, and become a published author at the same time. Some of our past contributors have launched writing and speaking careers from the publication of their stories in our books!

Our submission volume has been increasing steadily—the quality and quantity of your submissions has been fabulous. We only accept story submissions via our website. They are no longer accepted via mail or fax.

To contact us regarding other matters, please send us an e-mail through webmaster@chickensoupforthesoul.com, or fax or write us at:

Chicken Soup for the Soul
P.O. Box 700
Cos Cob, CT 06807-0700
Fax: 203-861-7194

One more note from your friends at Chicken Soup for the Soul: Occasionally, we receive an unsolicited book manuscript from one of our readers, and we would like to respectfully inform you that we do not accept unsolicited manuscripts and we must discard the ones that appear.

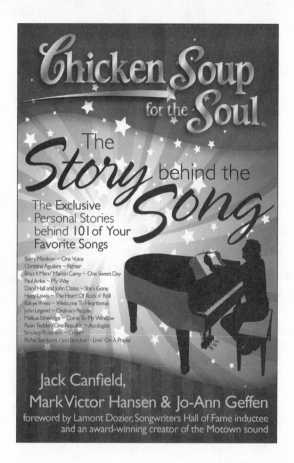

Ever wondered what inspired your favorite songs? What was going on in the songwriter's life at the time? Who those lyrics were really about? Did he really write the song on a napkin? Many of music's most famous names reveal the stories behind their best-known songs. Many of these exclusive stories are told for the first time. Photos and lyrics are included too. You will never listen to these songs the same way again. A great gift for anyone who loves music, any age.

978-1-935096-40-5

# *C*lassics for Music Lovers

www.chickensoup.com